IMAGES
of America

WAPAKONETA

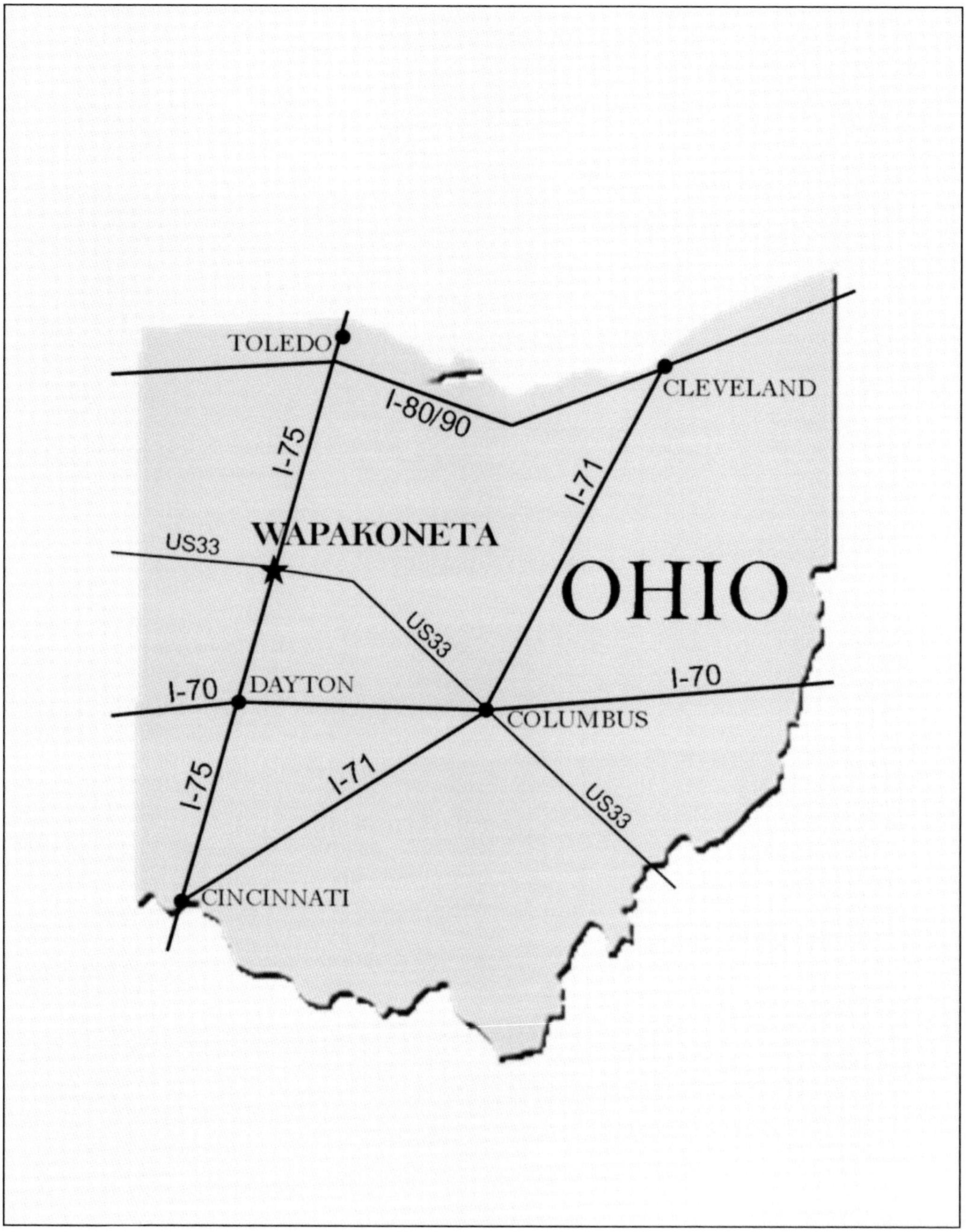

Wapakoneta is situated in Northwest Ohio at the crossroads of several major transportation routes. (Courtesy of the Downtown Wapakoneta Partnership.)

On the Cover: Taken about July 20, 1915, Wapakoneta postal carriers are, from left to right, Ferd Lanning, Frank Kerst, Charley Bush, Fred Swink, Almond Brown, postmaster Adam Schaffer, Fred Wiss, Earl Parish, Cornel Lanning, William Christler, Victor Fry, William L. Hasting, Henry Brockert, Howard Horn, Merle Kerst, and Albert J. "Dusty" Miller. (Courtesy of Eugene and Shirley Pohlable.)

IMAGES
of America

WAPAKONETA

Dianne Dodds Knipp with the
Downtown Wapakoneta Partnership

ARCADIA
PUBLISHING

ISBN 978-0-7385-7794-4

Published by Arcadia Publishing
Charleston, South Carolina

Printed in the United States of America

Library of Congress Control Number: 2009934668

For all general information contact Arcadia Publishing at:
Telephone 843-853-2070
Fax 843-853-0044
E-mail sales@arcadiapublishing.com
For customer service and orders:
Toll-Free 1-888-313-2665

Visit us on the Internet at www.arcadiapublishing.com

To Vernon, whose generous spirit and preservation of Wapakoneta's history have made this project a joy.

Contents

Acknowledgments 6

Introduction 7

1. Native Americans 9

2. City Structures 17

3. Industry and Enterprises 43

4. Recreations and Celebrations 73

5. A Community Kaleidoscope 93

6. Fame and Footprints 117

ACKNOWLEDGMENTS

The volunteers and collectors of Wapakoneta history have contributed to this collection with generosity and enthusiasm. It is impossible to thank everyone who volunteered their time and access to their collections; however, contributors have been noted with the images appearing in this book. Unless otherwise noted, images presented are from the author's collection or the Downtown Wapakoneta Partnership archives. It is with gratitude I thank Jon Anspaugh, Vernon E. Doenges, Erin Hollenbacher, Genelle Berry, John Zwez, Peggy Prater, Jim Bowsher, DeLynn Epperly, Mike Borges, Rachel Barber, Dan Bennett, Mary Beech, and Chris Niekamp for their hours of editorial contribution and committee work. In addition, the assistance of Joseph L. Bennett, the vice president at the Purdue Research Foundation, was most appreciated in providing technical information from the Neil A. Armstrong collection. Thank you also to Neil Bowsher, the Auglaize County Engineer's office, the Marilyn Henkener family, the late Jack Springer, Arcadia author Mark Camp, and local railroad historian Wayne York for the information they provided.

I would especially like to thank the Downtown Wapakoneta Partnership and the Auglaize County Historical Society for their support and encouragement in all things historical that formed the framework for this project. A special thank you is extended to Greg Myers for his guidance, interest, and encouragement in gathering this collection of stories and photographs that will add to the community's history.

This book wouldn't have been possible without the assistance of these prior works: *History of the Shawnee Indians: From the Year 1681 to 1854, Inclusive* by Henry Harvey; *Atlas of Auglaize County, Ohio* edited by H. G. Howland; *History of Auglaize County, Ohio* by William J. McMurray; *Atlas and History of Auglaize County with Biographical Sketches* by J. H. Meyer; *Early History of Auglaize County* by J. D. Simkins; *Atlas of Auglaize County with Historical and Biographical Sketches* edited by John Walsh; *The History of Western Ohio and Auglaize County* by C. W. Williamson; and *The Peace of Mad Anthony and the Treaty of Greenville* by Frazer Ells Wilson.

INTRODUCTION

Wapakoneta does not lack a rich and varied history. Local archeological evidence spans a time when prehistoric Native Americans found the area to be a rich hunting ground to the establishment of a modern space age history on July 20, 1969, when native Neil A. Armstrong, commander of *Apollo 11*, walked on the moon.

Long before the first settlers arrived in the Wapakoneta area, prehistoric Native Americans used the banks of the Auglaize River as a hunting camp and grounds. Early French fur traders also noted the existence of Wapakoneta on a map as early as 1748, but the site became better known as a council house of the Shawnee Indian Nation in the 1760s.

Wapakoneta later became the location of a Shawnee Indian Reserve established by the Treaty of Greenville in 1795, where it remained a center of Native American government until the Shawnee left for Kansas in fall 1832. Several Native American leaders like Blue Jacket, The Prophet, and Tecumseh, met at the Wapaughkonnetta council house, but the well respected leader Catahecassa, or Black Hoof, maintained a stable presence in guiding the Shawnee while learning to deal with European settlement influences.

An anecdote explaining why Chief Black Hoof agreed to the sale of reservation lands was recorded in the 1880 Atlas of Auglaize County. Black Hoof stated, "because the United States government wanted to buy and possess our lands, and remove us out of the way. I consented because I could not help myself, for I never knew them to undertake anything without accomplishing it. I knew that I might as well give up first as last, for they were determined to have our lands."

A firm business climate was established prior to Ohio becoming a state when Fort Auglaize was built near Wapakoneta as an outpost serving fur traders, government surveyors, and Native Americans. Organized industry became a greater part of Wapakoneta history in the early 1800s when members of the Friends (Quakers) church established a mission to serve the Shawnee Indians. Missionaries, under the direction of Isaac Harvey, built a gristmill and sawmill on the banks of the Auglaize River at the Wapakoneta Reserve after the War of 1812. Friends or Quakers, concerned about the losses of Native Americans, had established a mission for the purpose of education and support prior to the War of 1812 but were unable to maintain a presence at Wapakoneta until after that war ended. Thirty-six years later, Isaac Harvey's brother, Henry, wrote a book documenting Shawnee history.

As the frontier pushed westward, the land around the reservation was quickly settled, and as the Shawnee Indians prepared to leave after the sale of reservation lands in 1832, buyers were in line to purchase the remaining lands at Wapakoneta. The town was platted and established in early 1833.

Early settlers to the Wapakoneta area included German immigrants who purchased and cleared the land, established small businesses, and produced farm and industrial products, which were later distributed by rail throughout the country. Settlement began in the area by the 1830s when the Ohio canal system was completed from Cincinnati to Toledo by the Miami Erie Canal and further expanded in 1858 when the first rail system passed through town. The establishment of the railroad provided Wapakoneta businesses a direct route to distribute products and import goods via ports on Lake Erie and Cincinnati on the Ohio River.

Following the Civil War, commerce and industry continued to flourish, and reliable outlets for area products became secure when rail lines were expanded. Some of the products shipped nationwide were the M. Brown Company Bent Wood churns (at one time the largest producer in the country); Wapak Hollow Ware Company cast iron cookware; and industrial knives from the Wapakoneta Machine Company. The Charles Wintzer Tanning Company is only one example of a small mid–1800's industry that grew into G. A. Wintzer and Son, celebrating 160 years of continuous operation in 2008.

Established in 1848, Wapakoneta became the Auglaize County seat. The present courthouse, built in 1894, stands among the many fine examples of 1800s construction throughout the city. Many architecturally significant buildings in downtown Wapakoneta include a variety of churches and business establishments. The Wapakoneta Chamber of Commerce sponsors an architectural walking tour of the town in both the business and residential sectors. Architectural examples abound for the serious student or casual observer of fine workmanship in the historic downtown and especially along the Auglaize Street corridor.

Wapakoneta citizens are both industrious and fun loving. Over many years, the community has supported operas houses, theaters, and the arts. Establishing their home in Wapakoneta, Harry Shannon; his wife, Adelaide Stoutenburg Shannon; and their children, Harry Shannon Jr. and Hazel, formed the core of the Shannon Stock Company. The Shannon Players traveled throughout the region performing a variety of plays on stage and under tents but were especially loved by the residents of Wapakoneta from about 1915 to the mid–1930s.

Nationally famous citizens include Dudley Nichols, who received an Oscar in 1936 for his screenplay, *The Informer.* A founder of the Screen Writers Guild, Nichols made history by being the first to refuse an Oscar in protest of the Academy's treatment of independent actors and writers in their bid to form a recognized union. Having a diverse and prolific career, Nichols served in World War I, where he received a medal for inventing a device to remove mines from the water without them exploding. After the war, Nichols became a writer for a newspaper in New York City, moving to Hollywood in 1929. The Wapakoneta city walking tour includes the location of his grandfather's Victorian-style family home across the street from where Nichols grew to adulthood. An Ohio Historical Society marker on South Blackhoof Street documents his significance to Hollywood history.

Wapakoneta's most famous citizen, Neil A. Armstrong, made history by being the first person to walk on the surface of the moon. Alive in the memory of many townspeople, the city welcomed Armstrong and his family with a homecoming celebration in September 1969 after that famous *Apollo 11* flight. The Armstrong Air and Space Museum was established through a challenge in 1969 by former governor James A. Rhodes to establish a museum to honor all Ohioans who have defied gravity. The museum was designed by Wapakoneta native Arthur Klipfel, dedicated on July 20, 1972, and built as a State of Ohio collaboration using over 50 percent of local funds in the construction. Community children participated in a penny drive that formed the foundation of the funds collected. The museum is a symbol of city pride and grassroots accomplishment.

Wapakoneta remains a viable and productive city. The town history reflects the many local traditions and community-minded citizens of the past. On the banks of the Auglaize River, near the location of the original Friends mill, the downtown business district continues to be the heart of the city. A celebration of the town's 175th anniversary in 2008 featured a parade with 175 units, and special events for the 40th anniversary of Armstrong's moon walk contributed to the variety of cultural events offered by civic and private organizations to enrich the lives of all area residents.

One

Native Americans

Long before recorded time, Native Americans used the Auglaize River basin as their hunting grounds. Evidence of their presence is recorded by the many flint tools and weapons they used to hunt and gather food. Of special significance is the 1995 discovery of a log containing the spear point of a long ago missed shot by one of these early hunters in the area we now know as Wapakoneta, Ohio. One animal known to be hunted by these prehistoric people was the mastodon. Skeletal remains of several mastodons have been found near the city and on outlying farms, all in areas thought to have been bogs.

As history was recorded, Wapaughkonnetta was the site of a trading post, a Shawnee village, and the regional Native American council house, capital of the Shawnee. This favored location on the banks of the Auglaize River was first made known in 1748 by the French fur traders but became more widely known as a Shawnee town when they developed a foothold in the area upon the departure of other native tribes.

The early history of the Shawnee tribe was documented first by William Penn, who established a friendship with many leaders, and later by another Quaker (Society of Friends) missionary and author, Henry Harvey, who lived and worked with them at Wapakoneta beginning in 1819. Concerned about the disruption of war and losses of the Native American people, Quakers built a gristmill, sawmill, and school for the benefit of the Native Americans in Wapakoneta as early as 1810, although that endeavor was not well documented. After the War of 1812, a second attempt was successful.

Catahecassa, or Black Hoof, was a chief of the Wapakoneta Shawnee who had fought white encroachment into Native American lands in Ohio until the Treaty of Greenville. Thereafter, he adopted a more agrarian way of life, unlike the other Shawnee leaders, Tecumseh and his brother The Prophet, who favored resistance.

In 1831, the Shawnee ceded their lands at Wapakoneta to the U.S. government after many treaties, unsuccessful attempts to stop white settlement, and unfulfilled promises of the U.S. government and its agents.

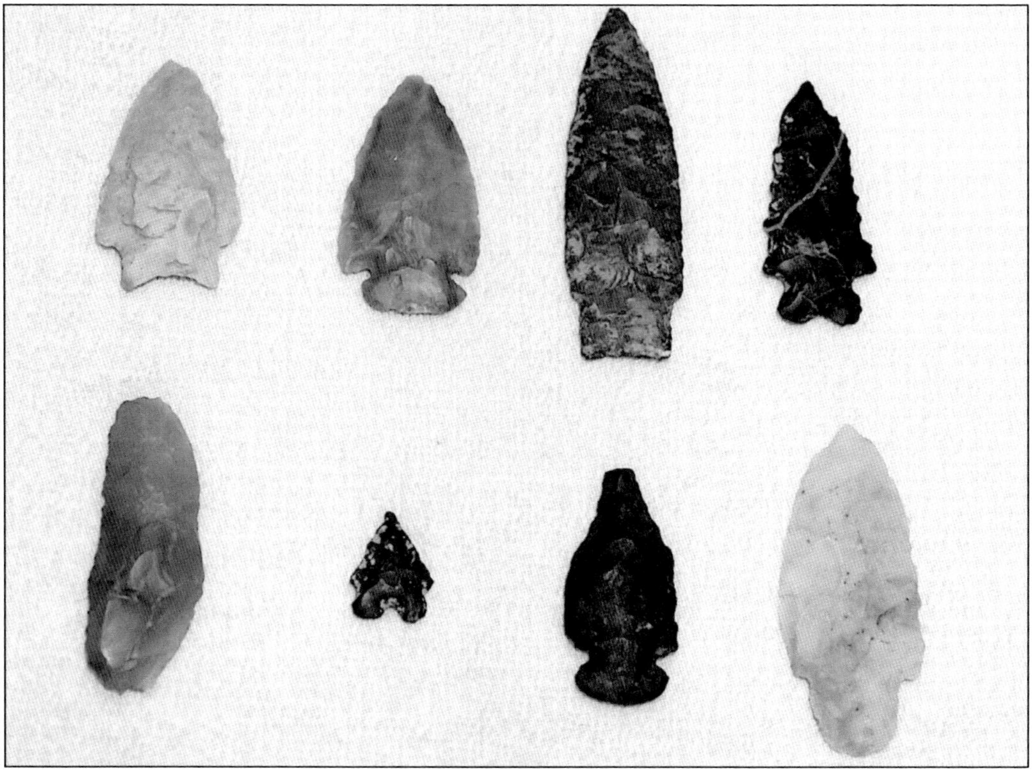

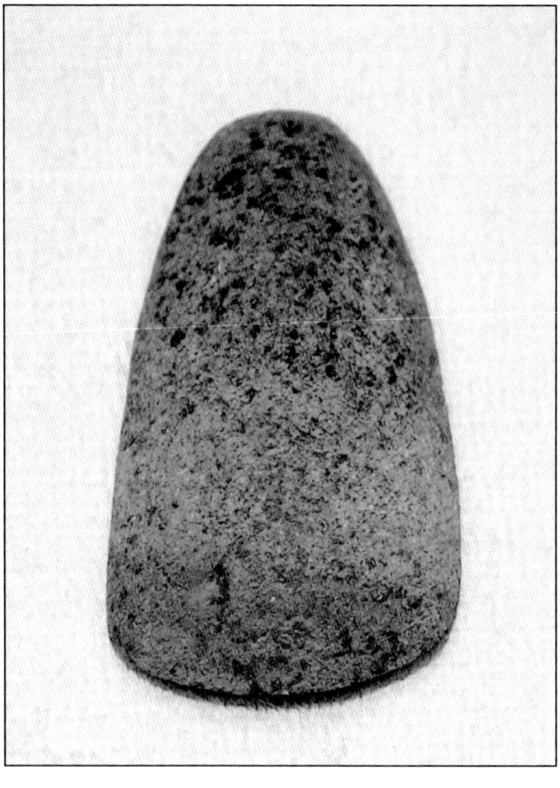

Prehistoric Native Americans had hunting camps throughout present day Ohio with archeological evidence placing Wapakoneta as a campsite. The flint tools and weapons above were found on the former William "Billy" Sammetinger farm on Pusheta Road. Specimens made of glacial drift rock, Licking County and Coshocton (Ohio) flint, scraping tools, knives, and lance points are all represented in this collection. (Courtesy of Paul F. Zwiebel and Jon Anspaugh.)

This archaic period stone tool made of glacial drift granite was found in a field near Pusheta Creek. Typical of ancient native artifacts found in the Wapakoneta area, a handle would have been lashed to the shaped stone by leather or strong reeds. Many other examples of prehistoric Native American tools and weapons were found on this farm. (Courtesy of Paul F. Zwiebel and Jon Anspaugh.)

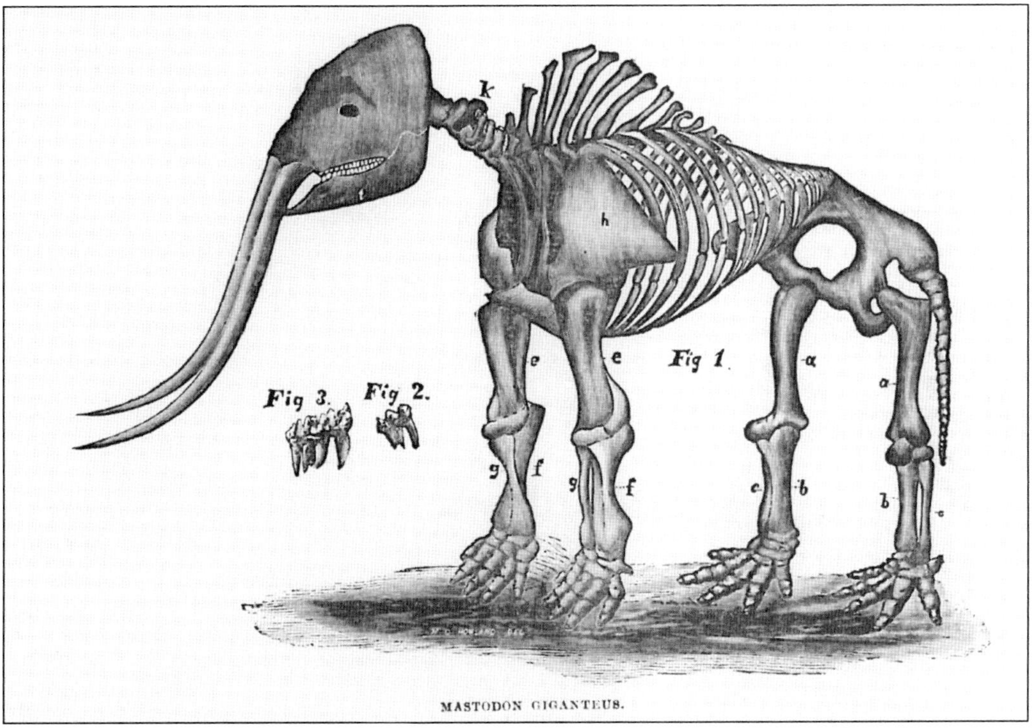

The first mastodon skeleton was discovered in Auglaize County near the village of St. Johns in 1870. The letters in the drawing indicate the parts found in this discovery. Located in areas that were thought to have been bogs, eight other partial mastodon and other prehistoric animal skeletons had been found by 1904. All skeletons were found very close to the city limits of Wapakoneta and in the surrounding countryside.

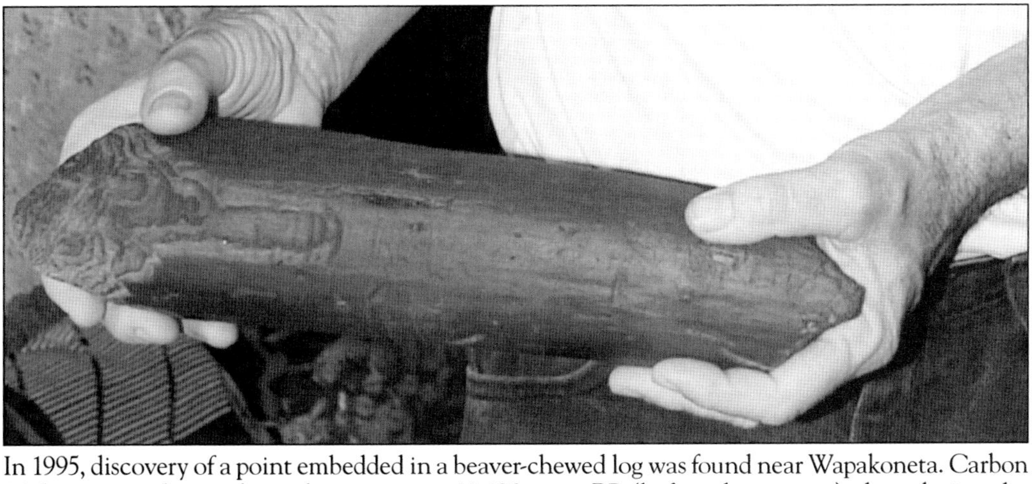

In 1995, discovery of a point embedded in a beaver-chewed log was found near Wapakoneta. Carbon 14 dating put the aged wood specimen at 11,490 years BP (before the present), thus placing the relic in the earliest phase of settlement in the region known as Ohio. In the 1998 summer issue of *Ohio Archaeology Magazine*, a full account is given of this discovery. (Courtesy of Jim and Neil Bowsher; photograph by John Zwez.)

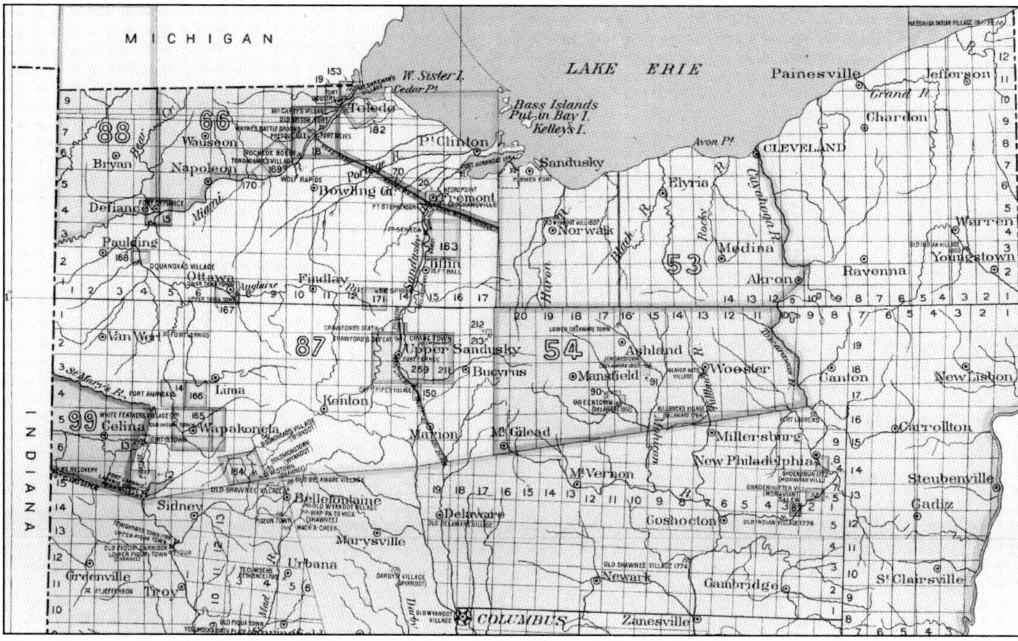

The Greenville Treaty, signed August 3, 1795, clearly established those lands that belonged to the Native Americans and those open for settlement after the Native American defeat at the Battle of Fallen Timbers near present-day Maumee. This treaty also established reservation lands north of the Greenville Treaty line, at which time, according to the treaty, an area "10 miles square" was established at the Wapakoneta village and council site. (Library of Congress Geography and Map Division.)

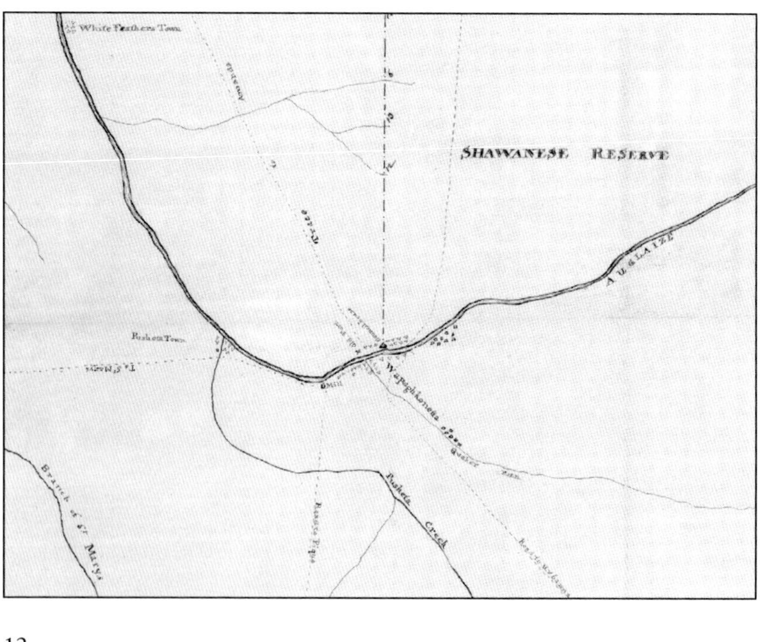

The map at left was drawn by John A. Fulton, D.S., in April 1819 as part of a government survey of the Wapakoneta Reserve established by the 1795 Greenville Treaty. Note the location of the old fort, mill, council house, and trails leading to other settlements. Native American homes are represented by the squares and triangles. (Courtesy of Ohio Historical Society.)

Catahecassa, or Black Hoof, the principle Native American chief at Wapakoneta, led his group of Shawnee to adopt a European way of life after the Greenville Treaty. He believed there was no hope of stopping white settlers and their influence on his people. Tecumseh's famous 1810 speech at the Wapakoneta Council House was unsuccessful in convincing Black Hoof's group to unite in a campaign against white settlers. (Courtesy of Ohio Historical Society.)

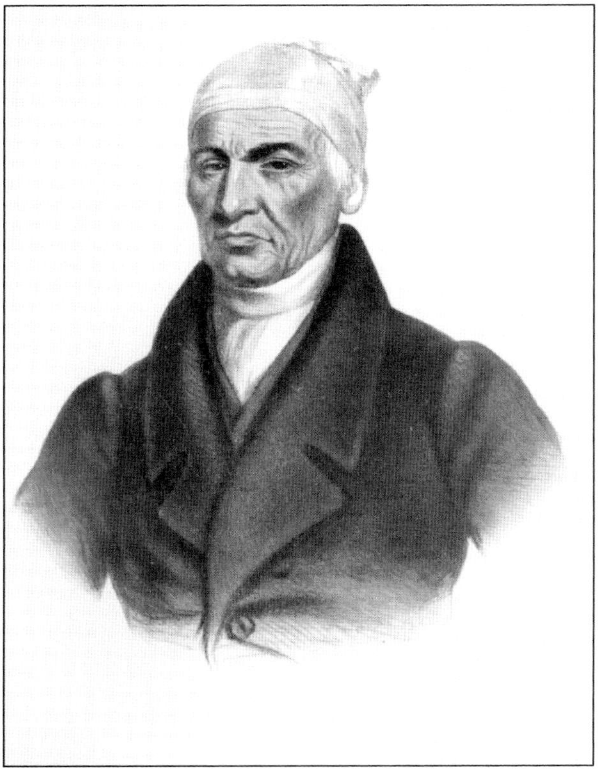

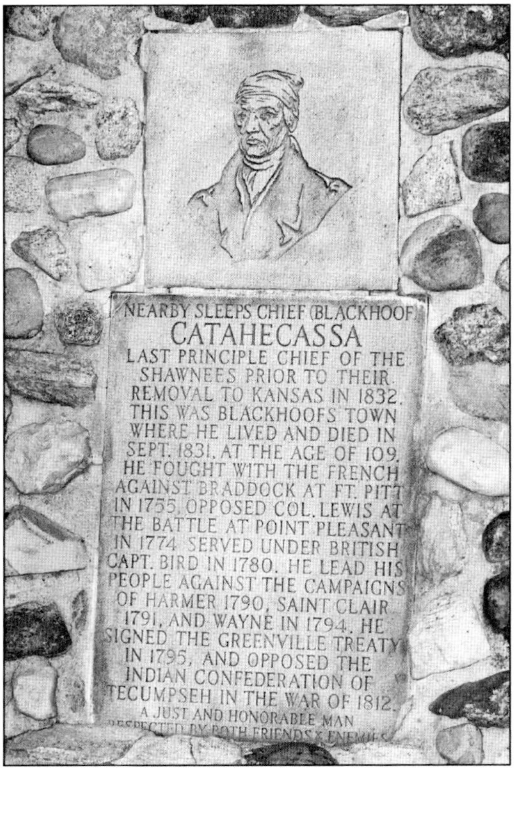

A memorial to the Native American leader Catahecassa is located at the St. Johns village cemetery along U.S. 33. Chief Black Hoof was reported to be 110 at the time of his death in 1831, prior to the tribe's relocation to Kansas in November 1832. The funeral was recorded in detail by the missionary Henry Harvey, who attended the solemn ceremony. (Photograph by and courtesy of John Zwez.)

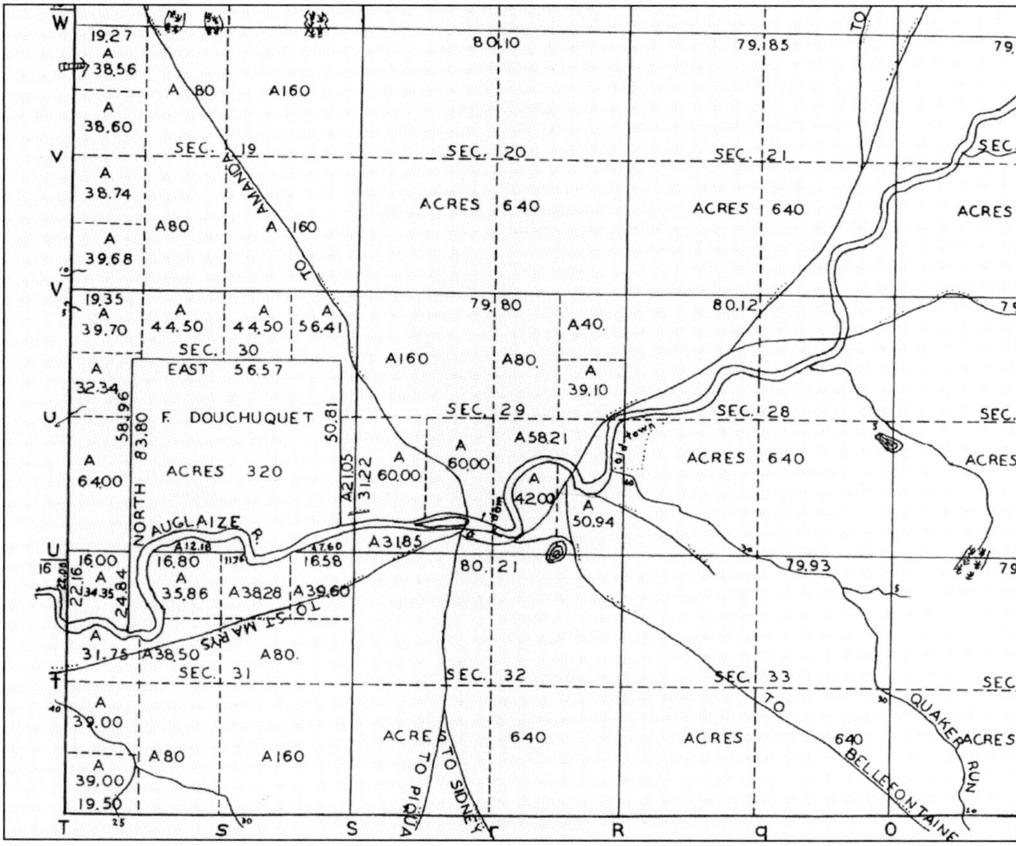

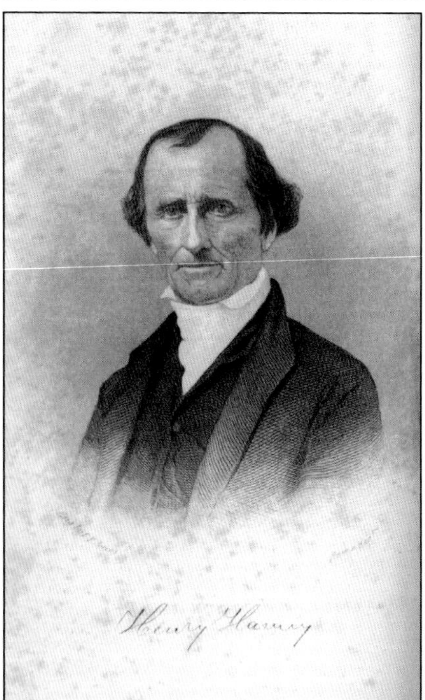

European influence was clearly established near Wapakoneta when French traders built a stockade known as Ft. Auglaize about 1748. Later a trader, Francis Duchouquet (born 1751) married a Shawnee woman and acted as a trusted local interpreter. As the map above shows, Duchouquet's position of respect prompted the Shawnee to give him part of their reserve (square at center left). The city of Wapakoneta lies within an Auglaize County township that also bears his name.

Henry Harvey, a Quaker missionary, came to work on the Shawnee Reserve about 1819. Harvey helped establish a gristmill, sawmill, and school for their children. He wrote *History of the Shawnee Indians* in 1855, documenting the culture and resettlement in Kansas. Harvey's respect and admiration for the Shawnee is evident in his writing as he gives a glimpse into the lives of these brave people. (Courtesy of Ohio Historical Society.)

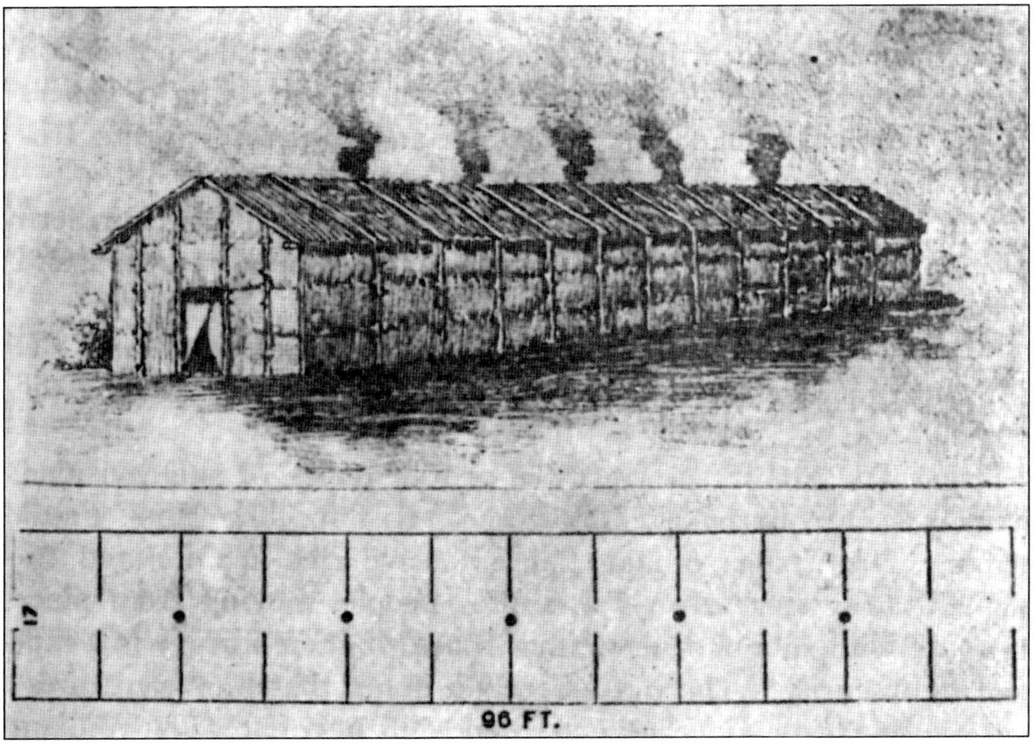

It was reported that the Shawnee lived in pole-structured wigwams covered with bark or skins and permanent, multiuse longhouse structures. The Shawnee were nomadic, but accounts in the late 1700s indicated the women maintained large fields of corn, squash, melons, and beans as well as groups of cattle. Sympathetic to the struggles of Native Americans, Quaker missionaries taught European farming (i.e., using horses for labor) and building methods.

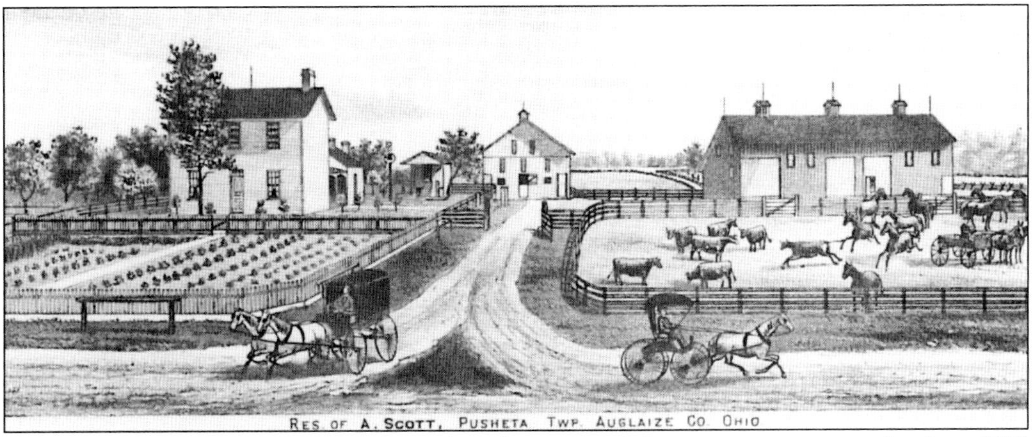

Due to growing Shawnee distrust of outside influences and changes on reservation lands, in 1825 the Quakers moved the location of the Wapakoneta Indian School to a farm location 5 miles south of town on the Hardin Pike trail. The school remained there until the Shawnee left for Kansas. This farm, later owned by A. Scott, was depicted in a drawing published in the *1880 Atlas of Auglaize County*.

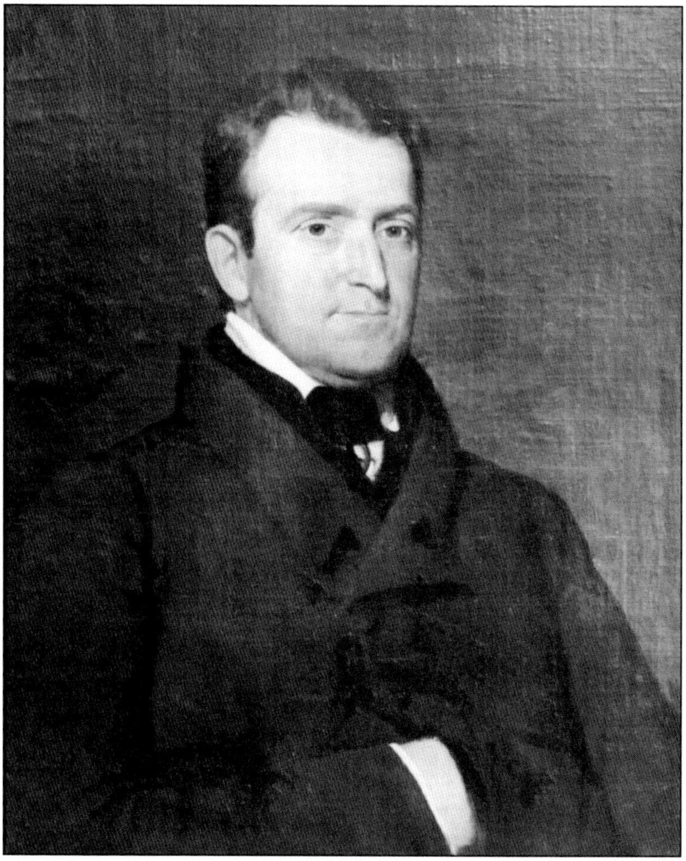

Irish born John Johnston became an Indian Agent at Piqua from 1812 to 1829, with Wapakoneta in his territory. His early government career was established by serving with Gen. Anthony Wayne. Johnston was well respected by the Shawnee, gaining trust when he helped organize a Shawnee party under Captain Logan to rescue captives at the siege of Ft. Wayne during the War of 1812. (Courtesy of Ohio Historical Society.)

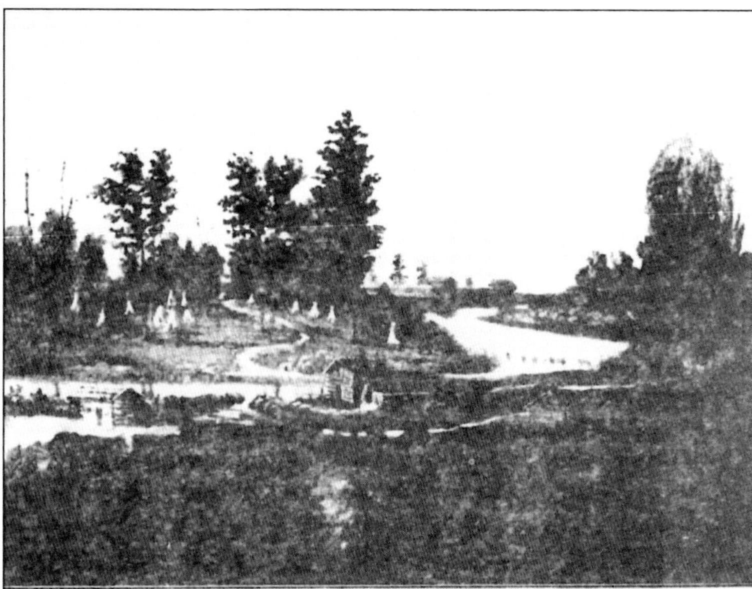

WAPAKONETA IN 1831.

322

Appearing in Charles W. Williamson's 1904 *History of Western Ohio*, this 1831 painting of Wapakoneta captures a romantic view of the city as it appeared just prior to the Shawnee removal to Kansas. The Quaker-established mill is at the center of this rendering, and a distillery is at the left. Old Ft. Auglaize is featured in the distance upriver.

Two

City Structures

Ohio became a state in 1803 and, with statehood settlers, began to spill westward across the landscape in record numbers. Although much of the state was wilderness at that time, a few towns were established long before white settlers arrived. Wapakoneta was one of those towns where, having first served as a Native American village, Indian Council House, and French fur trading post, government employees and frontiersmen had long-established business ties.

When the Shawnee Indians left the reservation for Kansas, pioneers eager to purchase formerly held reservation lands were waiting nearby. A federal land office, formerly at Piqua, was established at Wapakoneta to handle the sale of property, and in December 1832, the first purchases of previously held Native American lands were made.

Settlers quickly moved to establish a European-style town when Wapakoneta, at that time part of Allen County, was platted in January 1833. The surveyor for Allen County, John Jackson, laid out the streets and alleys for a handful of early residents, among them the land office register and merchants.

Churches and businesses dating from the earliest days of the city are still some of the oldest continually operating endeavors of the city. Originally part of Allen County, growth of Wapakoneta was tied to Dr. G. W. Holbrook's work in the establishment of Auglaize County in 1848 as well as his work to have a railroad pass through the city as it went north in the state from Dayton to Toledo in 1858.

Like many cities in northwestern Ohio, real growth and industry followed the Civil War. Wapakoneta became a more successful market and industrial town due to the rich farmland surrounding the city, the influx of industrious German immigrants, the established railroads, and a ready supply of lumber.

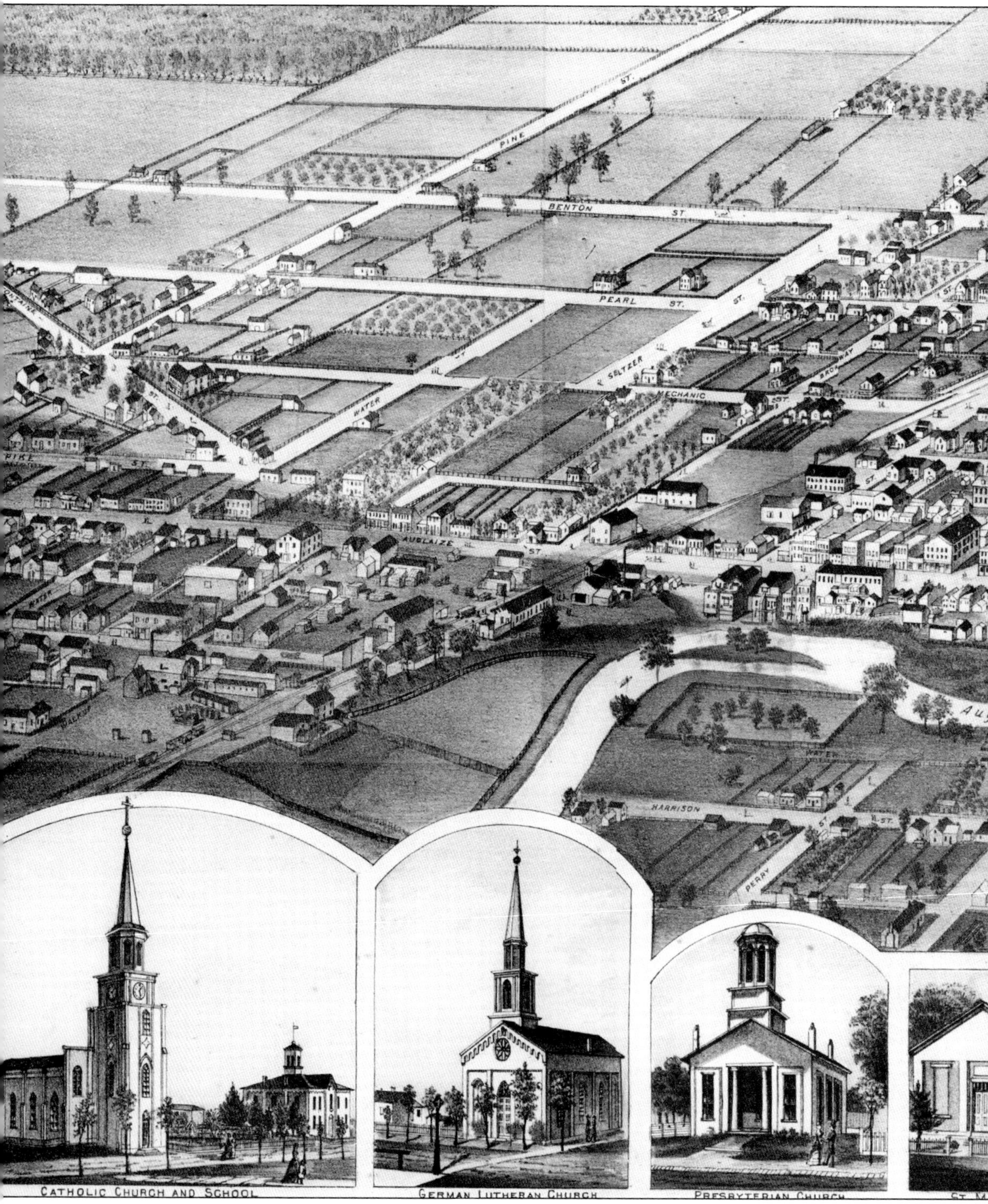

This bird's-eye view of Wapakoneta was originally published as a two-page, color feature in the *1880 Atlas of Auglaize County*. Note an island once graced the river, and the Blackhoof Street bridge was the only bridge access across the river. At this time, the river came very close to the back of the buildings downtown. The area behind the buildings was filled in during a Works

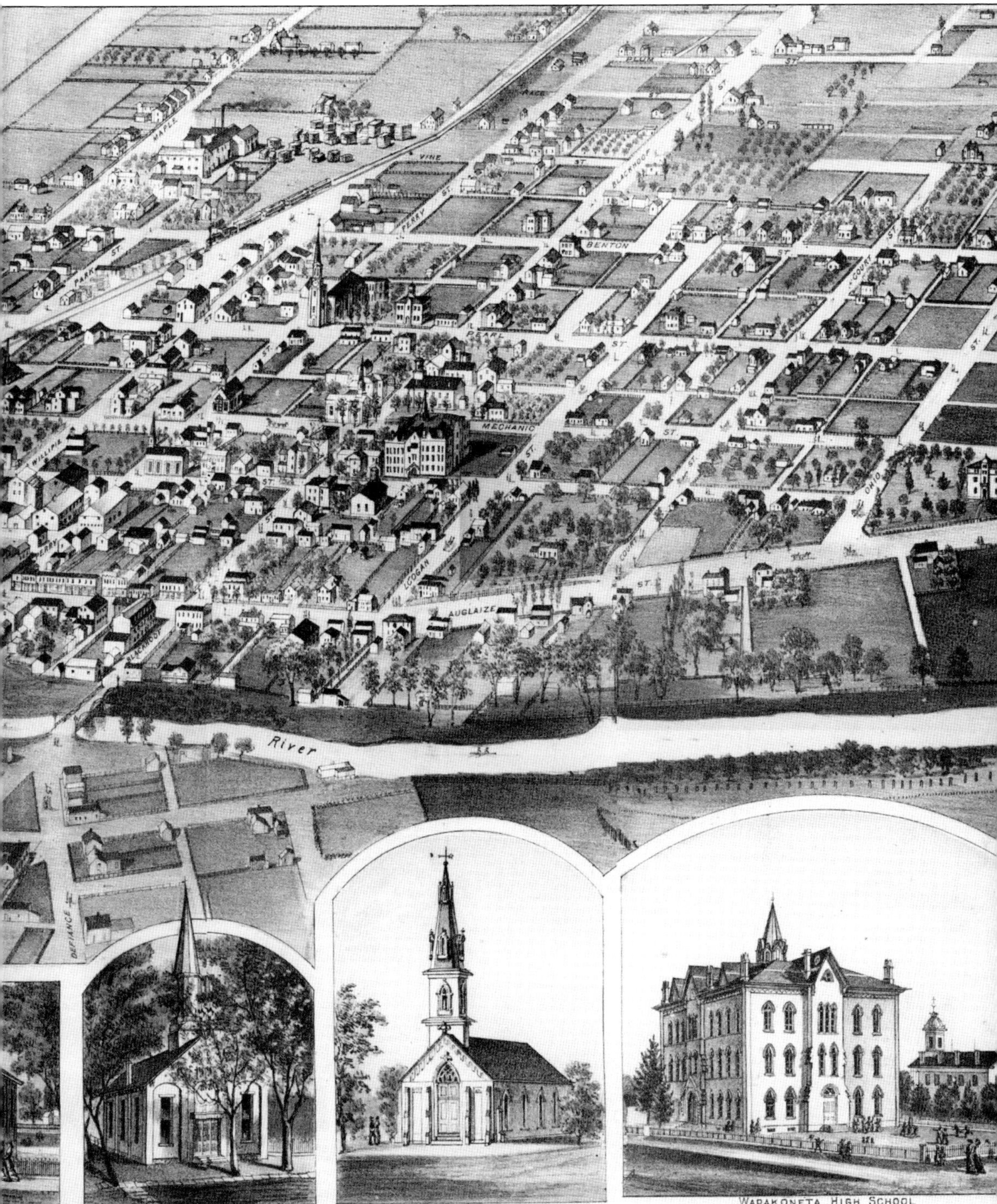

Progress Administration (WPA) project in the 1930s and the curve was made sharper. Auglaize Street is the wide street in the forefront, where it still remains the central artery. An enlarged copy of this drawing is on display at the Wapakoneta Area Chamber of Commerce offices. (Courtesy of Auglaize County Engineer.)

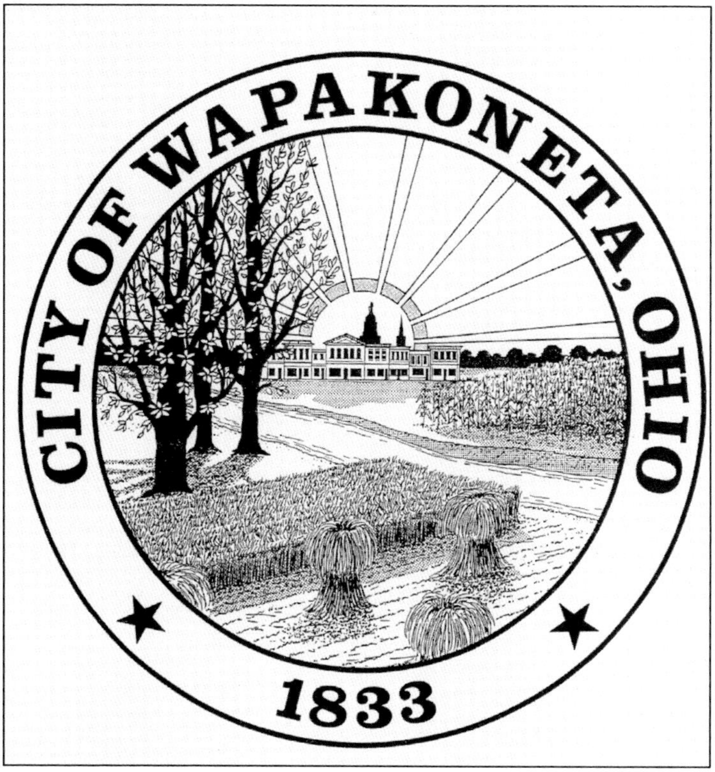

The Wapakoneta city seal, adopted on May 18, 1994, was originally designed as a high school art project by Brandi Geyer. Geyer imagined what her family may have seen in the early 1800s with woods to the north and farmland to the south of the city proper. The seal depicts the interdependence of agriculture and business to the growth and prosperity of the city. (Courtesy of City of Wapakoneta.)

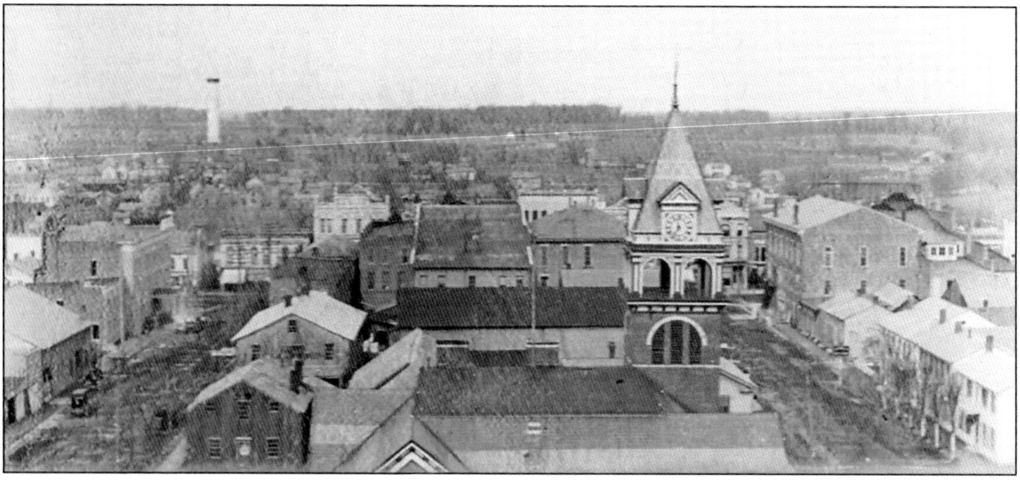

This aerial view of downtown Wapakoneta was taken from the courthouse tower. The clock tower on the City Building was intact in its original form at the time this photograph was taken. The Henry House Hotel can be seen in the lower right, and at the left, on Perry Street, is the livery stable behind the 1898 Hotel Steinberg. (Courtesy of Wapakoneta City Fire Department.)

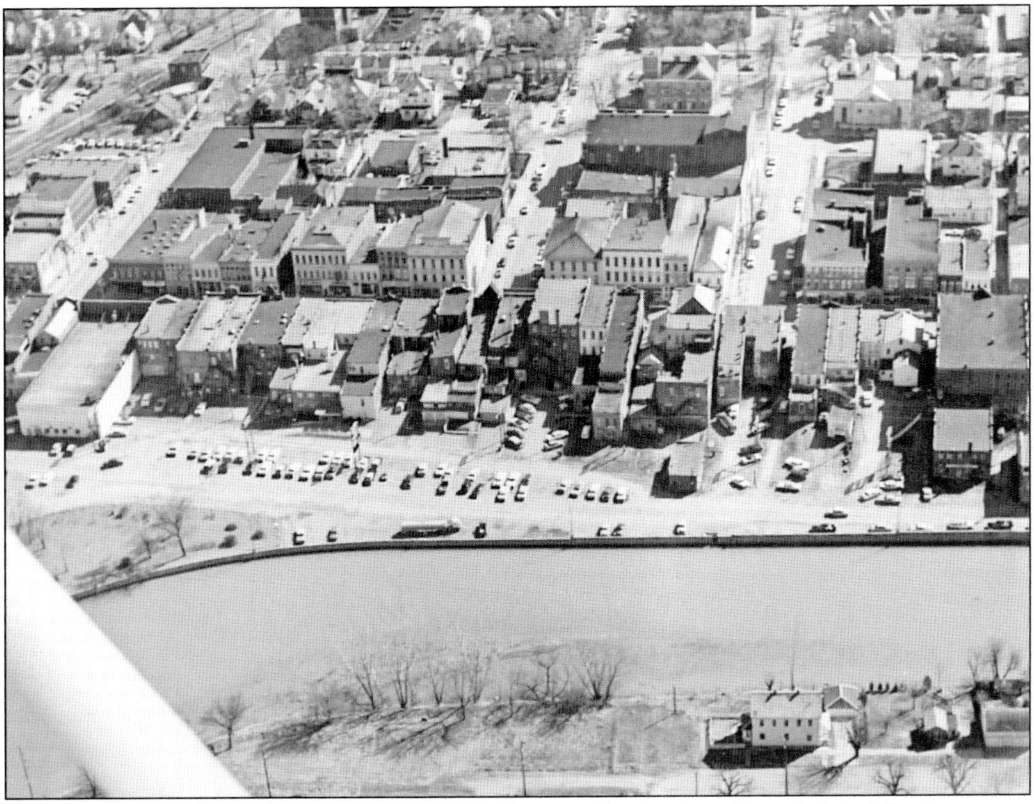

This aerial view of Wapakoneta, taken in 1961, features the Auglaize River behind the downtown business district. The trees in Heritage Park on the south shore of the river bend are small compared to the large trees enjoyed by Wapakoneta residents today. (Courtesy of Vernon E. Doenges.)

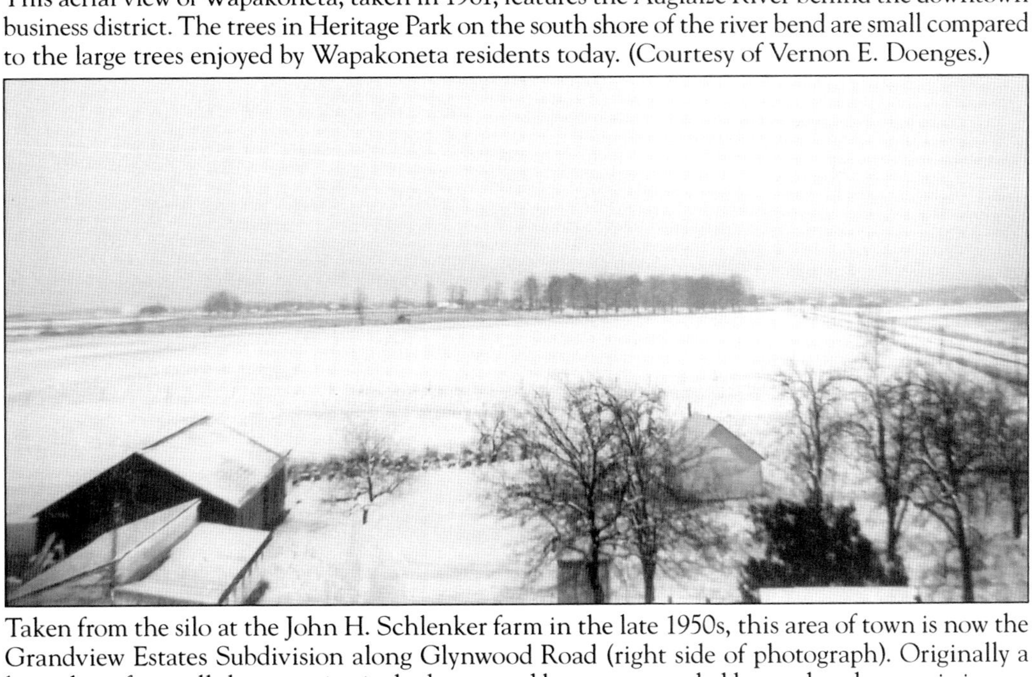

Taken from the silo at the John H. Schlenker farm in the late 1950s, this area of town is now the Grandview Estates Subdivision along Glynwood Road (right side of photograph). Originally a large dairy farm, all that remains is the house and barn, surrounded by modern homes sitting on what were previously rolling pastures. (Courtesy of Peggy Schlenker Prater.)

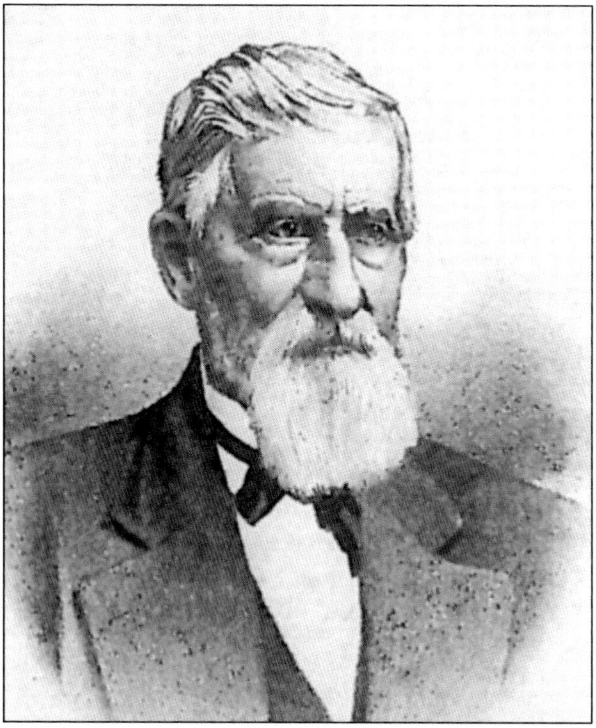

Dr. George Washington Holbrook, born in 1808 in Palmyra, New York, arrived in Wapakoneta to practice medicine in 1832. The first person to suggest the idea of Auglaize County, he developed a county plan in 1846. Using his own resources, Holbrook lobbied the Ohio legislature until the county was established in 1848. In the 1850s, he was a force of persuasion, placing Wapakoneta on the route of the Dayton and Michigan Railroad's extension northward.

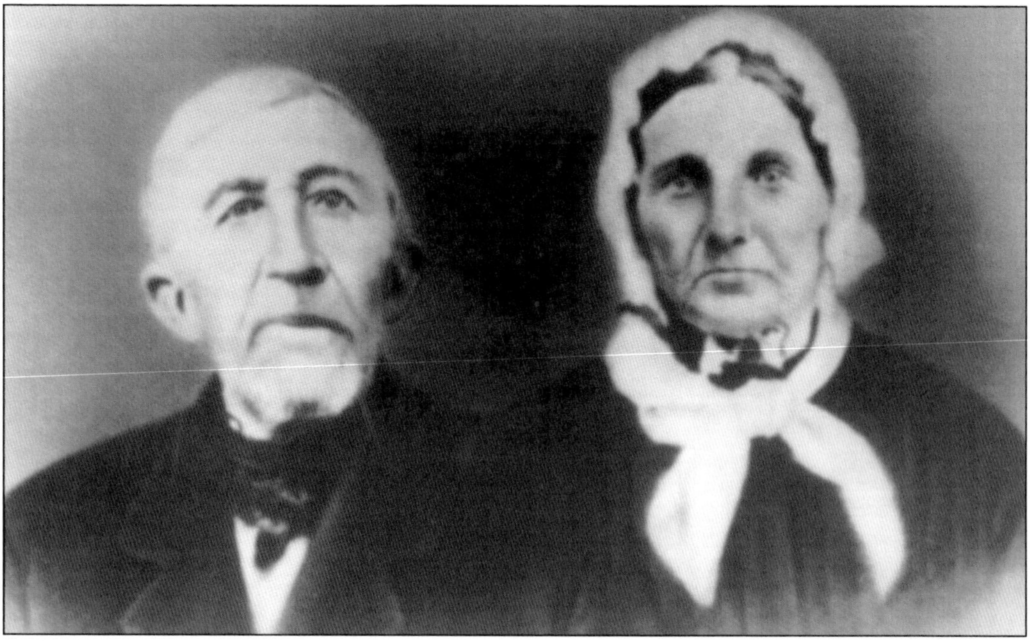

Ludwig and Christina Munch Helmlinger came from the Alsace-Lorraine area of Germany, settling near Wapakoneta about 1834, an experience typical of many Wapakoneta pioneers. Immigrants to the area were typically farmers and tradespeople, many possessing skills like wagon making. The children and grandchildren of the early pioneers developed an entrepreneurial spirit, becoming successful farmers and business owners and thus pushing the city into the industrial age. (Courtesy of Linda Knerr.)

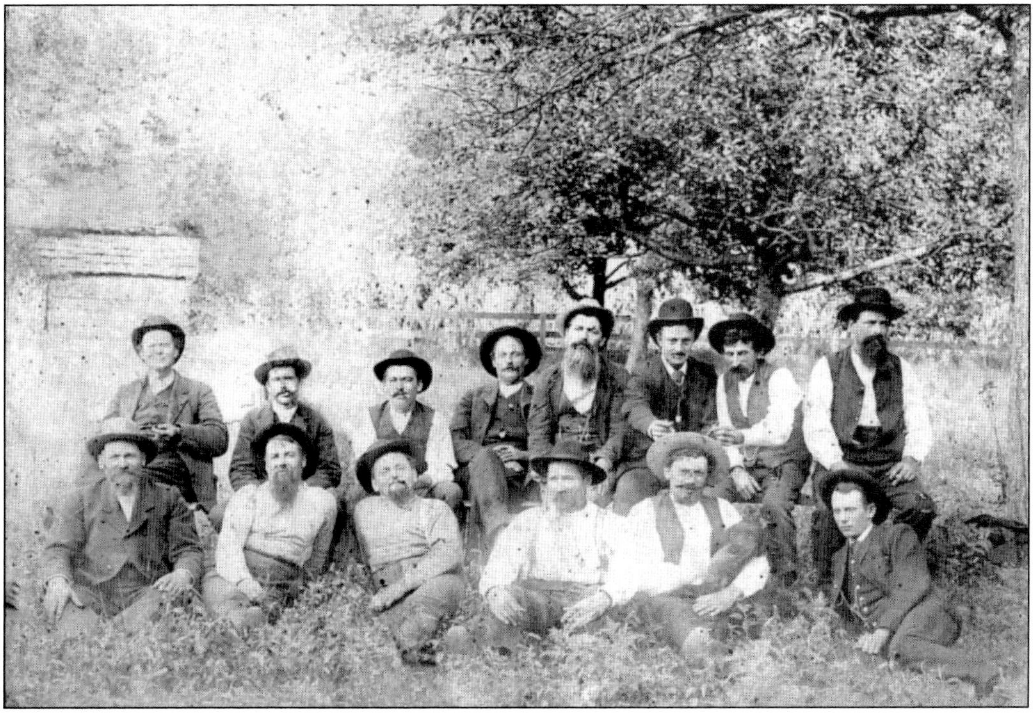

A large copy of this "Old Pioneers about 1875" photograph is housed in the Auglaize County Historical Society Museum. Although the men are not identified, the playful spirit of the cigar smokers helps us identify them with people we know today. (Courtesy of Vernon E. Doenges.)

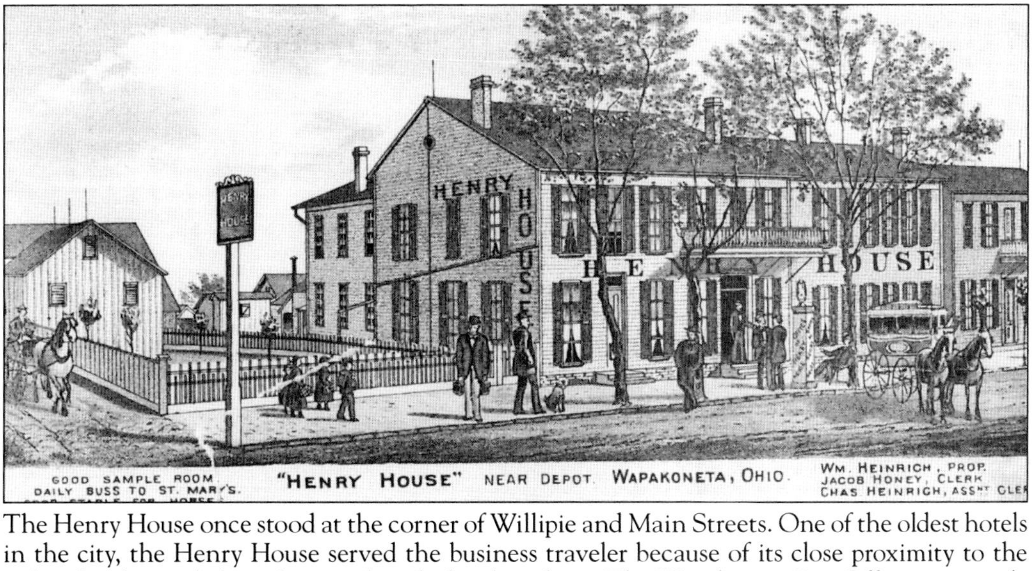

The Henry House once stood at the corner of Willipie and Main Streets. One of the oldest hotels in the city, the Henry House served the business traveler because of its close proximity to the railroad and provided a gathering place for local residents. The Wapakoneta Post Office is currently located on this site. This image was first printed in the *1880 Atlas of Auglaize County*.

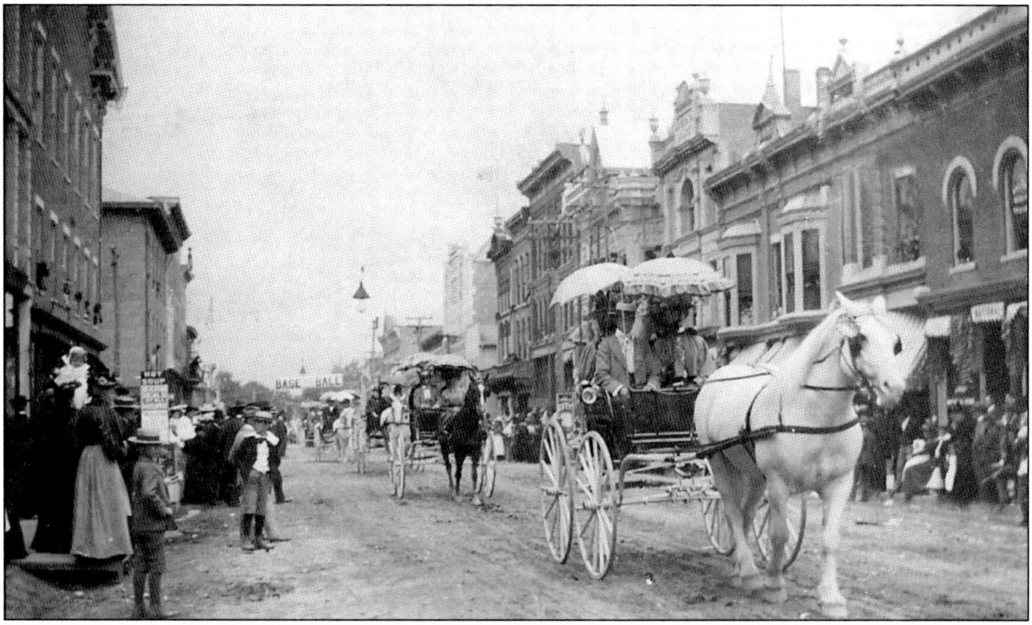

A parade on Auglaize Street at the turn of the 20th century shows a completed downtown business district in the background. Many buildings still retain the original architecture on the upper floors and are included in the National Historic Commercial District of downtown Wapakoneta. Note the photograph was taken before the street was bricked, and the baseball banner is reminiscent of the many banners we see across Auglaize Street today.

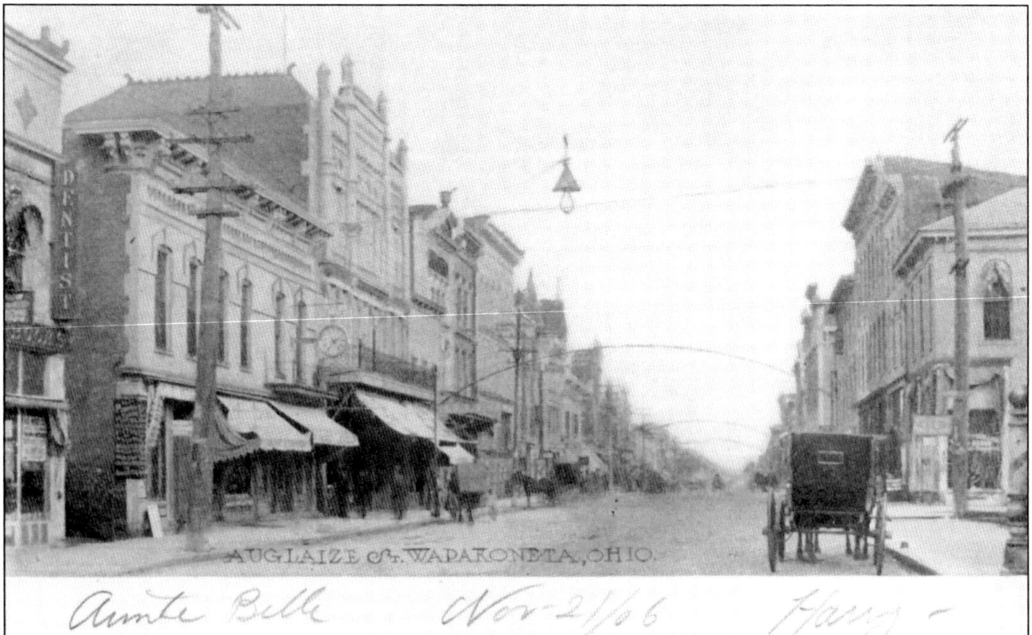

Auglaize Street in 1906 was a busy thoroughfare. The barber pole at the right was located in front of the barbershop at the Hotel Steinberg. This view, facing east, indicates the early establishment of the completed business district we now enjoy. You can even imagine the twitter of chimney swift (birds), which glide overhead in the downtown area during the summer months.

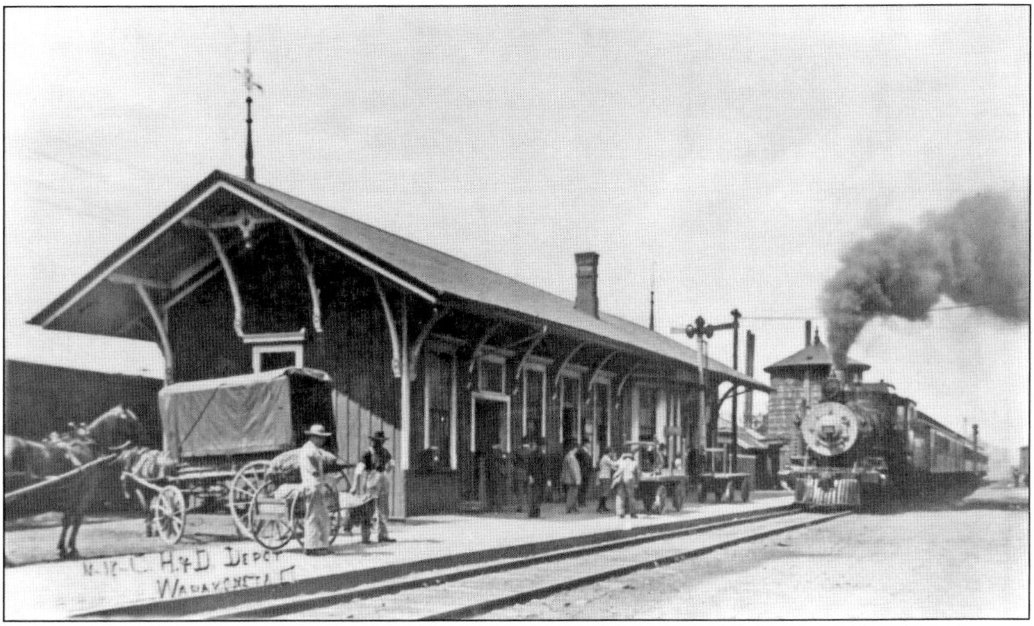

The Dayton and Michigan Railroad, established in 1858, connected Dayton and Toledo by way of Sidney, Wapakoneta, and Lima, giving the region access to a Lake Erie port. In 1863, this line became part of the Cincinnati, Hamilton, and Dayton Railway (CH&D). The depot pictured above was replaced by a brick structure when it became the Baltimore and Ohio Railroad (B&O). (Courtesy of Vernon E. Doenges.)

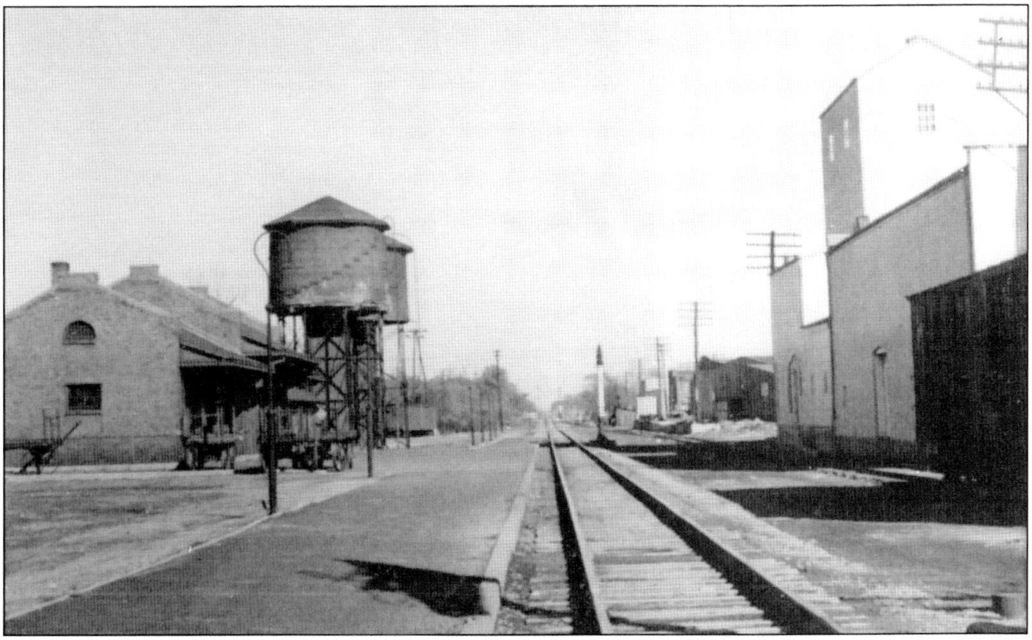

The brick structure at the left is the B&O passenger depot that replaced the CH&D about 1917. The water towers were removed when diesel replaced steam locomotives. The structure originally had a lobby, baggage room, and ticket office. This view of the depot is facing northeast towards Cridersville and Lima. (Courtesy of Vernon E. Doenges.)

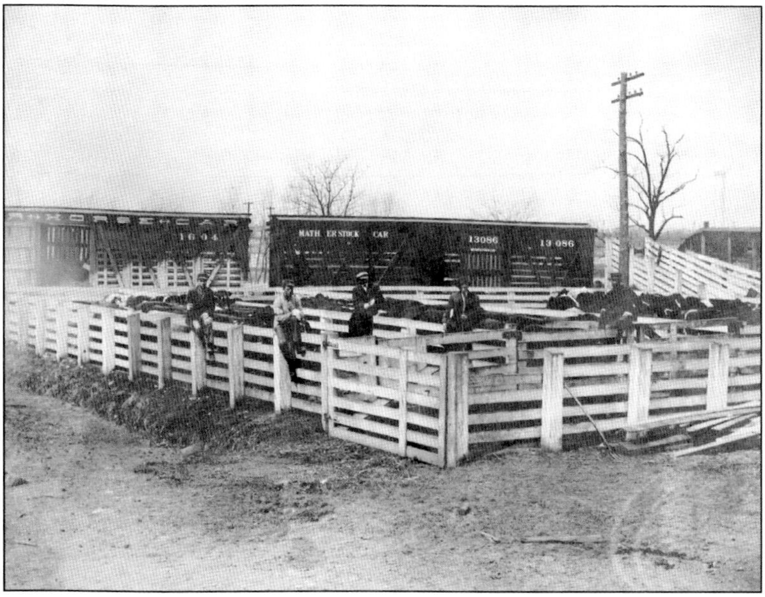

The livestock holding pens on the east side of the B&O railroad and north of Auglaize Street provide a glimpse of how this small area was used to load rail cars. The water standpipe north of the city is barely visible at the upper right. (Courtesy of Jim Bowsher.)

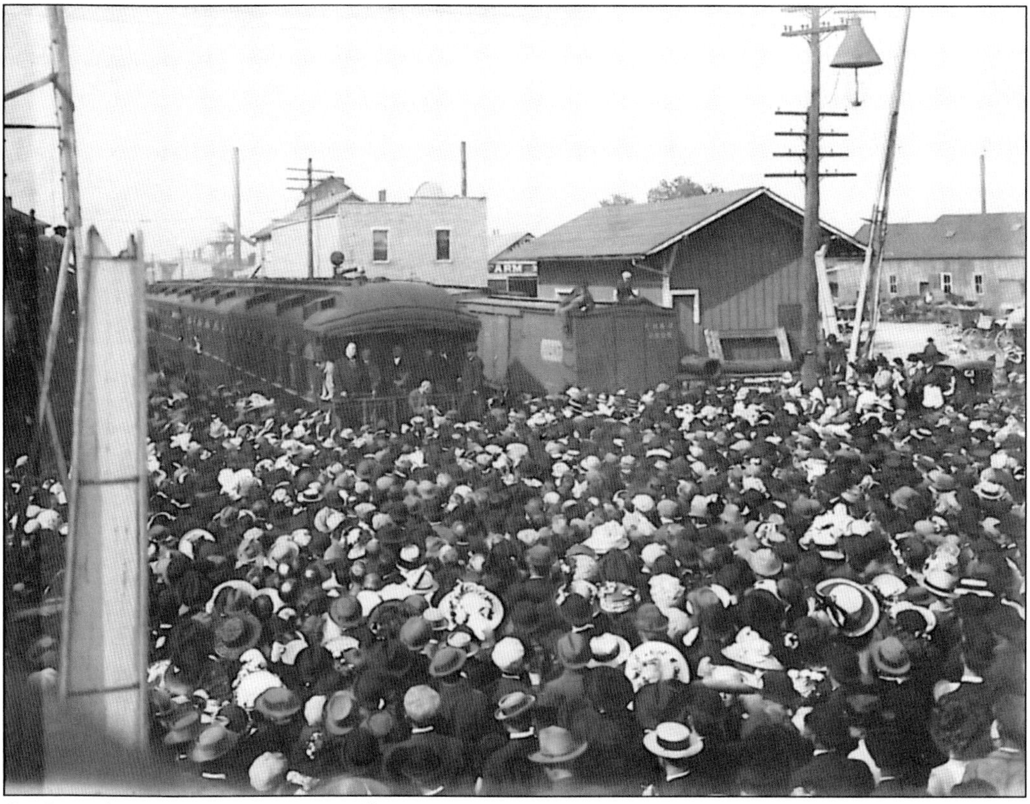

On Saturday, May 18, 1912, Pres. William Howard Taft became the first president to visit Wapakoneta. This election year campaign produced exciting events for residents when William Jennings Bryan spoke on the steps of the courthouse on May 7 and former president Theodore Roosevelt visited May 16. The battle between Taft and Roosevelt split the Republican party, allowing Democrat Woodrow Wilson the presidential victory that fall. (Courtesy of Combs Printing.)

A railway accident on the B&O in October 1950 shows a northbound 1926 freight steam locomotive lying on its side at the intersection of the two rail lines that passed through the city. Note the crossing tower located at the New York Central (T&OC) adjacent to Willipie Street. In 1957, the last steam locomotives operated through Wapakoneta connecting Cincinnati, Toledo, and Detroit. (Courtesy of Loren Stemen.)

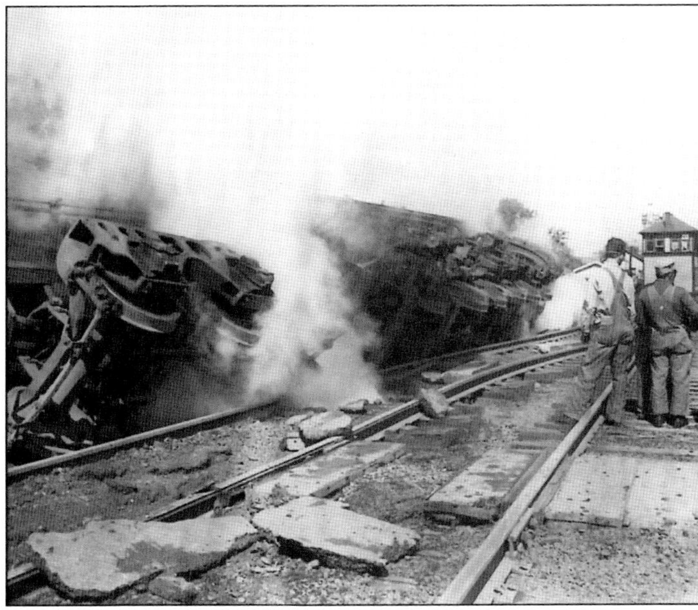

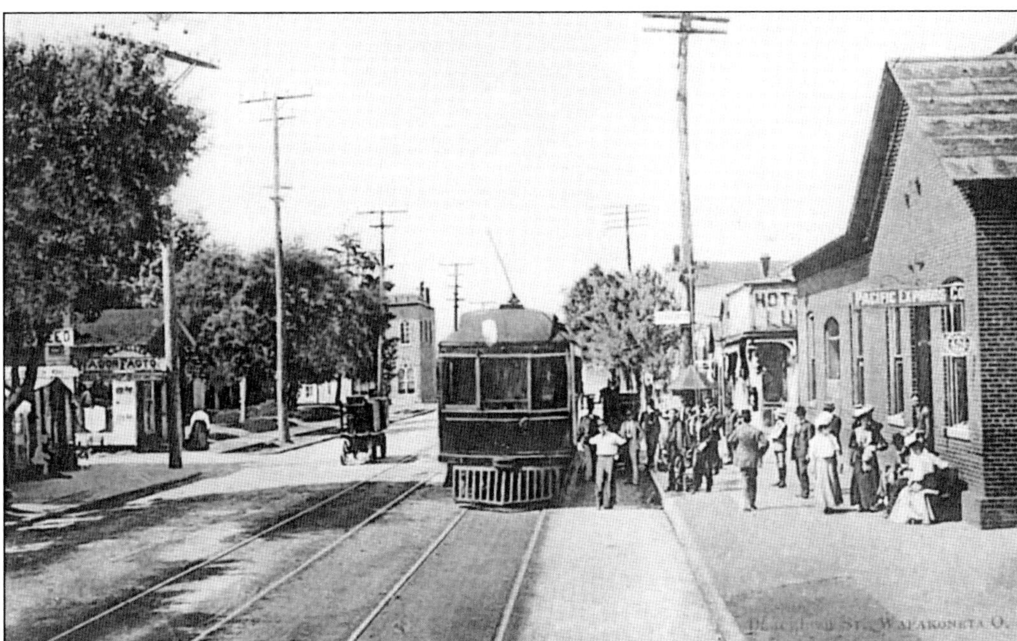

The electrically powered trains that connected communities in the early 1900s, known as the interurban railway, maintained a division headquarters in Wapakoneta. This Blackhoof Street scene was only one of many lines crisscrossing Ohio by World War I, when 2,798 miles of train track was recorded. The advent of automobiles for the average family made the interurban lines nearly obsolete, and the Great Depression stopped the remaining lines by 1932. (Courtesy of Vernon E. Doenges.)

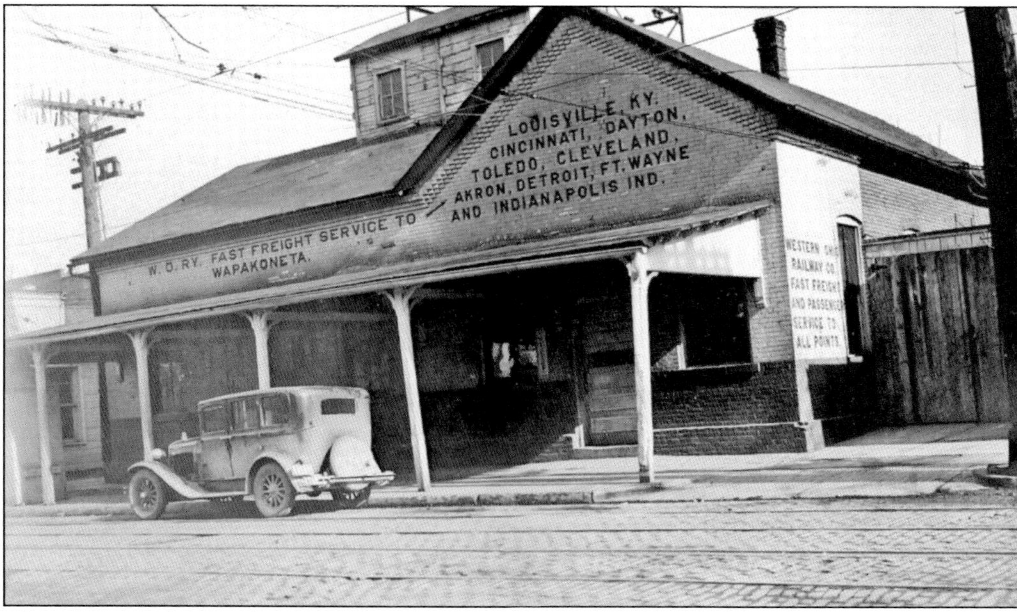

The Western Ohio Railway Depot on South Blackhoof Street was a hub of activity for passengers and freight. This 1930s photograph features a covered passenger area. The interurban was located in Wapakoneta 27 years before being abandoned. The last car made a run to Lima on January 16, 1932, piloted by "Chip" Koehl, who had been a motorman on the line throughout its history. (Courtesy of Allen County Historical Society.)

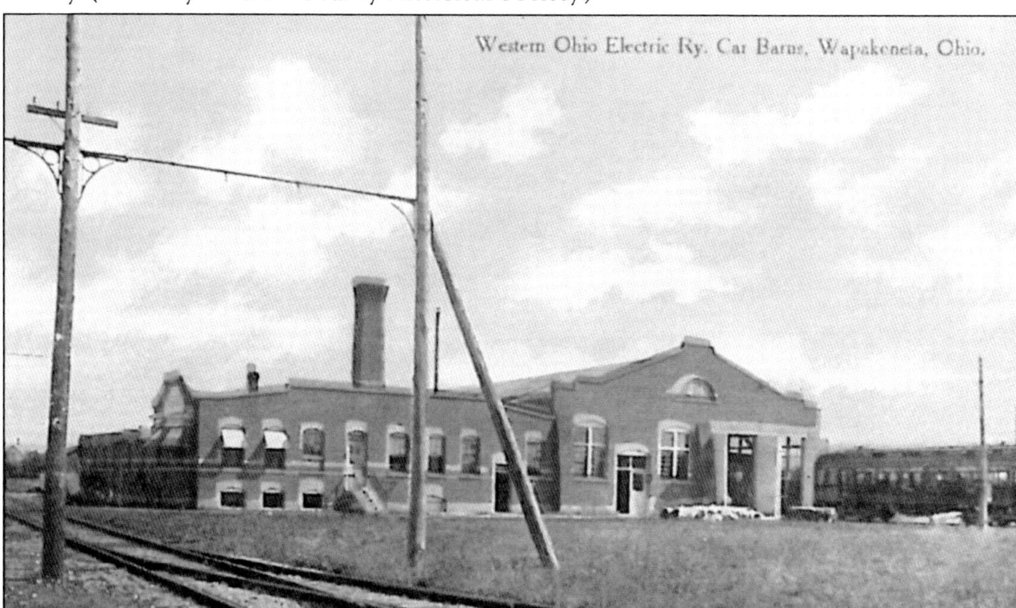

The car barns for the Western Ohio Railway were acquired by the Ohio State Highway Department after the railway was abandoned in 1932. Overhead trolley lines, rails, and equipment were removed by CWA workers in 1934 when the last of the rails were pulled from the brick pavement on Blackhoof Street. In 2003 the buildings were transferred to the Auglaize County Highway Department. (Courtesy of Vernon E. Doenges.)

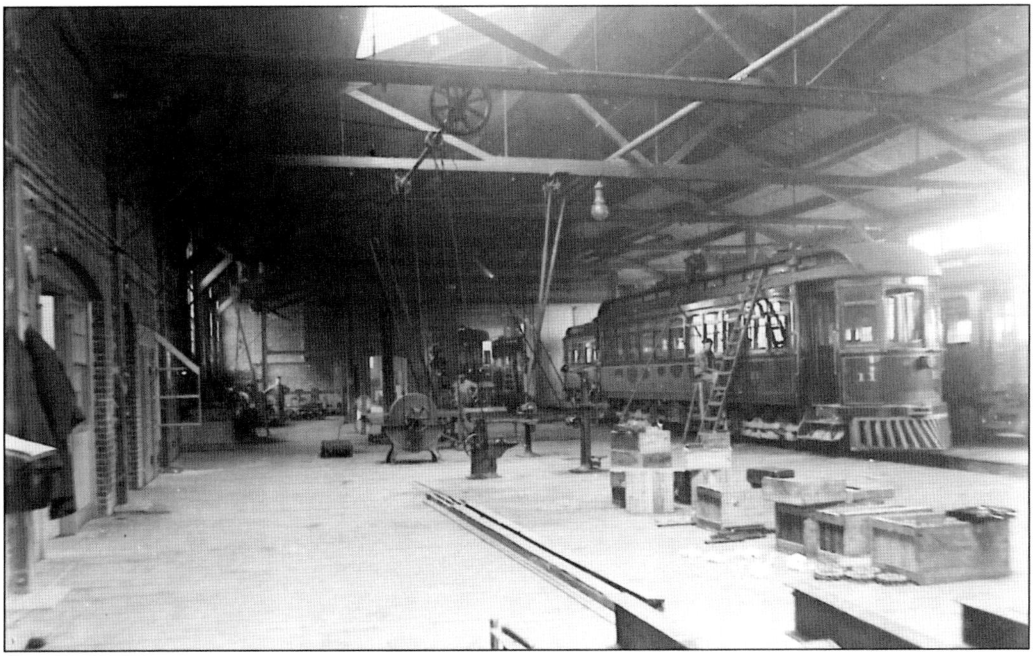

The Wapakoneta car barns of the Western Ohio Railway housed the maintenance equipment and were used to build and repair freight cars throughout the railway history. This photograph inside the car barns gives a glimpse of the magnificent design of the railway cars. Note the overhead belt drive system used to power the shop machinery. (Courtesy of Combs Printing.)

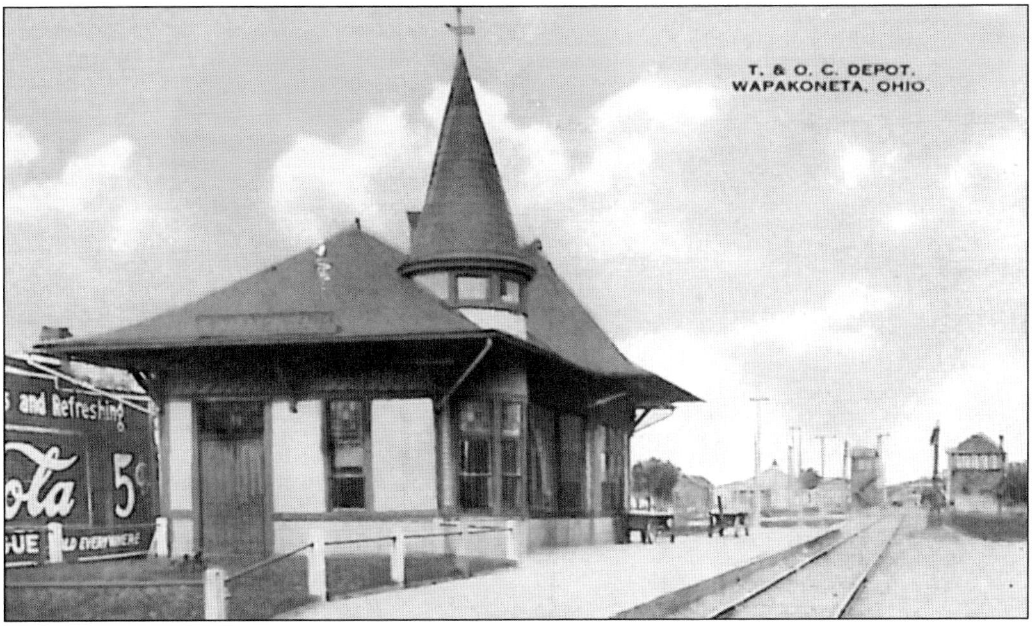

This passenger depot in Wapakoneta was built for the Columbus and Northwestern Railroad traveling from Columbus through Wapakoneta and on to St. Louis. By World War I, it became the Toledo and Ohio Central (T&OC.) The crossing tower (right at tracks) protected the trains at the north-south intersection of the CH&D (later known as the B&O) railroad, which carried more traffic. (Courtesy of Vernon E. Doenges.)

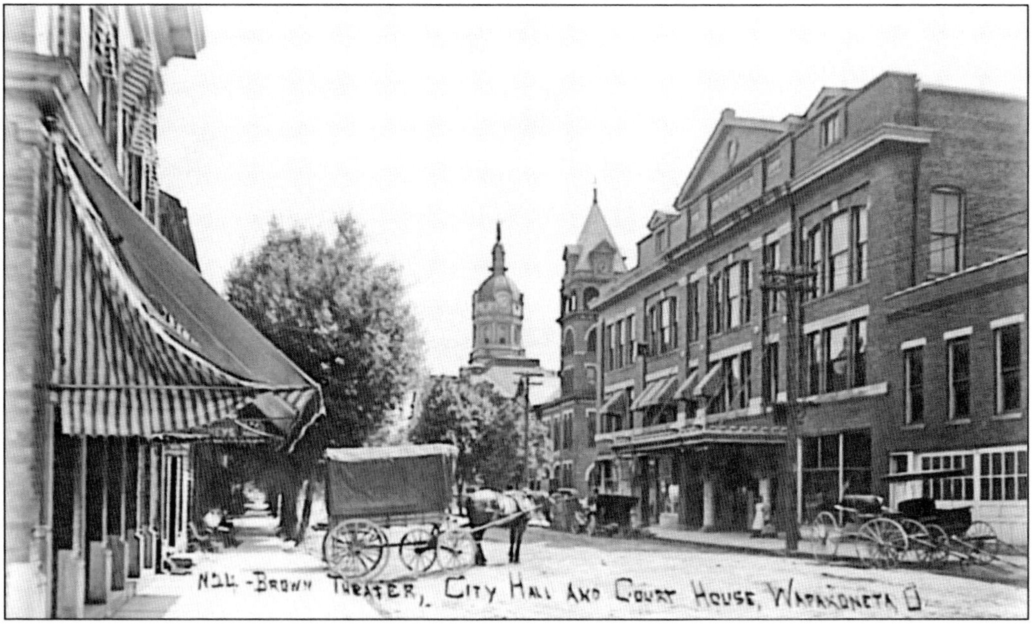

In 1910, Willipie Street looked remarkably as it does today. Builder Michael Brown dedicated the 1904 Brown Theater building to the citizens of Wapakoneta. The ground level housed the post office with business offices and lodge rooms above. Early theater advertisements touted a good view from any of the 1050 seats, electric lights for stage enhancements, and a curtain containing asbestos for the safety of the patrons.

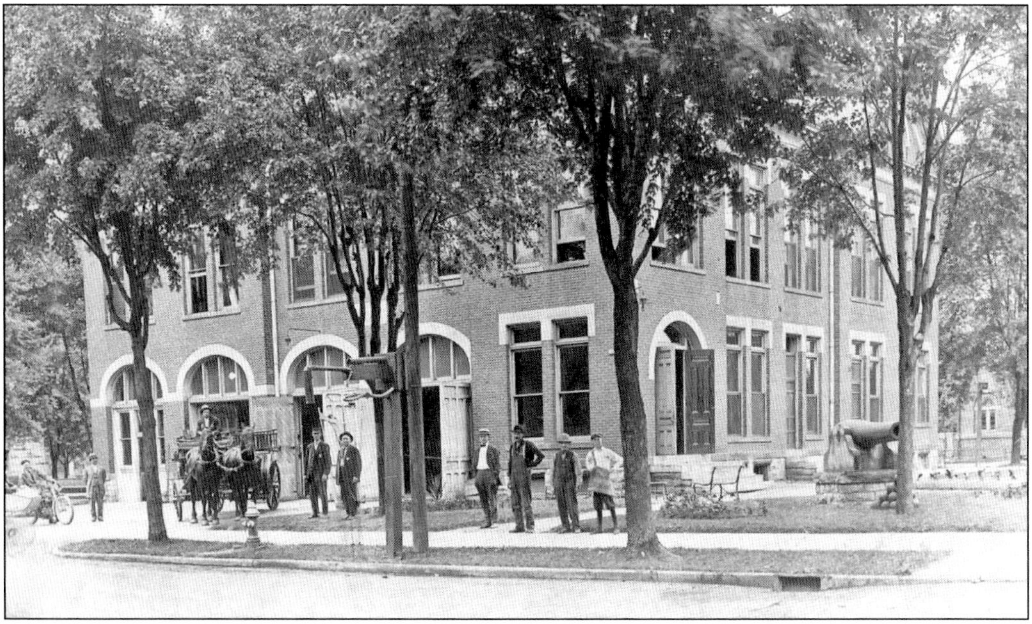

The Wapakoneta City Building continues to house the local fire department at 103 Willipie Street. Although a portion of the tower has been removed and the cannon was donated to a World War II scrap drive, the exterior structure otherwise remains unaltered. One of the most picturesque buildings of the city, the Romanesque Revival architecture is exemplified by the round, arched windows. (Courtesy of Wapakoneta City Fire Department.)

The first motorized fire apparatus of the Wapakoneta Fire Department was used until 1968. The 1917 American LaFrance engine had a tiller at the back to help the steel-wheeled truck negotiate turns since the front and back wheels worked independently. (Courtesy of Wapakoneta City Fire Department.)

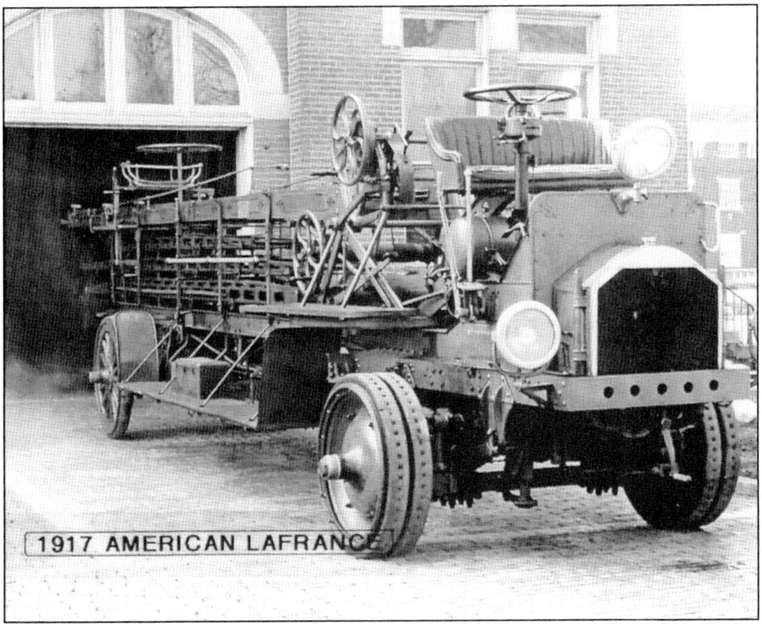

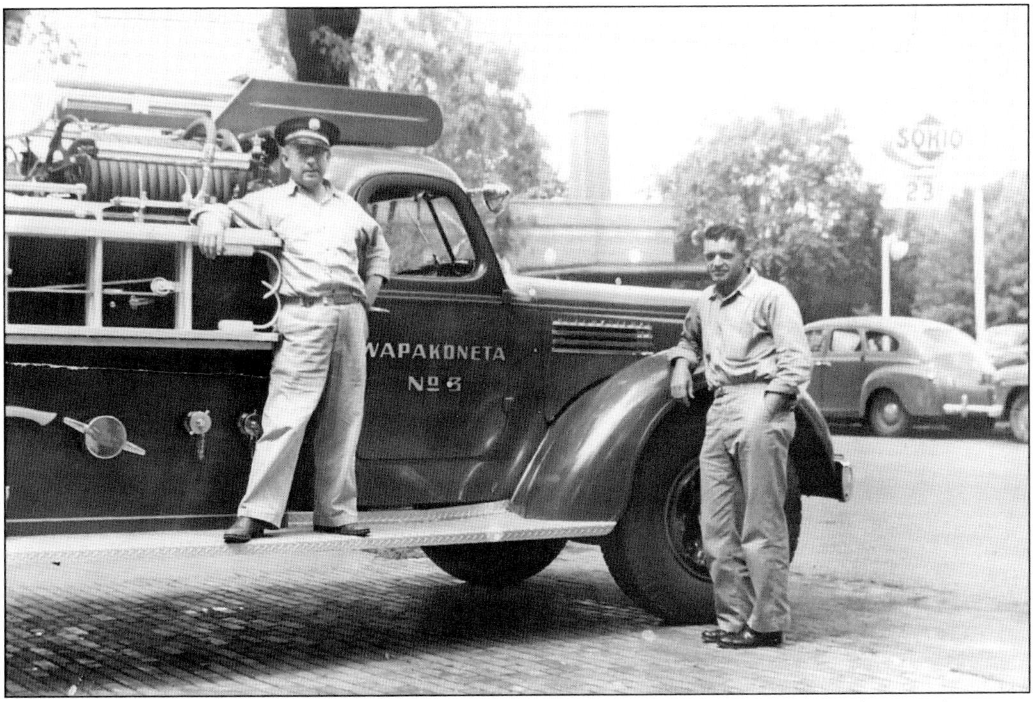

Sam Foos, fire chief, stands on the running board of this Wapakoneta International engine/pumper. Taken about 1952, fireman Alfred (Bud) Zink leans against the front fender. Zink, who served as assistant fire chief and jack-of-all-trades, was instrumental in modernizing the City Building interior. The Sohio Service Station across the street from the City Building was removed in the 1970s. (Courtesy of Wapakoneta City Fire Department.)

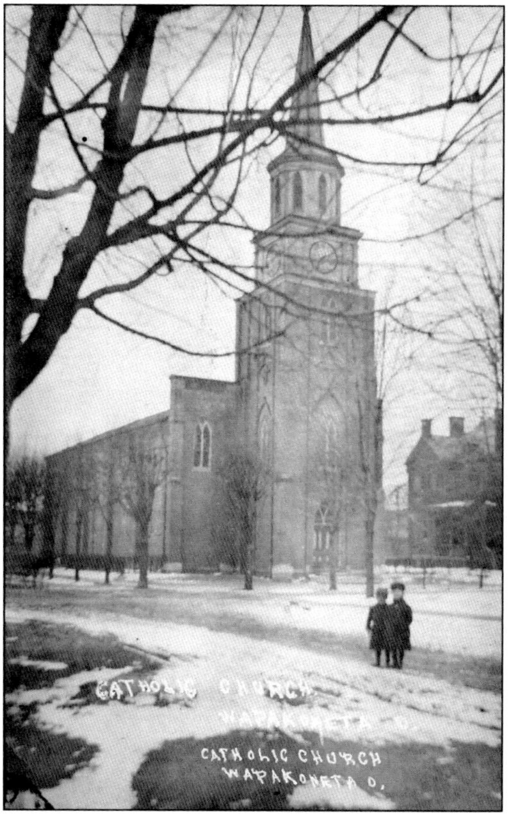

The Catholic church, dedicated to St. Joseph, was originally erected in 1858 after many years of planning. A brick school near the church was built in 1869 for a sum of $4,000. The school was replaced in 1899 at the same location, which remains in use today as a parish services building. (Courtesy of Scott Knerr.)

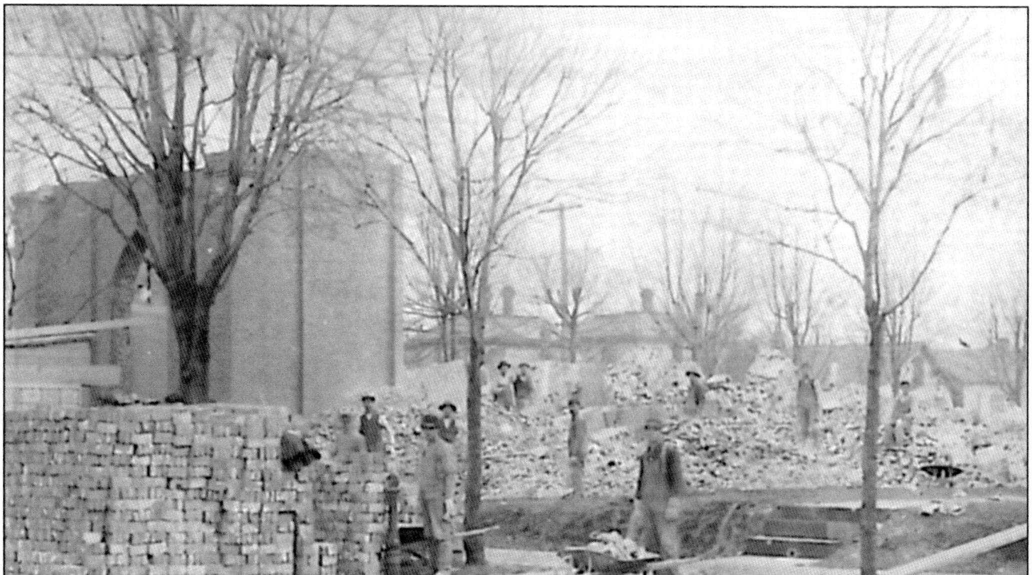

As the St. Joseph's congregation grew, the church became too small for the parish and a larger church with two steeples was built in 1911 at the same location. As the original brick parish church was torn down to make way for a larger church, laborers carried the bricks by hand as the old church was dismantled. (Courtesy of Vernon E. Doenges.)

One of the oldest churches in the city, The First Presbyterian Church was built in 1862. Located at 206 West Main Street, the building is now the location of the Wapakoneta Museum of the Auglaize County Historical Society. Architecturally significant, this Greek Revival building is only one of many stops on a popular Wapakoneta city self-guided walking tour. (Courtesy of Auglaize County Historical Society.)

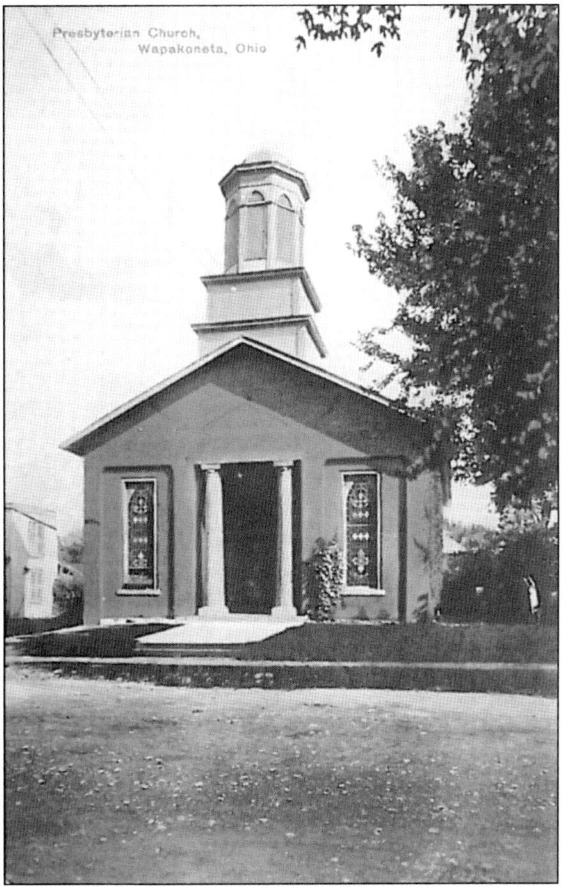

Organized as a congregation in 1833, the Methodist church in Wapakoneta served as a school and courthouse until the Auglaize County Courthouse was built in 1850. Built on the same lot, the 1906 building (pictured below) served the congregation until 1958, when a new church was built on Glynwood Road. The 1959 Auglaize County Public Library was built on this site at Perry and Mechanic Streets. (Courtesy of Scott Knerr.)

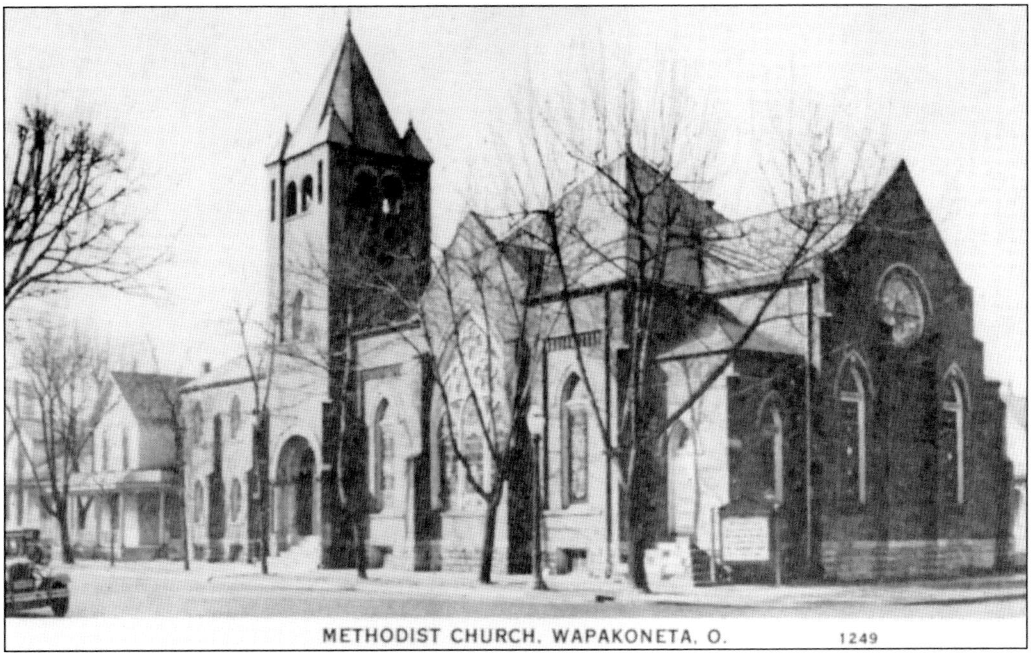

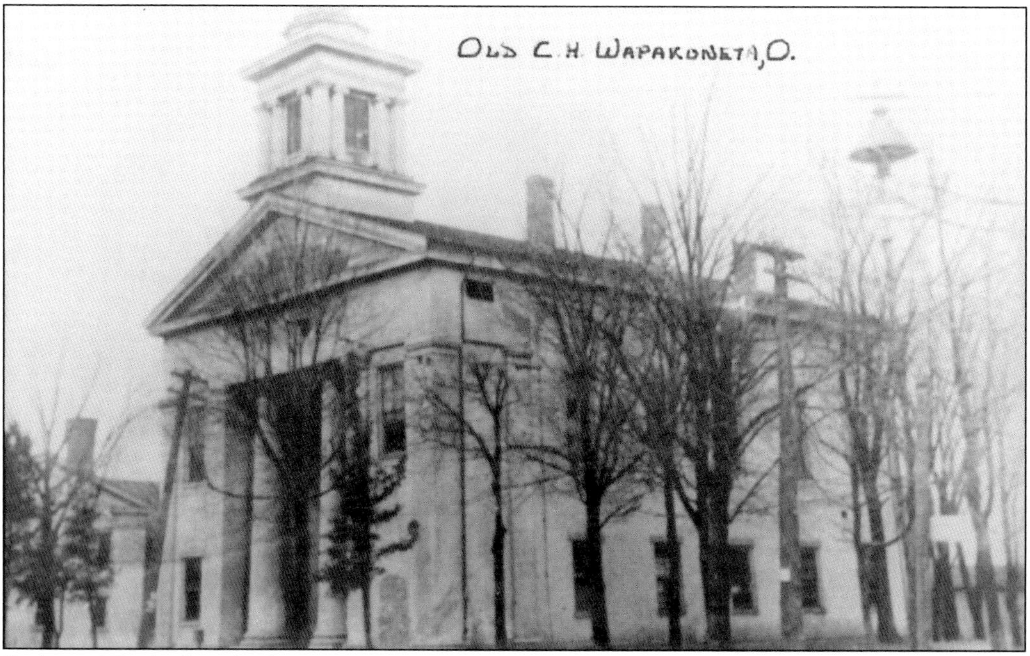

Built in 1850, the first Auglaize County Courthouse was also the first public building in Wapakoneta. The Greek Revival building, located in the 200 block of South Blackhoof Street, was erected for a cost of $11,499 by builders James Elliott and Sobert Scott. This courthouse was used for all county offices until a new, larger, and more modern courthouse was completed in 1894. (Courtesy of Scott Knerr.)

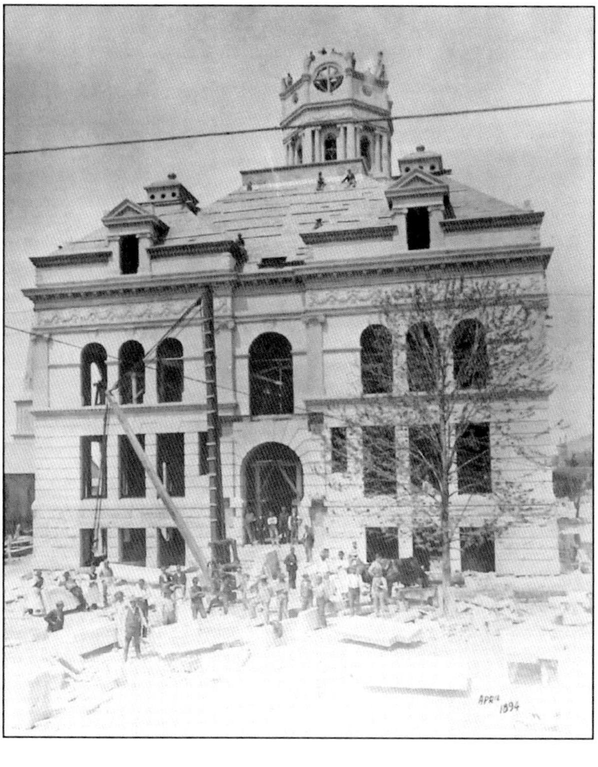

Built of Berea sandstone, the current Auglaize County Courthouse was completed in 1894. Some workers earned $1.50 per day at the construction site with $259,481.00 being the completed building cost. This photograph shows the hard work in progress as the slabs of sandstone are hoisted into place. Note the workers on the roof and atop the uncompleted clock tower. (Courtesy of Auglaize County Commissioners.)

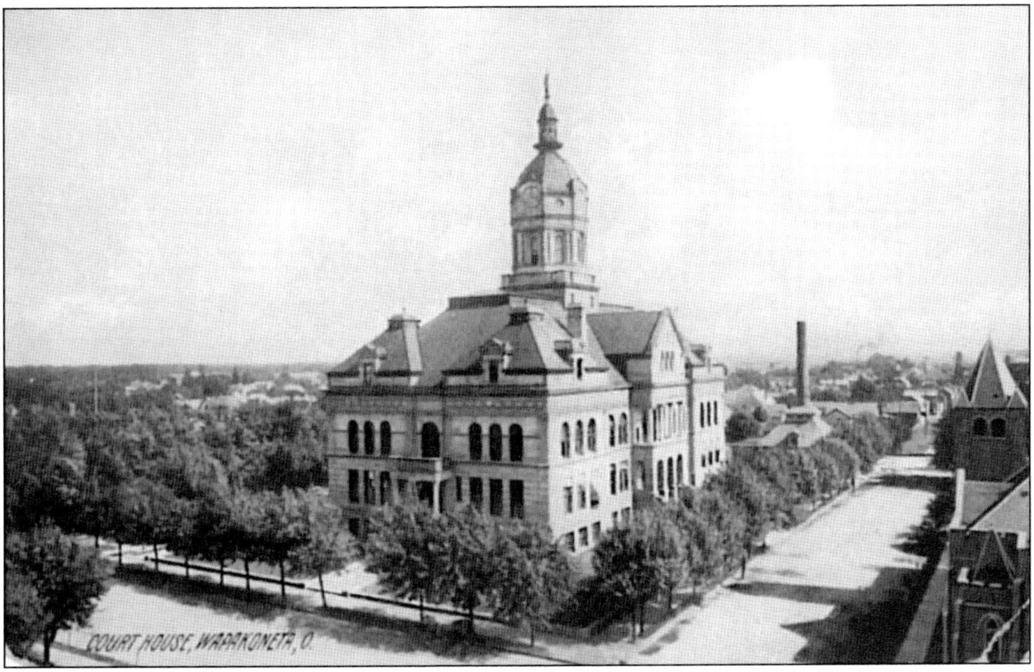

The Auglaize County Courthouse retains much of its original architectural detail, including stained glass skylights, decorative tile work, and furniture. The copper *Statue of Justice*, which originally stood atop the tower, is now on display in the lobby. (Courtesy of Vernon E. Doenges.)

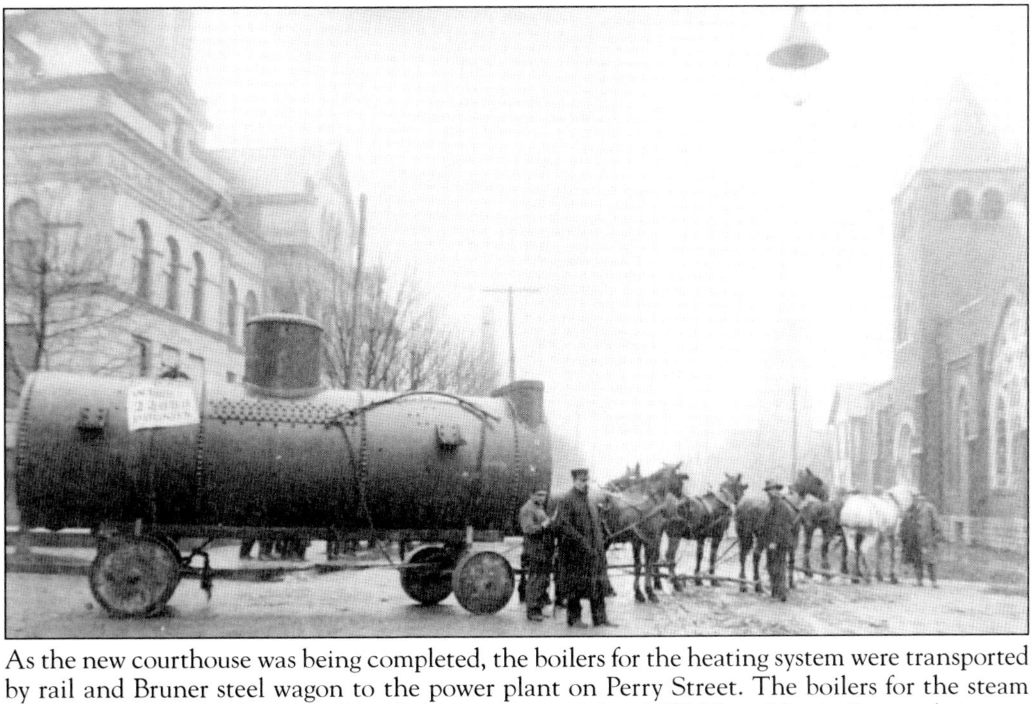

As the new courthouse was being completed, the boilers for the heating system were transported by rail and Bruner steel wagon to the power plant on Perry Street. The boilers for the steam heating system are still in use. From left to right are Adam J. Walther, Martin Bruner (patentee of the steel wagon made in Buckland), George Hager, and unidentified. (Courtesy of Auglaize County Commissioners.)

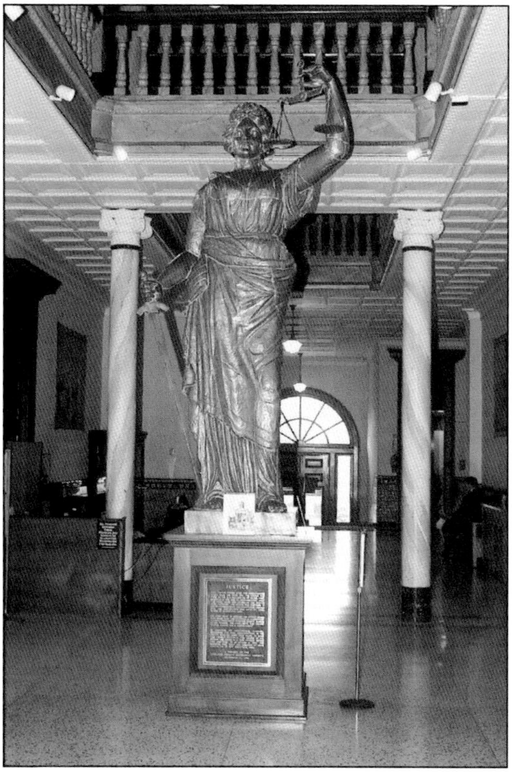

The *Statue of Justice*, once on the courthouse tower, was removed in the 1950s due to deterioration. The Auglaize County Historical Society restored the statue for the 1994 Courthouse Centennial Celebration. Local schoolchildren helped with the restoration by participating in a Copper Pennies For A Copper Lady campaign. (Photograph by and courtesy of John Zwez.)

The steps of the courthouse have been a popular place for photographs and gatherings from the beginning of its history. Note the stack of ladies bonnets and personal items at the sides. A lady at the right front holds a megaphone, possibly to organize the group for the photograph. (Courtesy of Combs Printing.)

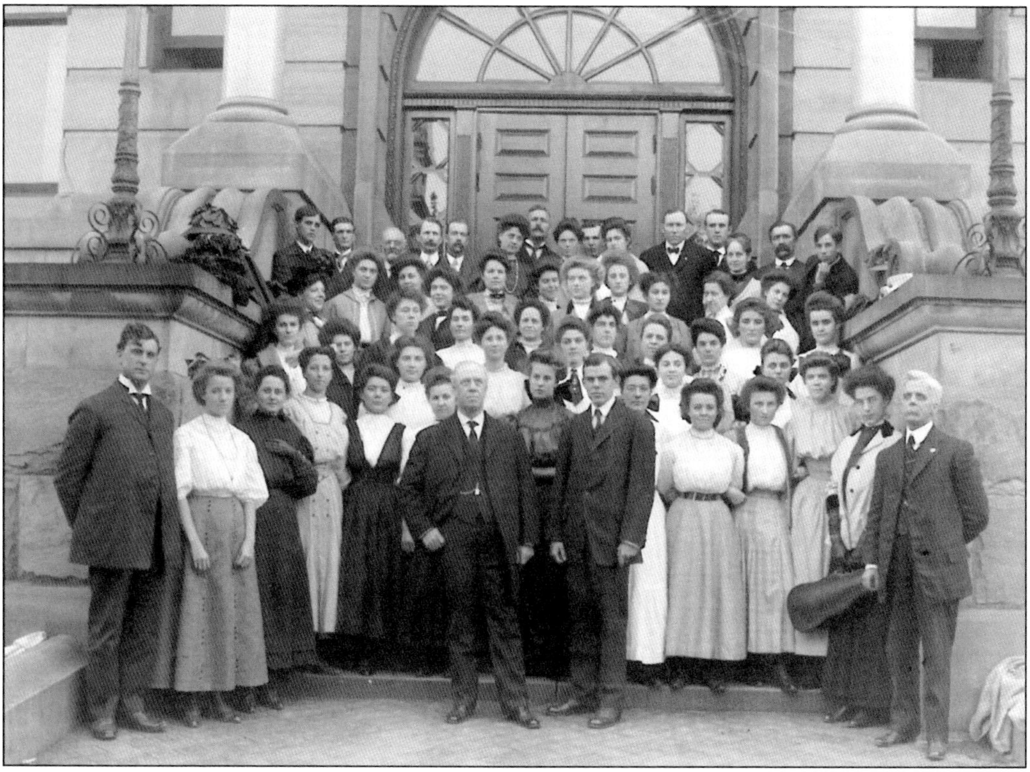

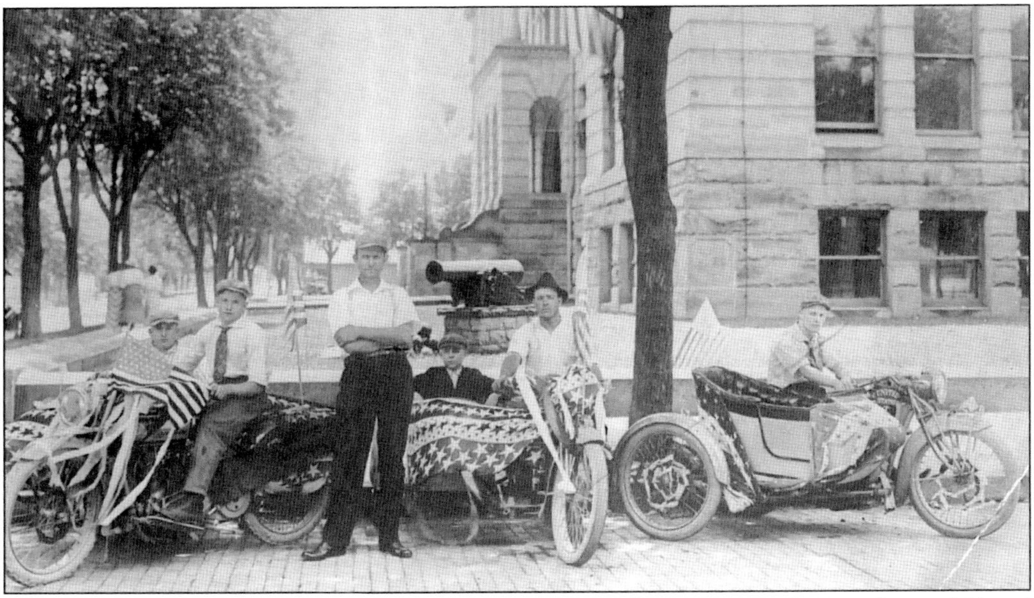

Parade routes often began at the courthouse area on Willipie Street. The parade would head north, turn left on Auglaize, and end at the fairgrounds or Greenlawn Cemetery, especially on Memorial Day. Photographed about 1912, members of the parade unit are, from left to right, Hubert Zimmerman in the sidecar, Bernie Oen, Ed Rehn standing, David Reynolds in the sidecar, Harley Moore, and Earl Orphal. (Courtesy of Vernon E. Doenges.)

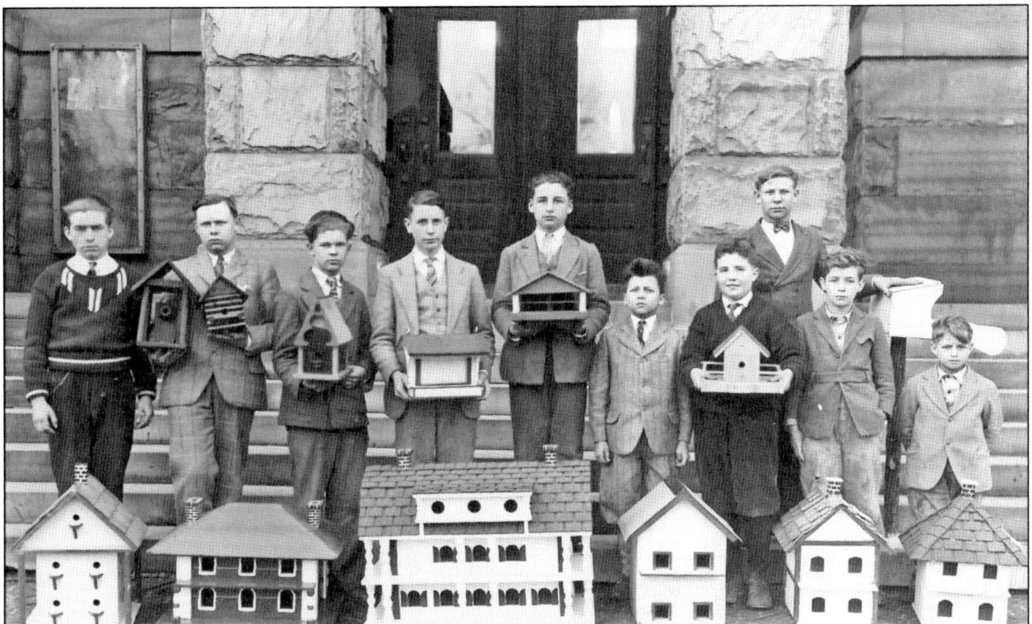

The Auglaize County Courthouse has been a landmark and source of pride, providing a beautiful backdrop to document local events. The March 1928 Kiwanis Club birdhouse contest for youngsters records the winners, from left to right, as Bud Heinl, John Churchill, Willy Diegel, John Waldman, Clarence Miller, Bill Disney, Ned Nichols, Kenneth Graf, and Eddie Graf. The gentleman in the back is unidentified. (Courtesy of Dan Graf.)

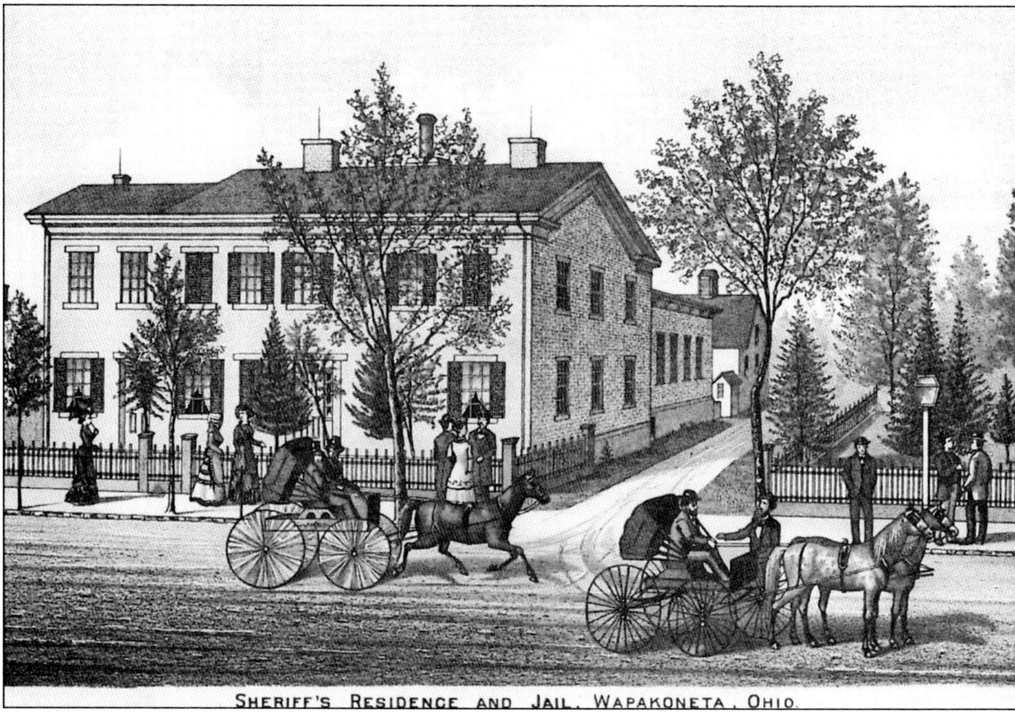

The Auglaize County Jail, pictured in the *1880 Atlas of Auglaize County*, was used for that purpose until 1998. Gaining the construction contract in 1850, Dr. G. W. Holbrook built the first county jail and sheriff's residence for $3,950. In 1873, it was reconstructed and improved for a cost of $15,098.

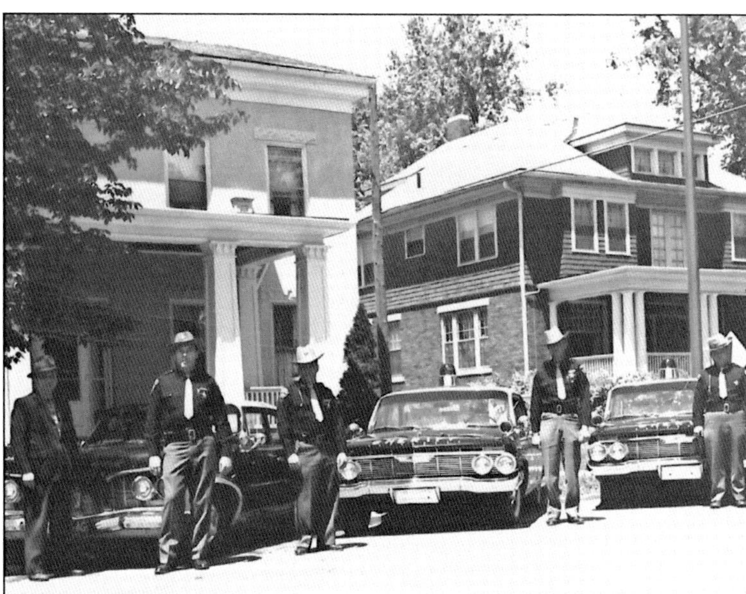

The 1961 Auglaize County Jail and Sheriff's Office (with a porch addition) is pictured at the left. This building was razed, and later the new Auglaize County Administration building was erected on the site. Deputies are, from left to right, Jim Goetz, Louis Bowersock, Jim Knoch, Al Bishop, and Larry Musser. (Courtesy of Vernon E. Doenges; photograph by William Rickert.)

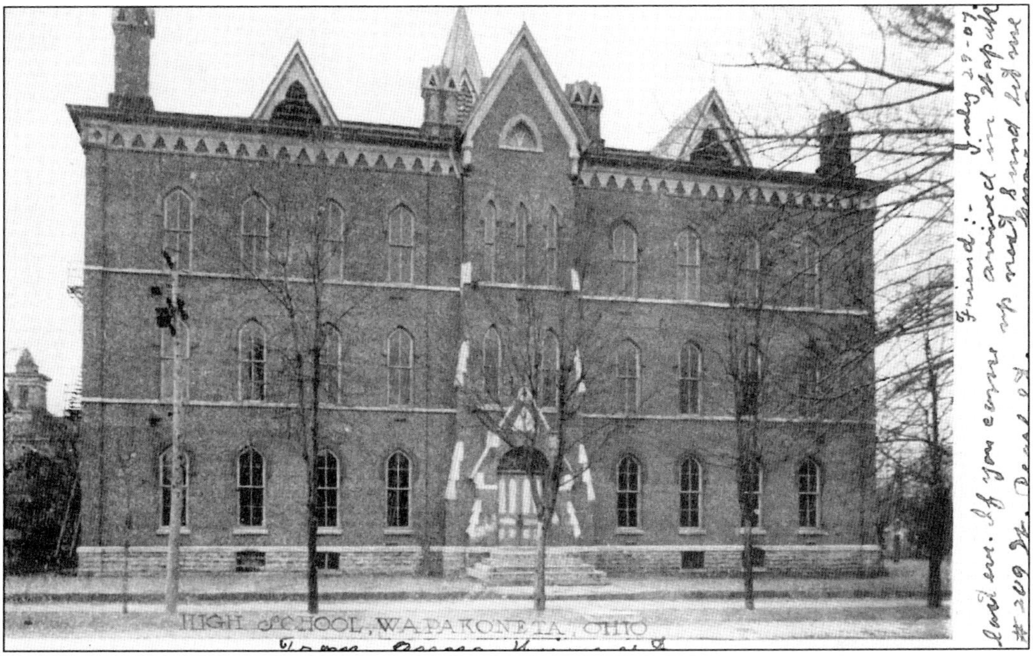

The Wapakoneta Union School was built in 1875 for $28,000 to serve 400 students. Later known as the Third Ward or Williamson School, it was named to honor Prof. C. W. Williamson—a well-respected, long-serving superintendent of Wapakoneta City Schools. The building became an elementary school when Blume High School was built in 1907. (Courtesy of Janet Schuler.)

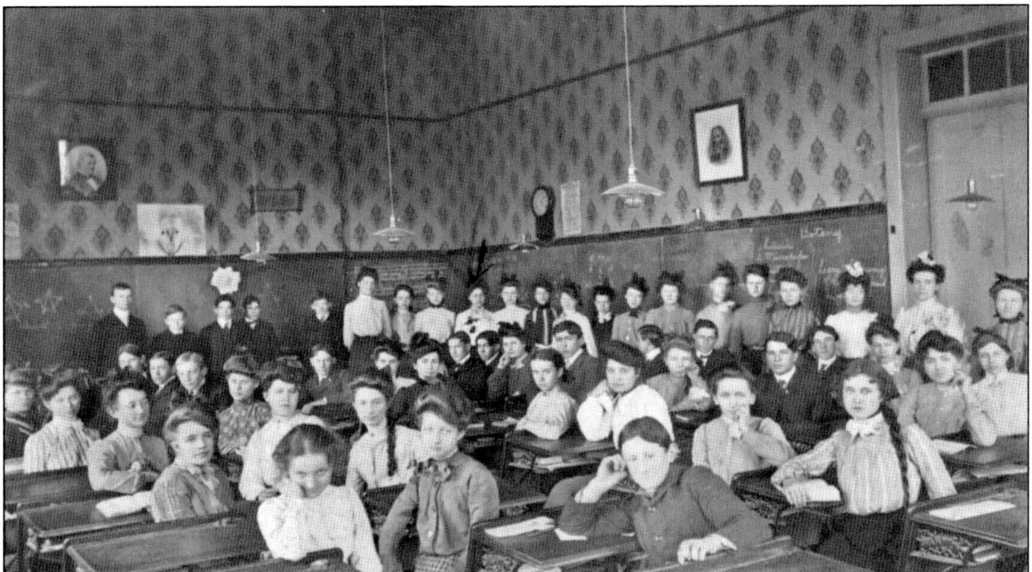

The camera has recorded a moment at Wapakoneta Union High School in 1903. The school contained a small natural history museum (where local historical artifacts were stored) and a third-floor gymnasium. (Courtesy of Auglaize County Historical Society.)

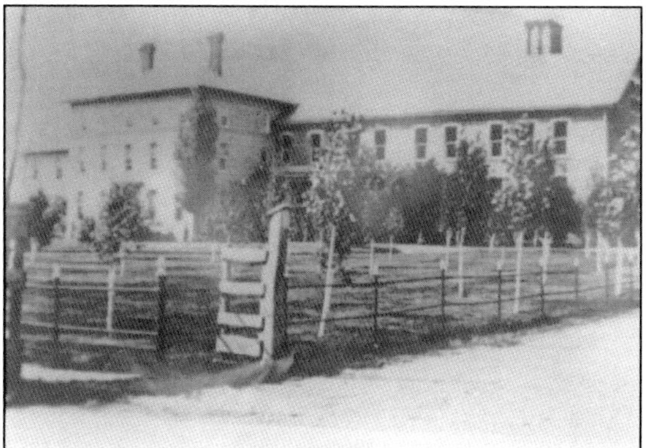

Auglaize County has had an infirmary since 1857 when a farm was purchased by commissioners for that purpose. When the 19th-century structure was destroyed by fire in 1907, a new infirmary was built in 1913 for $100,344.08. The new structure, still used today, employed the latest fireproofing methods, laundry plant, walls of reinforced brick and concrete, and steel framing structures. (Courtesy of Vernon E. Doenges.)

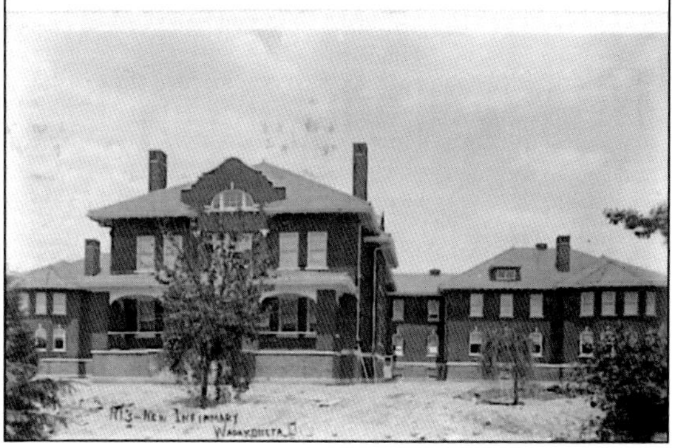

In the early 1900s, Auglaize Street is torn up for the construction of a paved street. The bricks are stacked along the sidewalks as construction crews prepare the roadbed for a smooth base. Looking west, the Kahn Building at 30 East Auglaize is the first building with awnings on the north side of Auglaize Street. (Courtesy of Ray Smallwood.)

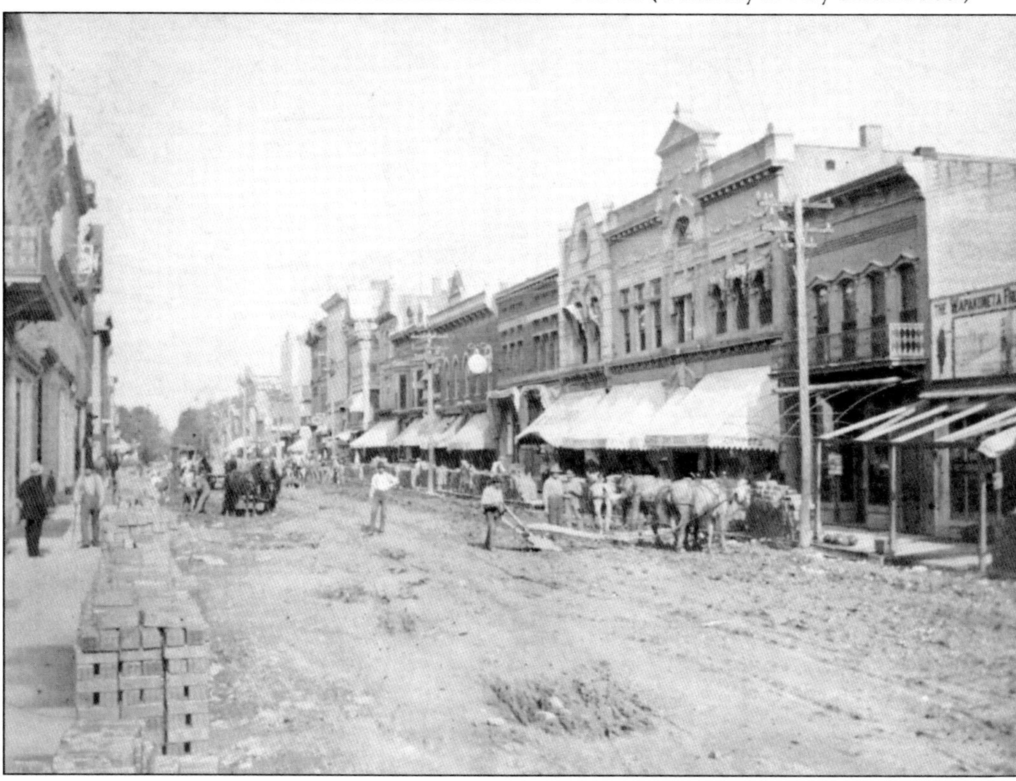

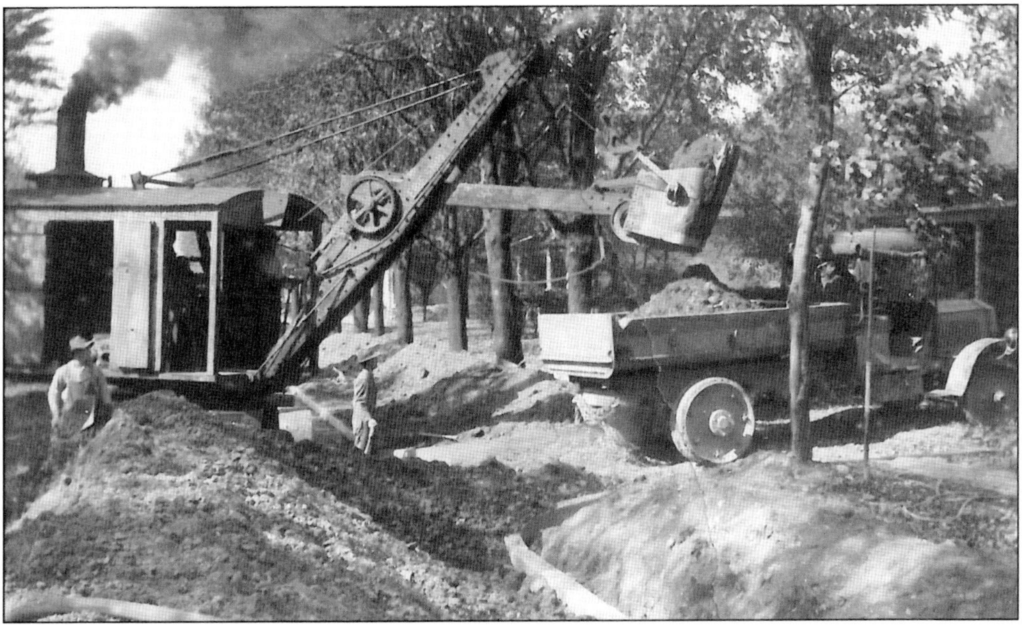

These 1920 photographs taken on West Benton Street provide an indication of the rapid growth of the city in providing infrastructure and modern city streets. With the more widespread use of automobiles, better streets and roadways were important for the growth of the city. In older residential sections, some city streets, such as Court Street, retain the original brick pavement. (Courtesy of Janet Schuler.)

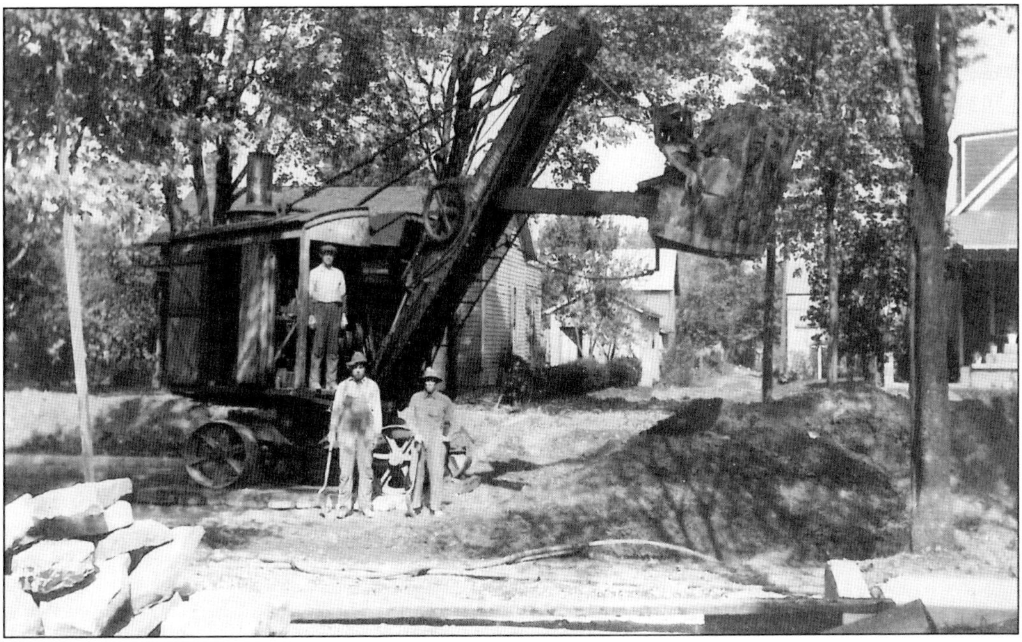

The steam shovel and dump truck remind us of the many changes in technology that were taking place during this time period. The steam powered shovel is caught in mid-puff as work for sewers and roadbed is constructed. (Courtesy of Janet Schuler.)

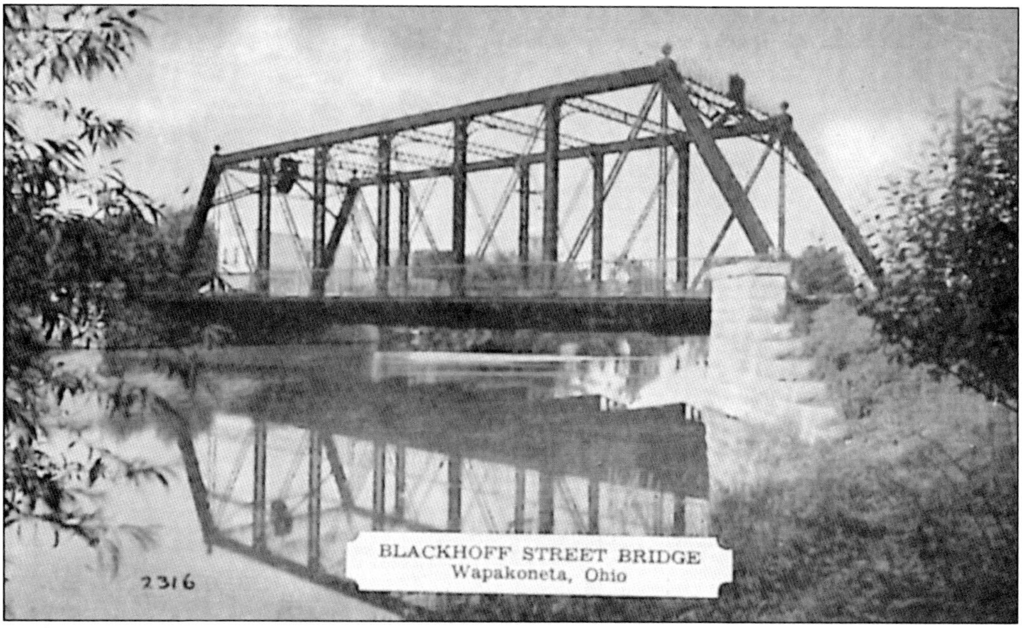

In the 1840s, a wood bridge was constructed across the Auglaize River connecting Blackhoof Street with the long-established Defiance Trail. The *1880 Atlas of Auglaize County* shows an 1864 three-span, wrought iron bridge at this location. Built in 1894, a single span through truss bridge (pictured above) also carried the cars of the Western Ohio Electric Railway toward Cridersville. (Courtesy of Janet Schuler.)

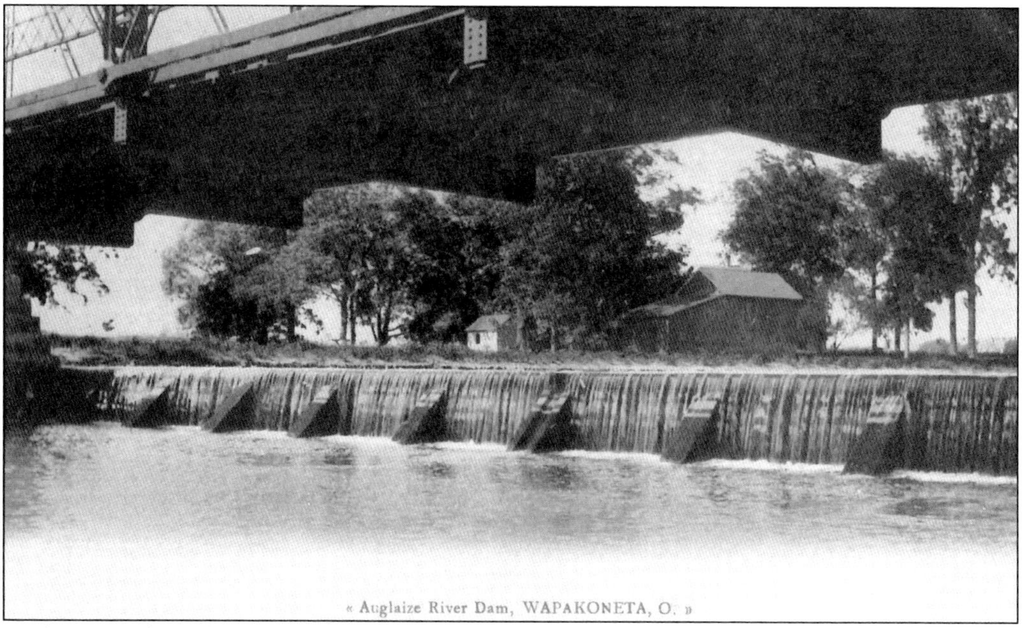

Looking east from the south side of the Auglaize River, the dam under the Hamilton Street Bridge is shown before the development of Harmon Park. The 2008 Wapakoneta Water Park would be at the location of the house and buildings. In 1908, Wapakoneta City Council gave a contract to contractors Smith and Dury for their bid of $2,795 for the building of an Auglaize River dam. (Courtesy of Scott Knerr.)

Three

Industry and Enterprises

Wapakoneta has always served the community as a reliable business town. Through the years, enterprising and energetic people have strived to provide a variety of manufacturing interests while providing employment opportunities and quality merchandise for area residents and the nation beyond. The *1880 Atlas of Auglaize County* lists many business enterprises including carriage makers, cigar manufacturers, and jewelers.

In the early days of the city, a steady supply of lumber in the county supported the numerous lumber mills, wheel and spoke factories, wagon makers, and production of well-known products like the Bent Wood butter churn. Vastly forested farmland was cleared, with lumber becoming the basis for industrial production in these marketable goods. It is difficult to determine how agrarian and entrepreneurial Wapakoneta became so interdependent in the 19th century. Originally a trading post, the town began to thrive when markets outside the region were established by the arrival of the railroad. In those early days, the business community was more local in character, but once the railroad was established and the Civil War ended, Wapakoneta flourished. Useful wooden products such as the broom, implement handle, churn, millwork, wagon, and wheel factories quickly emerged. Later, early 20th century technology developed into light industrial and technology-based enterprises. The interdependence of farm and manufacturing enterprises continue as agricultural and industrial interests headquarter in and around the city.

Wapakoneta celebrates the industrious past that has formed the basis of the modern work force available today. The craftsmanship of the past is also evident in the lasting structures of the city buildings, residences, and businesses that have withstood many economic changes. Throughout the Wapakoneta area, innovative business leaders have counted on hard-working craftsmen of German extraction and other industrious immigrants for their dedication to excellence, which was needed to compete in the national markets during the 19th century.

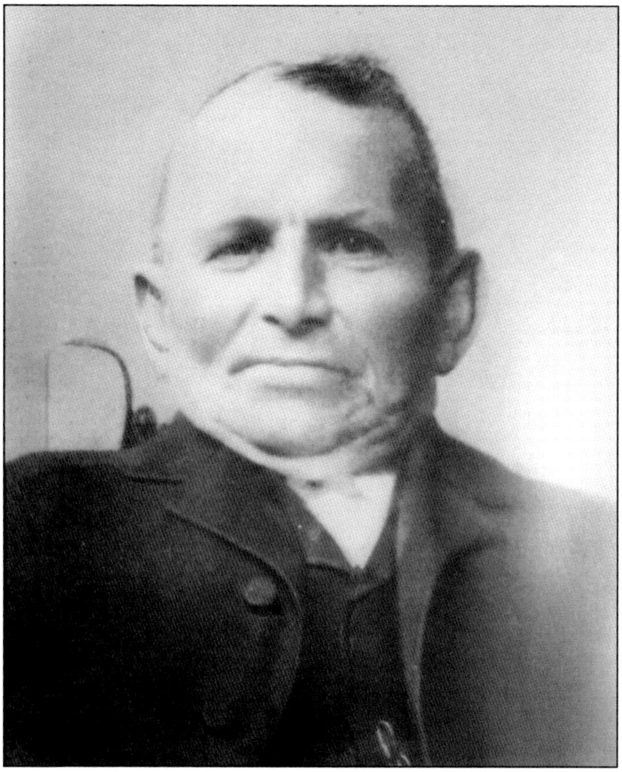

German-born Charles "Karl" Wintzer, a Wapakoneta pioneer and owner of Charles Wintzer Tanning Company (oldest continuous business in Auglaize County), immigrated at 14 to work for his uncle, Gottlieb Machetanz, in the hide business. In 1857, Wintzer became owner after his uncle's death, and he laid the groundwork for a company that remains a vital part of the business community today. (Courtesy of G. A. Wintzer and Son.)

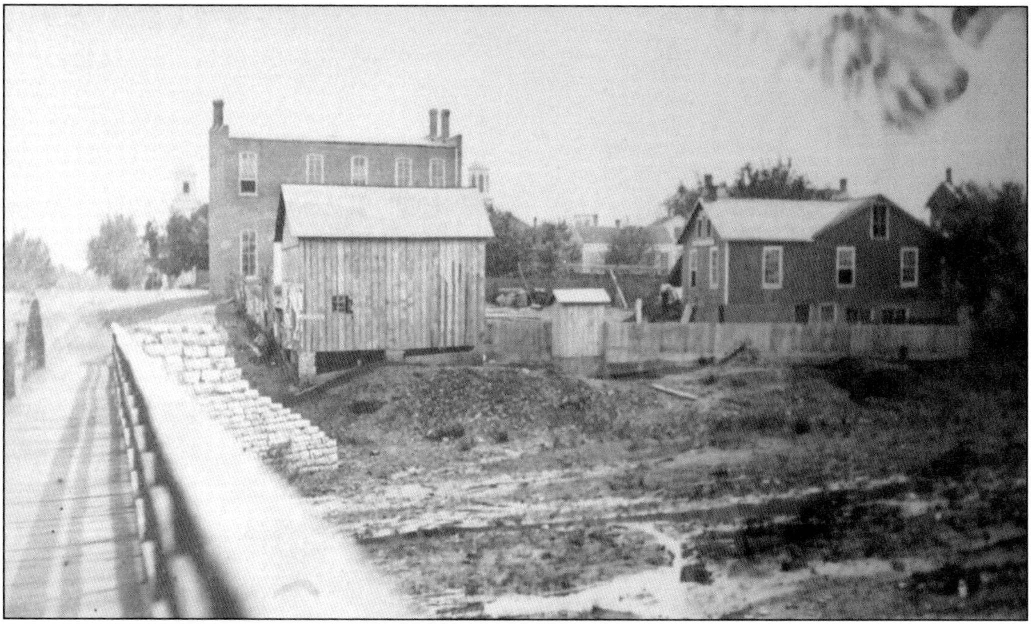

Charles "Karl" Wintzer established the Charles Wintzer Tanning Company, which became G. A. Wintzer and Son Company in the 1920s. The tannery engaged in the purchase and tanning of hides and skins to manufacture strap leather products from their home and business at 202 West Auglaize Street. This view of the tannery, taken from the Blackhoof Street bridge, includes the rear of the leather shop and home. (Courtesy of G. A. Wintzer and Son.)

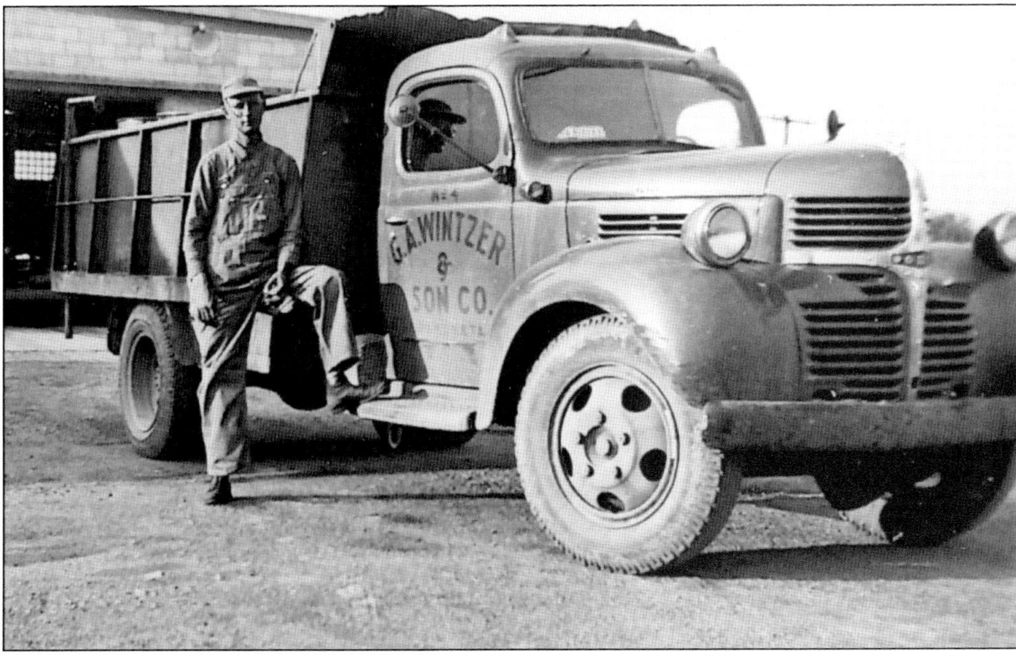

Employee Everett Zwez poses by the distinctively orange 1950s Wintzer Company truck. Similar trucks can still be seen throughout the region collecting hides for salting and fats for reprocessing. The internationally known company specializes in recycled fats and oils, poultry meal from meat and bone, and poultry processing. Five generations of the Wintzer family have been actively engaged in the business and community. (Courtesy of G. A. Wintzer and Son.)

John Henry Doering (center left with beard) established a hardware business in Wapakoneta in 1866. Doering Hardware began in a small brick building on the site of a Native American council house in Wapakoneta. This structure, located on the same site and shown in the *1898 Atlas of Auglaize County*, is located at 19 East Auglaize Street, now part of the Eagles Lodge. Doering was active in city business and civic endeavors.

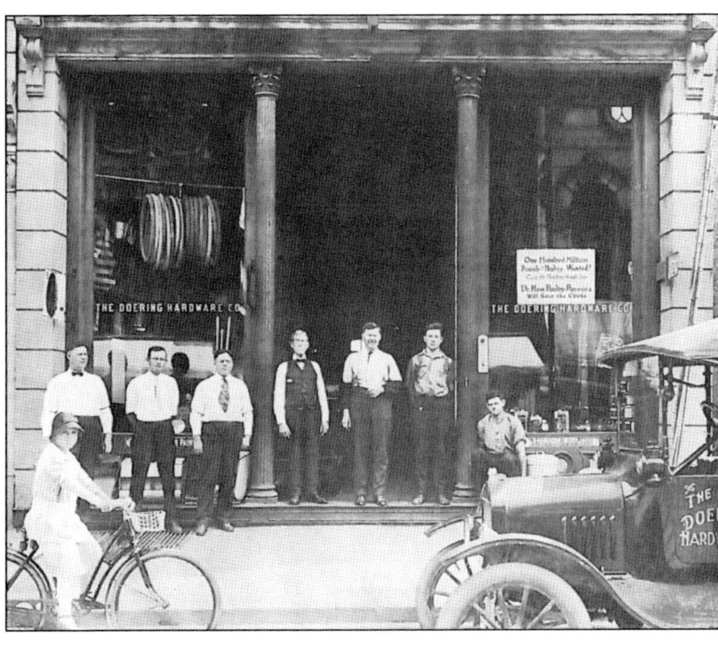

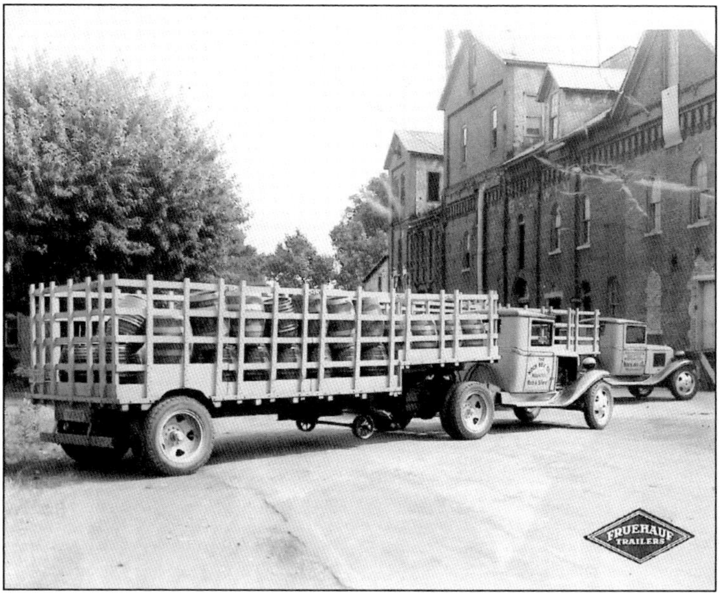

Although a small malt beverage production was begun in 1862 near the Auglaize River, C. T. Kolter became the first organized brewery in Auglaize County in 1868. Reorganizing in 1895 near the corner of Water and Harrison Streets, C. T. Kolter and Henry Koch merged to form the KK Bottling Works, evolving into the City Brewing Company by 1912 when the trademark then became "KK." (Courtesy of Becky Maxson.)

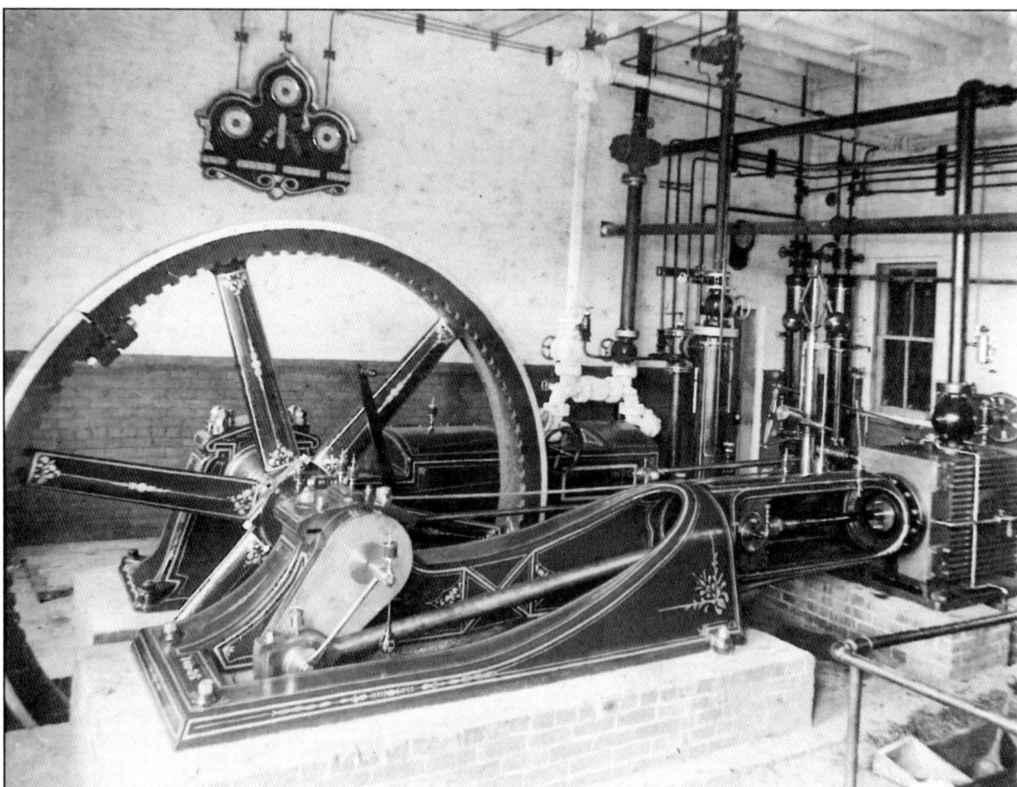

The ice machine pictured here supplied the city and surrounding territory with a steady supply of clean ice from the City Brewing Company (KK). During the Prohibition years, KK bottling works produced seltzer and soda waters like root beer, orangeade, ginger ale, sarsaparilla, and cream soda. After Prohibition, they once again produced beer under the name Old Vienna until they closed in 1951. (Courtesy of Combs Printing.)

The Kreitzer Buggy Works located at 4-6 Park Street manufactured buggies from the top floor down. As the buggy was nearing completion and becoming heavier, it also approached a point of departure on the ground level. The *1880 Atlas of Auglaize County* listed two other carriage factories in the city. The Kreitzer Buggy Works was a successful endeavor for many years and also sold chassis for industrial uses.

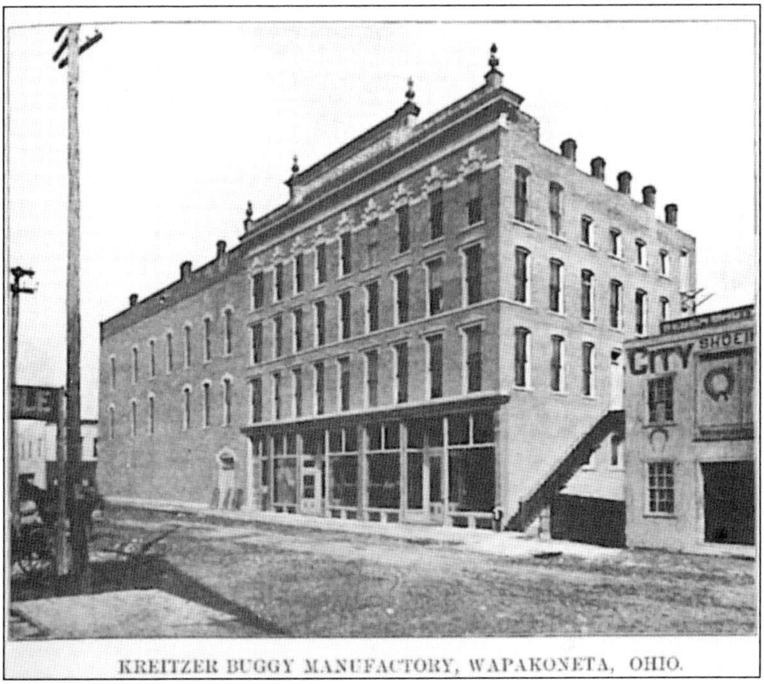

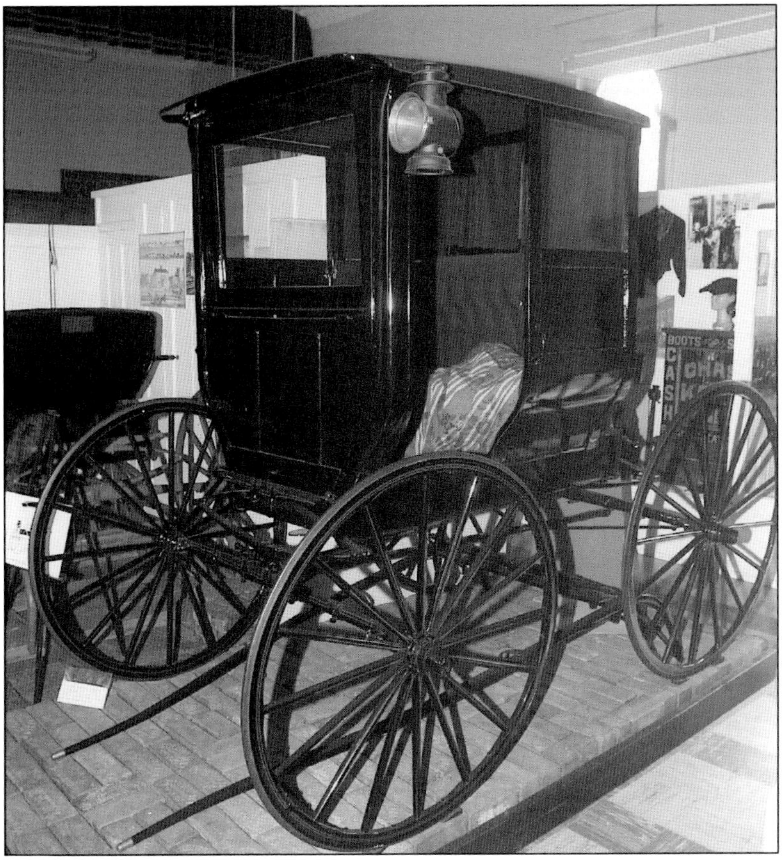

A restored Kreitzer storm buggy is on display at the Wapakoneta Museum of the Auglaize County Historical Society. (Courtesy of Auglaize County Historical Society; photograph by John Zwez.)

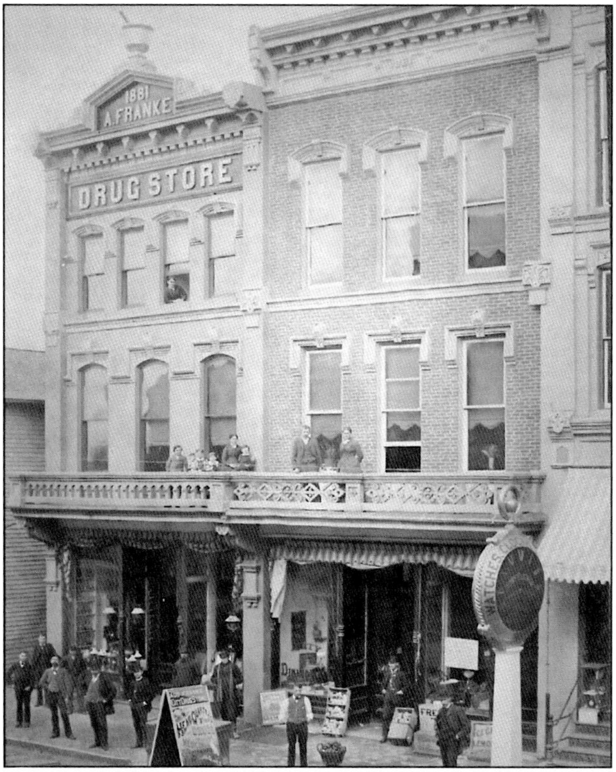

German immigrant August Franke built a drugstore at 18 West Auglaize Street in 1881; note the mortar and pestle atop the building. The well-known businessman came to Wapakoneta in 1867 and served residents until his death in 1899. Both buildings in this photograph, constructed in 1881, feature a fanciful balcony adding to the charm of the street until the 1940s. (Courtesy of Mike and Pam Doepker.)

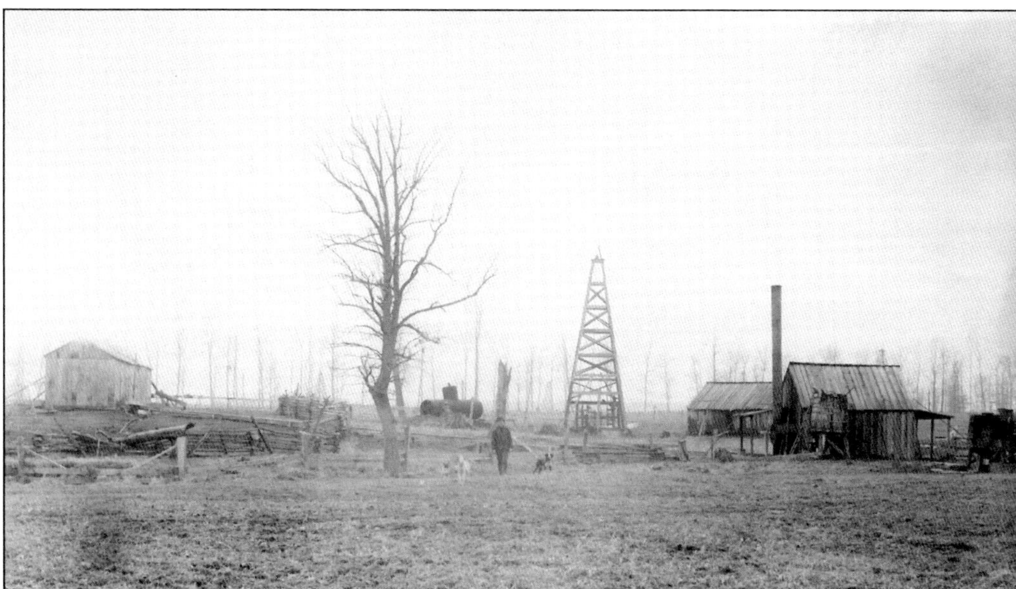

Oil boom days occurred in the Wapakoneta area after gas and oil were discovered near Cridersville. The oil field pictured here is located at the William J. Hasting farm at Two Mile, the area where the present day Wapakoneta Country Club now sits. A map of Duchouquet Township oil well locations in 1898 indicates numerous active wells in the vicinity. (Courtesy of Eugene and Shirley Pohlable.)

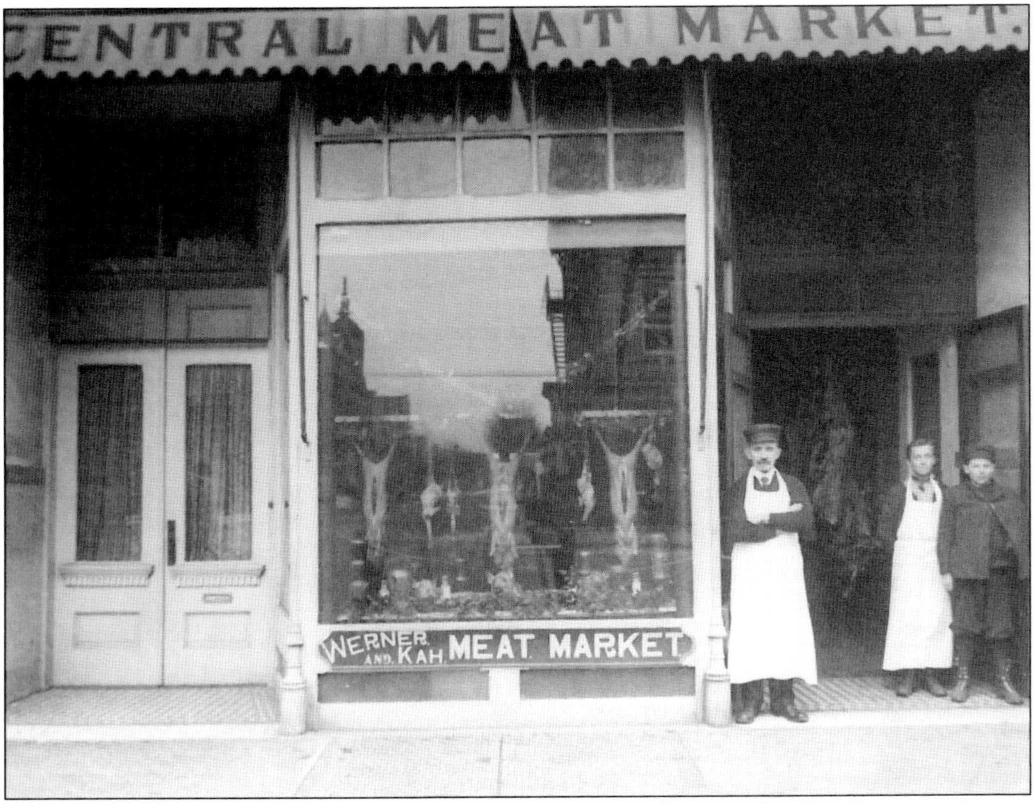

Harry Kah and Jacob Werner formed a partnership in 1894, locating their butchering and meat market at a variety of locations along Auglaize Street. This Distelrath Block photograph presents a unique image of the courthouse in the Werner and Kah Meat Market window reflection. Kah Meats continues to operate under the guidance of fifth generation family members on Keller Drive. (Courtesy of Linda Knerr.)

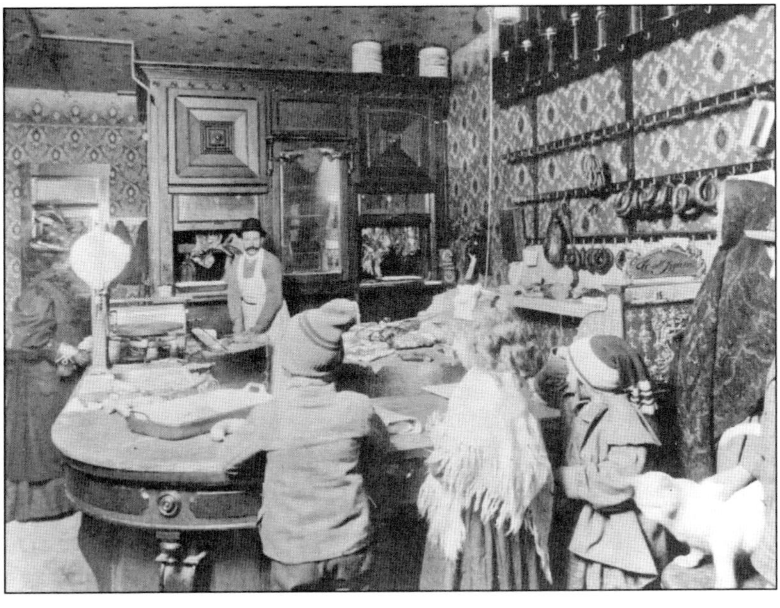

In this photograph taken of the Werner and Kah Meat Market near the end of the 19th century, a glimpse is provided inside a retail shop of that era. Sausages hang on the wall at the right, and large chunks of meat on the chopping block are ready for custom orders. (Courtesy of Linda Knerr and Auglaize County Historical Society.)

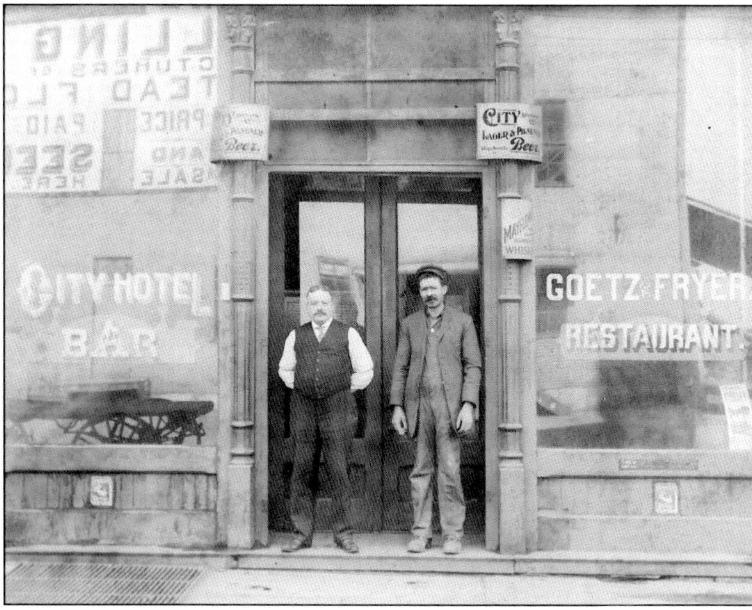

In 1899, there were 20 citizens engaged in the saloon business in Wapakoneta, many of them in the downtown business district. Once called saloons and sample rooms, these establishments were later called cafes, taverns, nightclubs, and bars. Taken after 1900, the City Hotel Bar windows reflects buildings across the street (Home Milling at 116 East Auglaize Street). (Courtesy of Jim Bowsher.)

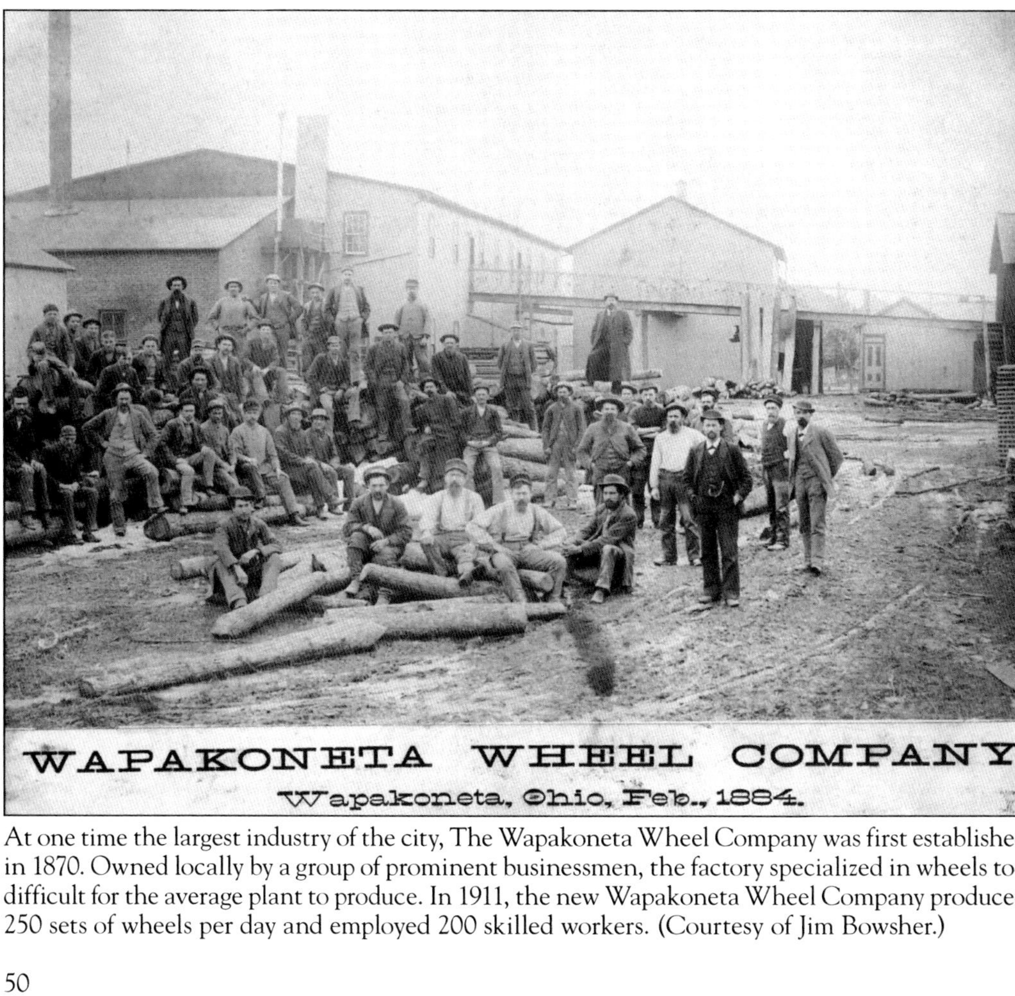

At one time the largest industry of the city, The Wapakoneta Wheel Company was first established in 1870. Owned locally by a group of prominent businessmen, the factory specialized in wheels too difficult for the average plant to produce. In 1911, the new Wapakoneta Wheel Company produced 250 sets of wheels per day and employed 200 skilled workers. (Courtesy of Jim Bowsher.)

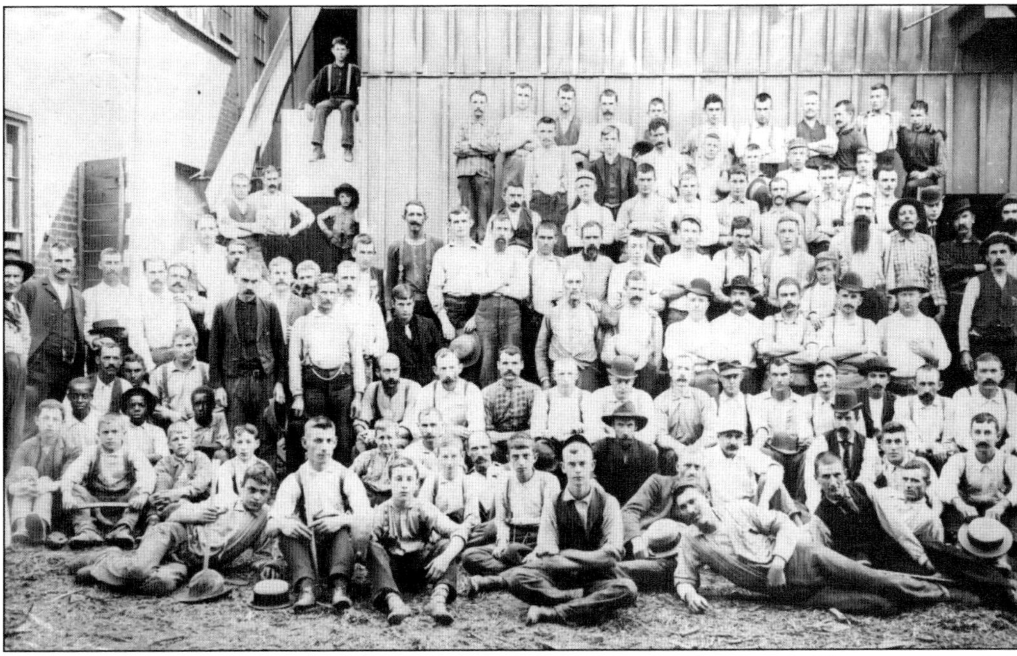

Workers at the Wapakoneta Wheel Company pose for a company photograph. The young boys hold spokes that they likely made. At the time, it was common for the youngest of wheel factory workers to shave the wood into spokes, becoming known as "little shavers." (Courtesy of Jim Bowsher.)

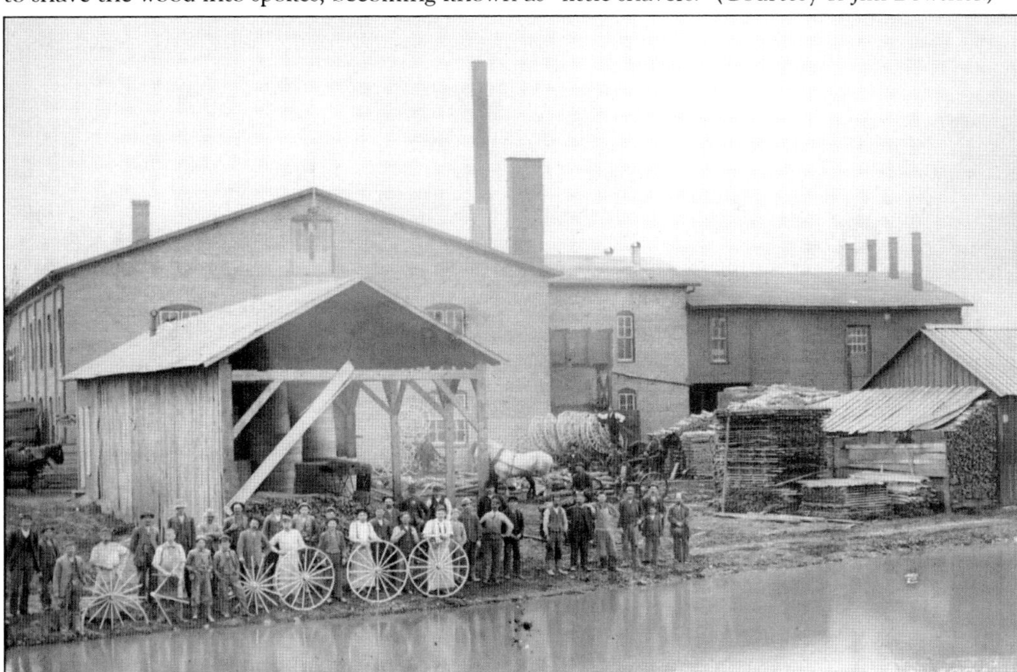

The New Wapakoneta Wheel Company, reorganized in 1910, manufactured all kinds of horse-drawn vehicle wheels, from the average farm wagon to special monster circus wagon wheels. Note the workers displaying the steps in wheel construction and the large wheels stacked against the building. (Courtesy of Jim Bowsher.)

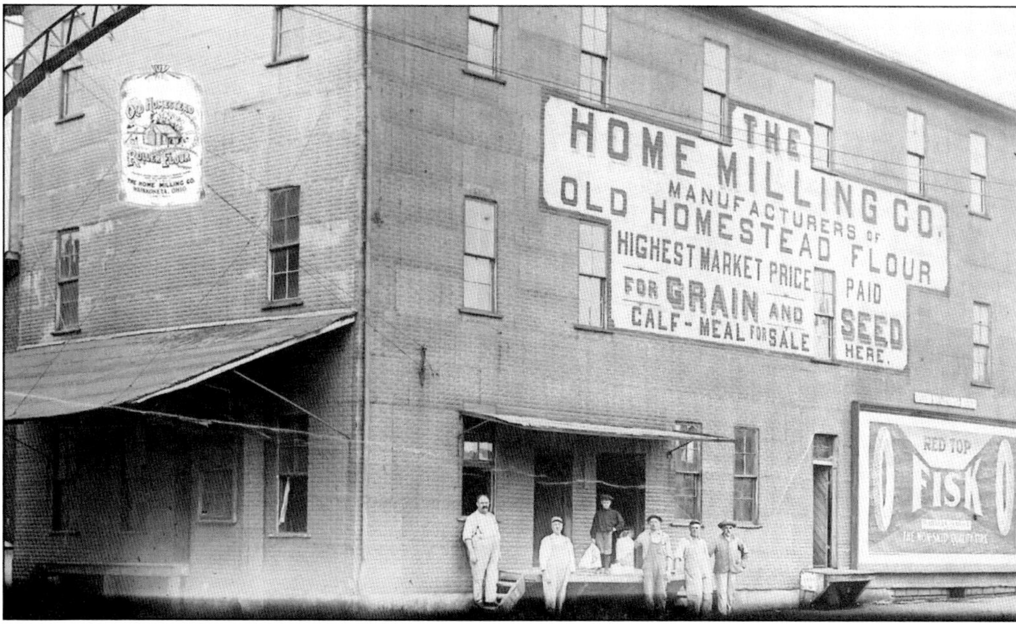

The Home Milling Company began operation after the Civil War when millstones were used to grind the grain. In 1893, the mill was remodeled using a rolling mill to produce high-grade all-purpose flour. By 1915, their winter wheat flour was widely known and sold. Advertising of the day claimed, "Old Homestead is sold by nearly every grocer and flour distributor in the territory." (Courtesy of Norma Rickert.)

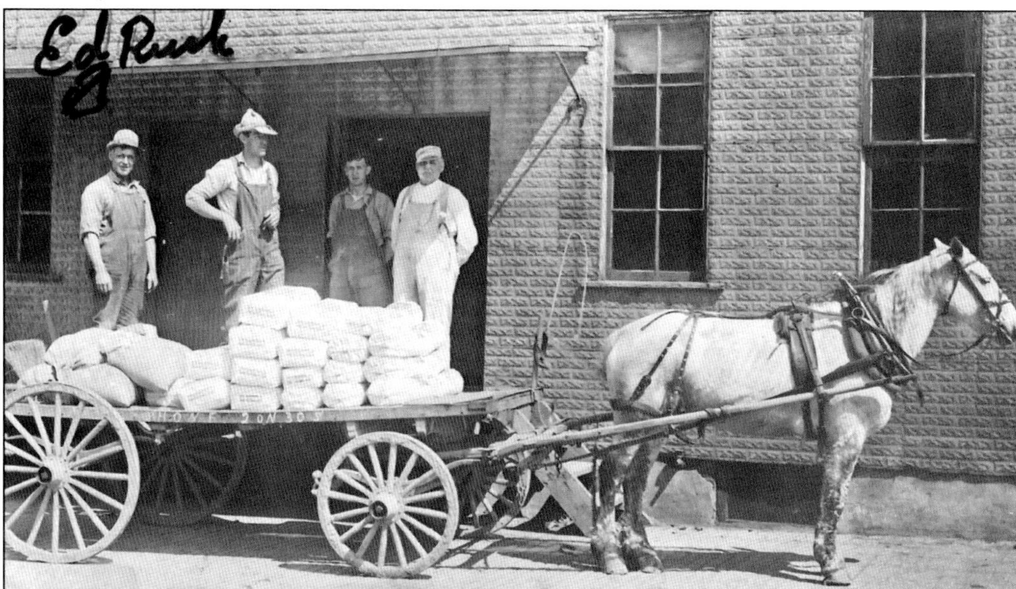

The Home Milling Company was centrally located opposite the B&O (CH&D) Railroad Depot. The mill was also a heavy buyer of wheat, corn, and oats directly from local farmers to sell on the national grain markets. Taken before 1900, employees pose by bags of grain for local delivery. Ed Ruck, second from the left, worked as an engineer at the mill for nearly 30 years. (Courtesy of Norma Rickert.)

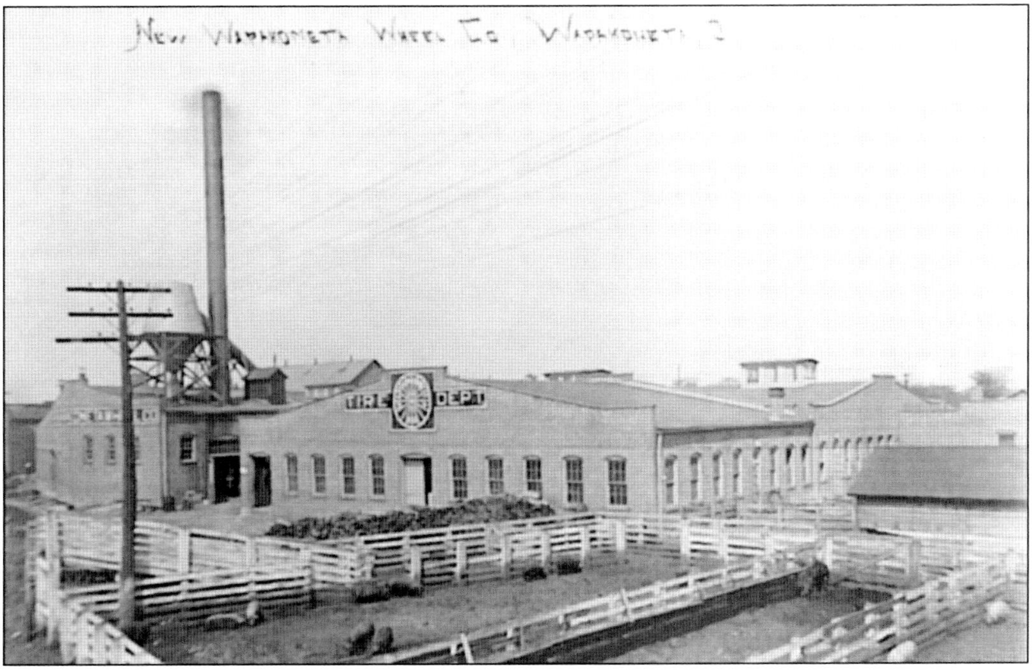

The stockyard holding pens, adjacent to the New Wapakoneta Wheel Company, were wedged into an area on the east side of the B&O (CH&D) Railroad depot near Auglaize Street. In the 1940s, the building housed the Sheets Furniture Company. (Courtesy of Vernon E. Doenges.)

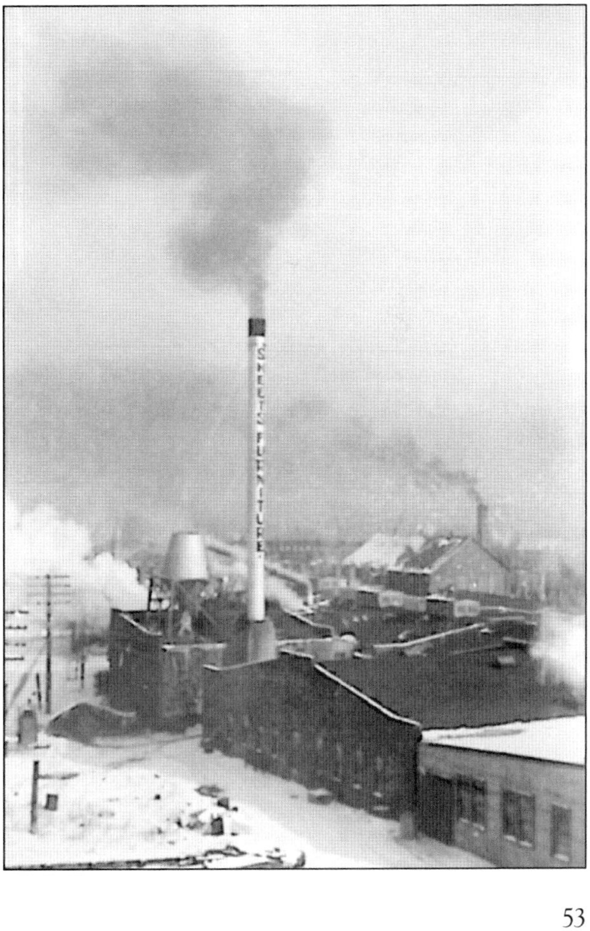

A look at industrial Wapakoneta in the 1940s shows the Sheets Furniture Company in the foreground and Wapakoneta Machine Company in the background. This view was taken from the Detjen Grain Elevator, where it also shows the area that once held the stock pens. (Courtesy of Lawrence Dietz.)

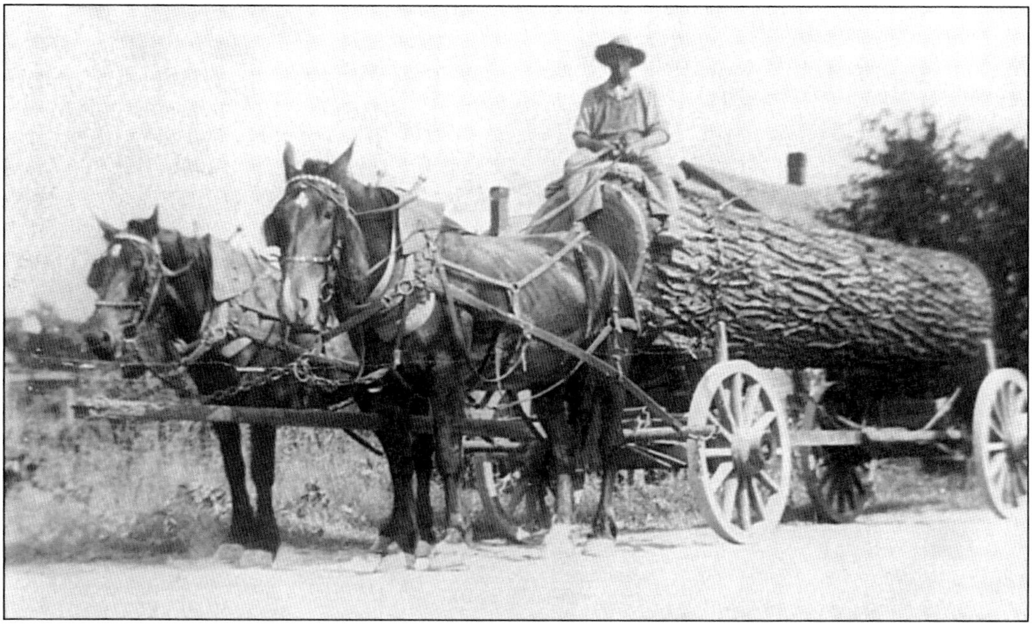

Wholesale and retail mills supplied hardwood lumber from large stands of timber surrounding the city. As the city grew, local lumber suppliers provided fence posts, porch columns and rails, screen doors, and windows. In a c. 1912 city business directory, the John C. Burden Sawmill advertised "lumber cut from oak, hickory, beech, elm, and ash which is bought from nearby farmers." (Courtesy of Linda Knerr.)

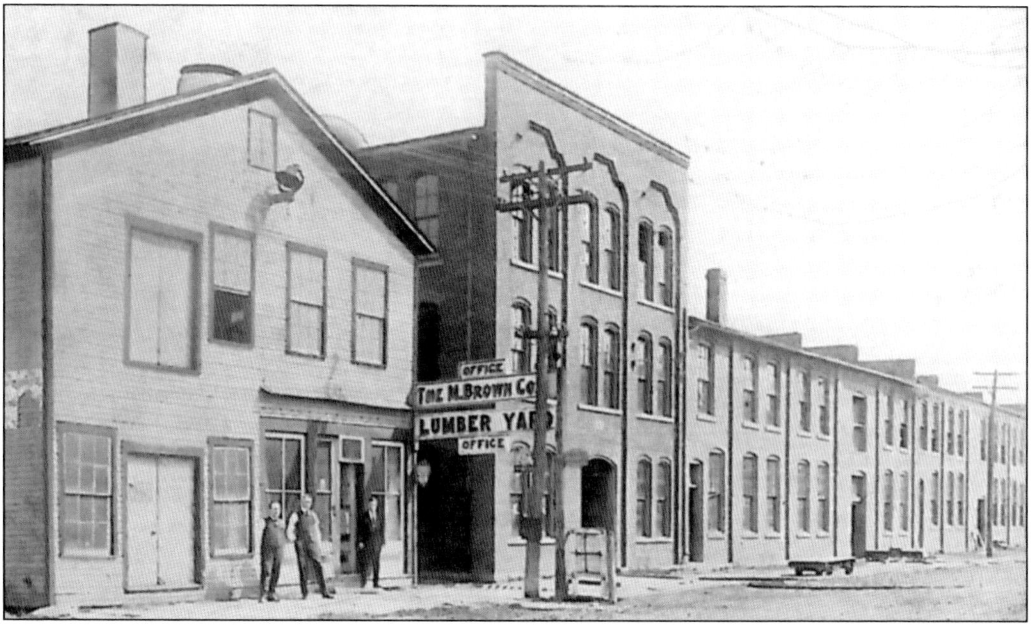

The Brown Lumber Company and M. Brown Company were located on South Park Street. The M. Brown Company produced the famous Bent Wood butter churn sold nationwide, obtaining a patent August 7, 1877. The patent provided a new way of forming the U-shaped box and improving the lid mechanism for a better seal. The churn legs (on each side) were also made from a single piece of bent wood.

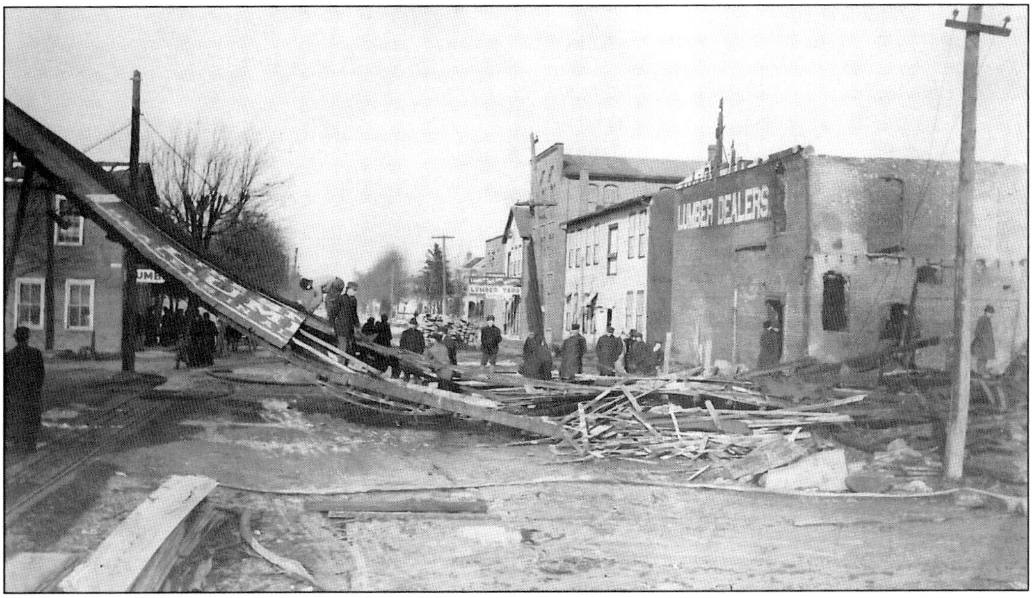

The M. Brown Company produced Bent Wood and dasher churns, wood measures, and the Ohio Washing Machine. Fire destroyed a portion of Brown Lumber, and production of the Bent Wood churn ended in 1912. The Standard Churn Company, a competitor, began in 1886 at Lima and Stelzer Streets. They produced the Anti-Bent Wood Churn when the patent of the Bent Wood churn ran out. (Courtesy of Vernon E. Doenges.)

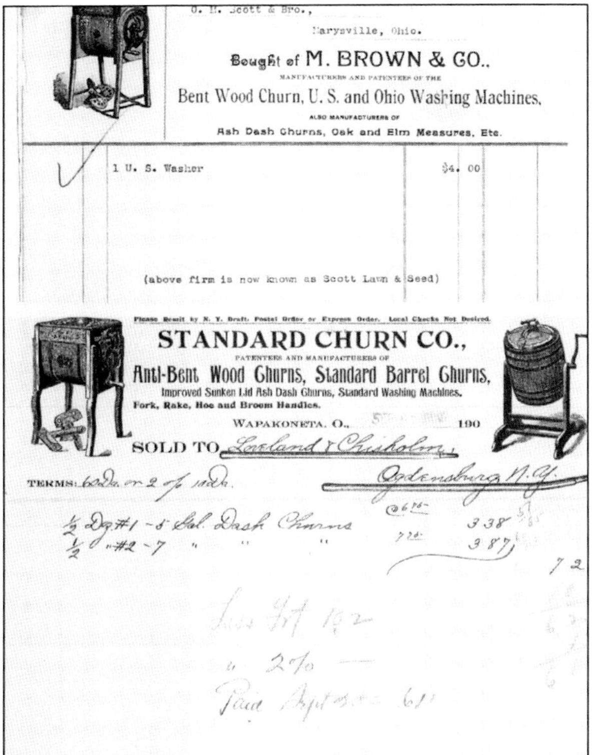

O. M. Scott & Bro.,
Marysville, Ohio.

Bought of M. BROWN & CO.,
MANUFACTURERS AND PATENTEES OF THE
Bent Wood Churn, U. S. and Ohio Washing Machines,
ALSO MANUFACTURERS OF
Ash Dash Churns, Oak and Elm Measures, Etc.

1 U. S. Washer $4. 00

(above firm is now known as Scott Lawn & Seed)

Please Remit by N. Y. Draft, Postal Order or Express Order. Local Checks Not Desired.

STANDARD CHURN CO.,
PATENTEES AND MANUFACTURERS OF
Anti-Bent Wood Churns, Standard Barrel Churns,
Improved Sunken Lid Ash Dash Churns, Standard Washing Machines.
Fork, Rake, Hoe and Broom Handles.

WAPAKONETA, O., 190

SOLD TO Loveland & Chisholm
Ogdensburg, N.Y.
TERMS: 60 da. or 2% 10 da.

½ Dz. #1 - 5 Gal. Dash Churns
½ " #2 - 7 " " "

The two Wapakoneta churn companies' products, popular with antiques collectors, can be confusing to the casual observer. The two invoices at right offer a glimpse at those differences; one being that the Anti-Bent Wood Churn had four separate legs. The churn dashers are displayed beneath the churn boxes for comparison. (Courtesy of Vernon E. Doenges and Auglaize County Historical Society.)

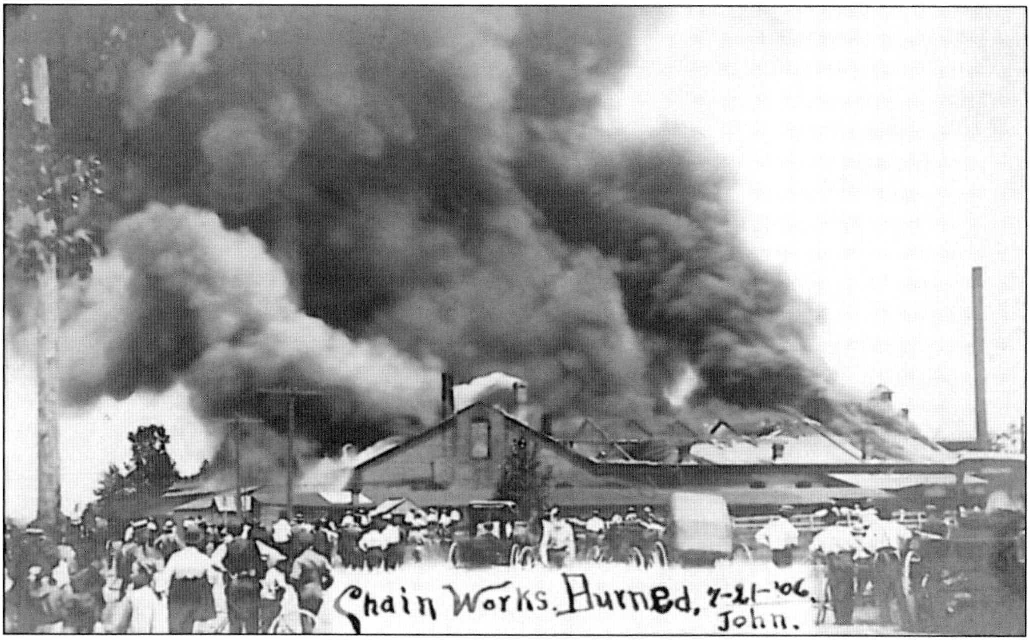

Rebuilt and reorganized after this 1906 fire, the Krein Manufacturing Company made welded chains for wagons, railroads, logging, and automobiles until the 1930s. The company, located on Krein Street, was known for high-quality, durable chains and advertised nationwide in trade and industrial publications. (Courtesy of Vernon E. Doenges.)

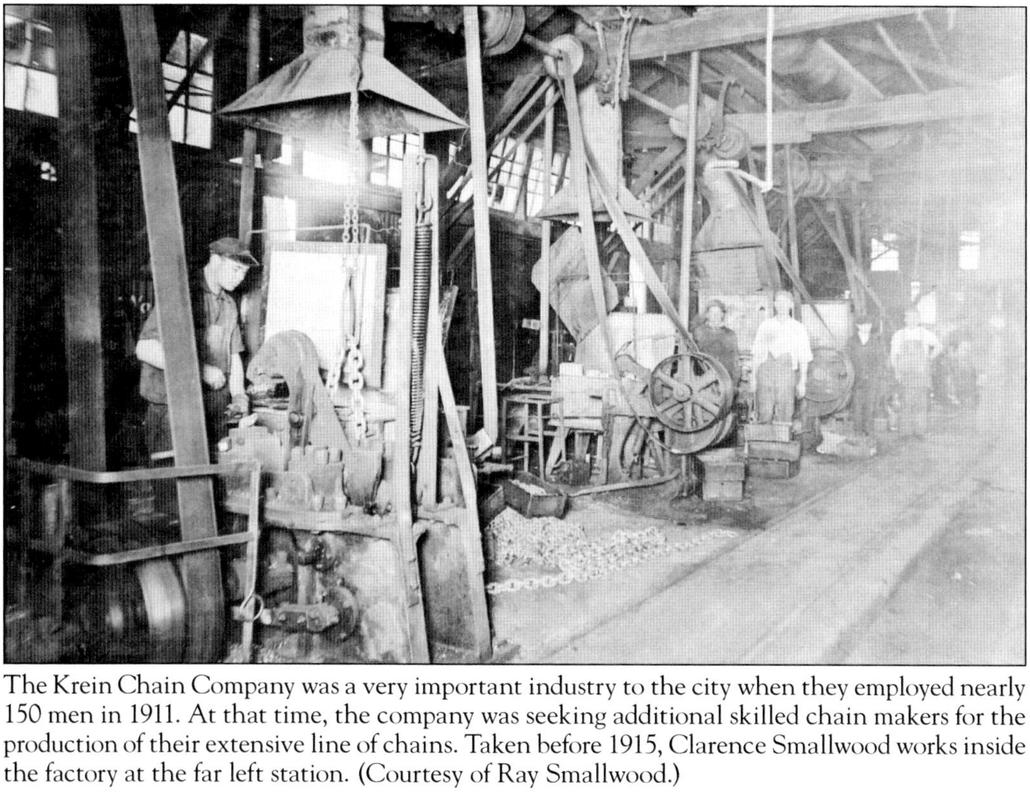

The Krein Chain Company was a very important industry to the city when they employed nearly 150 men in 1911. At that time, the company was seeking additional skilled chain makers for the production of their extensive line of chains. Taken before 1915, Clarence Smallwood works inside the factory at the far left station. (Courtesy of Ray Smallwood.)

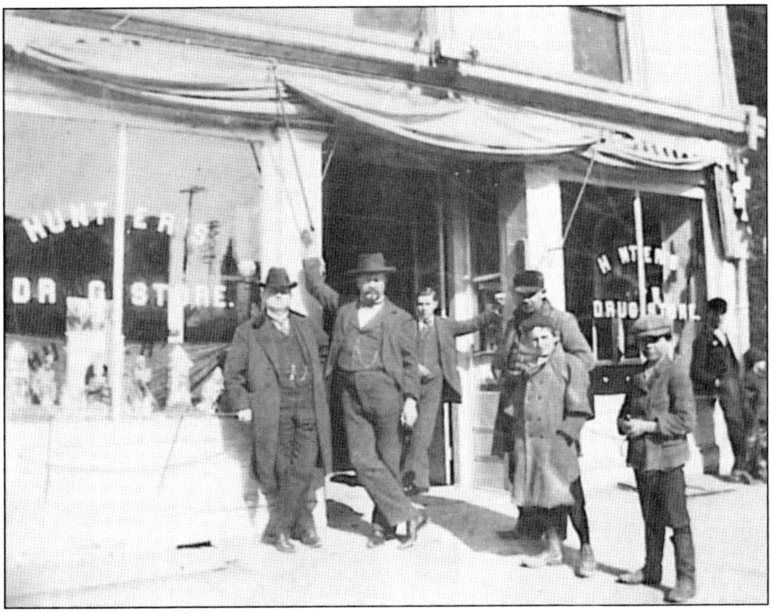

Dr. Franklin Crittenden Hunter (second from left) was a prominent local physician and pharmacist. His drugstore was located at 102 West Auglaize Street, where it continued in later years as Herwig Drug. Dr. Hunter solicited for the first local telephone service in Wapakoneta and signed up 50 subscribers. (Courtesy of Vernon E. Doenges.)

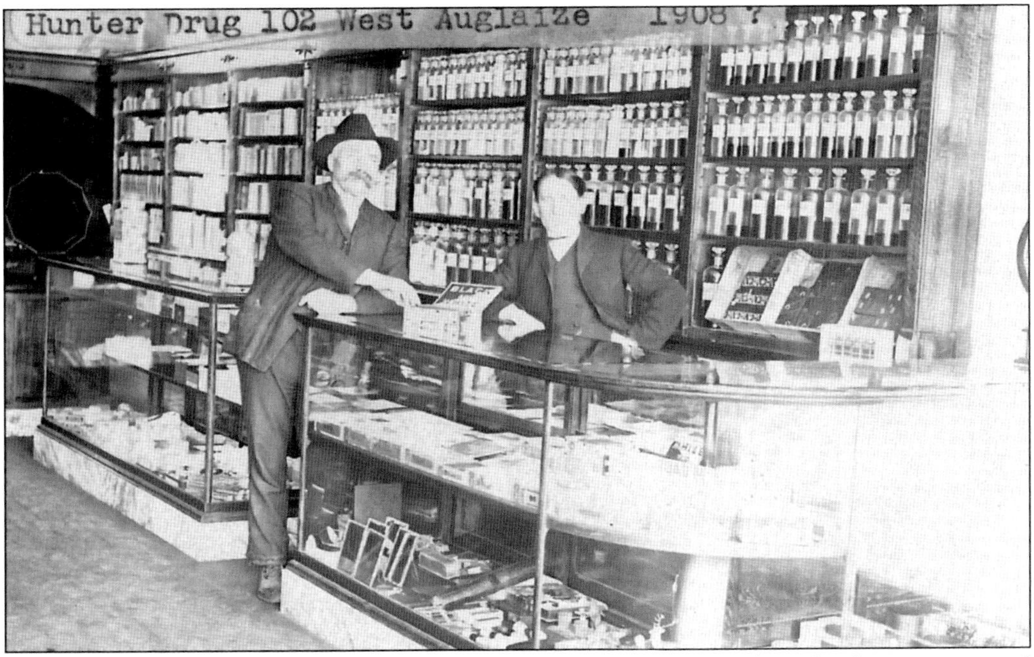

Inside Hunter Drug, *c.* 1910, bulk products can be seen from a time when the druggist prepared prescriptions according to a formula. Dr. Franklin C. Hunter, at the end of the counter, proudly offers the viewer a cigar. Look inside the cases for a snapshot of merchandise offered in that era. Can you find the reindeer? (Courtesy of Vernon E. Doenges.)

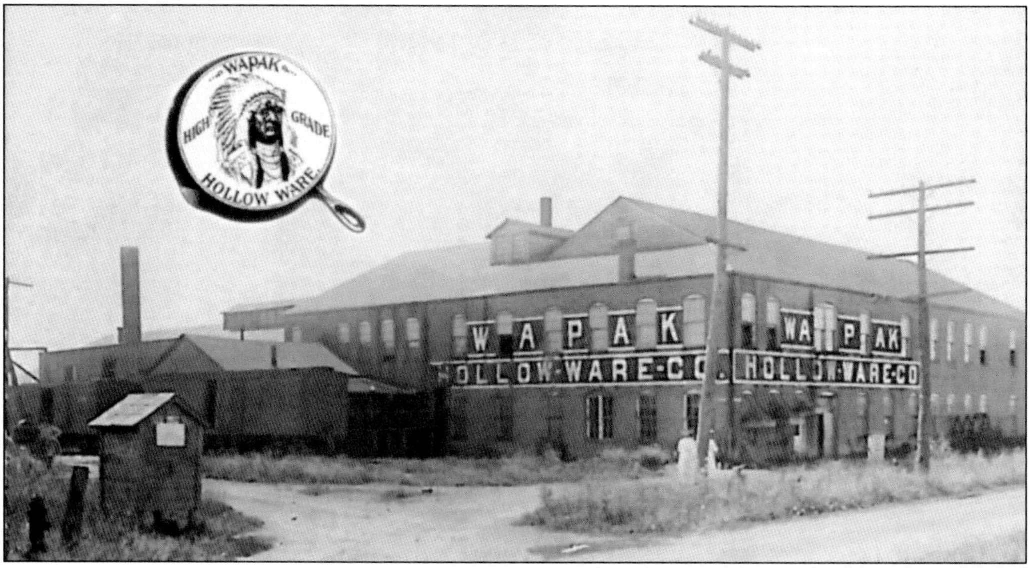

Wapak Hollow Ware Company began in 1903 with these assets: machinery $10,132.82, plant $8250.25, fixtures $108.65, and $5,000 cash. Located at Krein and Willipie Streets, the foundry made quality cast iron skillets, irons, urns, feed boxes, watering toughs, manufacturing kettles, industrial doors, and grates. Using this logo, Wapak Hollow Ware became well known when large, national catalog companies sold a variety of their products. (Courtesy of Vernon E. Doenges.)

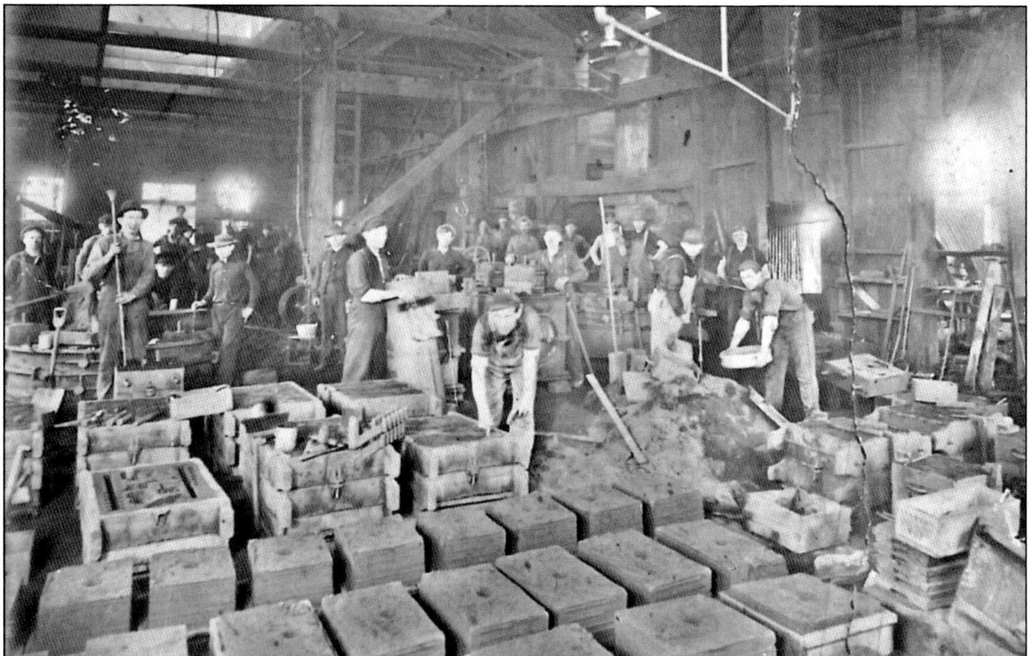

Taken inside the Wapak Hollow Ware foundry, boxes hold casting sand for stove grates. Several models of iron stove grates and repair pieces were available in their catalog. A wide variety of items were produced, but the company was better known for cooking utensils and sad irons. Many foundry pieces were marked "WAPAK," but the Wapak Indian Head skillet has only a 2.25-inch Indian medallion on the bottom. (Courtesy of Combs Printing.)

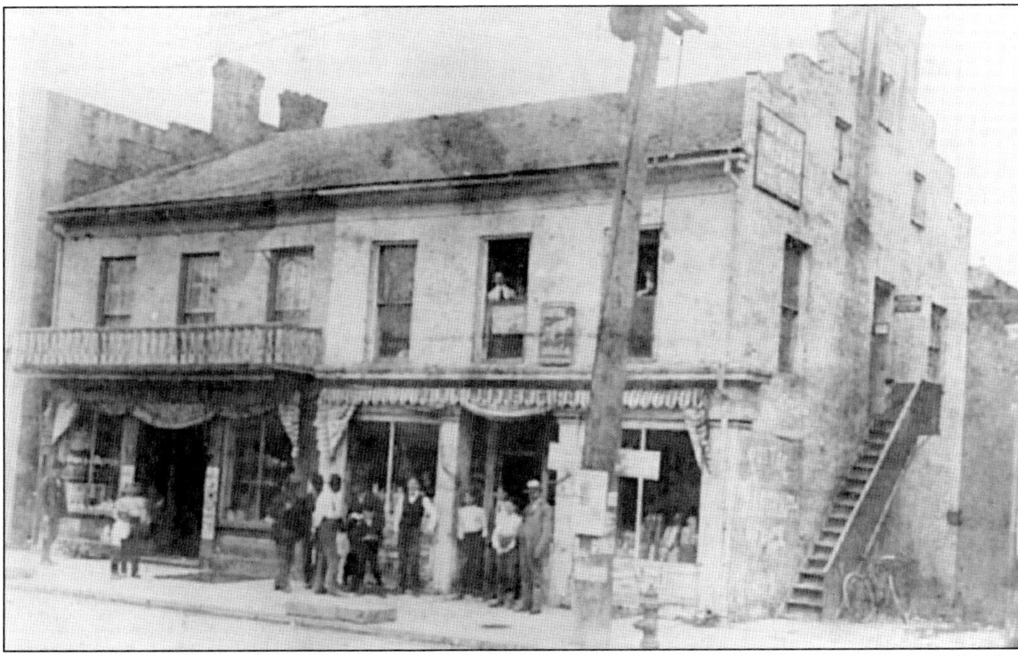

The Wapakoneta Telephone Company was formed on July 12, 1895. George Andregg had the first telephone at his laundry and his number was 5. The first telephone company office was in this building on the southeast corner of Perry and Auglaize Streets. A small office with one operator was located on the second floor. (Courtesy of Telephone Service Company.)

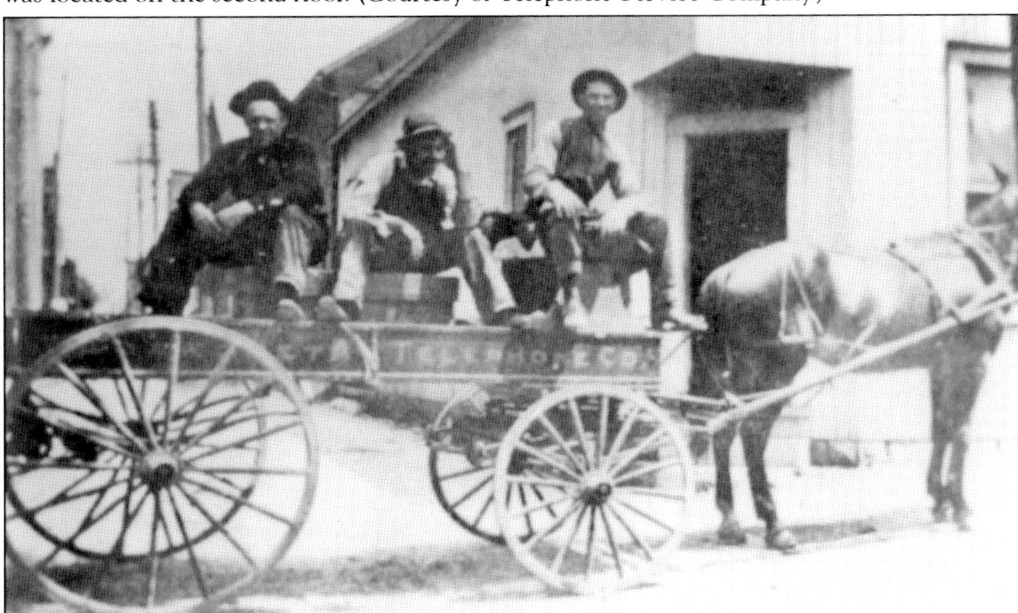

Employees Mike Kantner, Brandy Kettering, and an unidentified person pose with the very first maintenance vehicle owned by the Wapakoneta Telephone Company. In the background is Dr. Martin's office, located in the alley behind what is now the Bookmark Bookstore on Blackhoof Street. Traveling down the alley, the angled door of Dr. Martin's office can still be identified. (Courtesy of Telephone Service Company.)

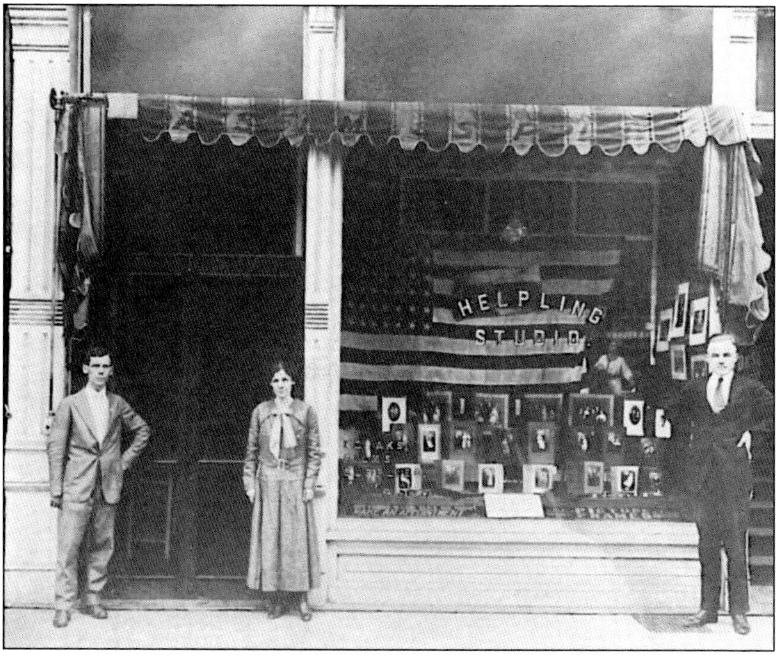

Lewis Helpling purchased a photography studio in 1908 from W. E. Potter, who had a photography business for 25 years prior. The Helpling Studio had been recognized by art critics of the day as one of the best photography studios in western Ohio. The Helpling Studio documented the flood of 1913 and important events in the lives of area citizens.

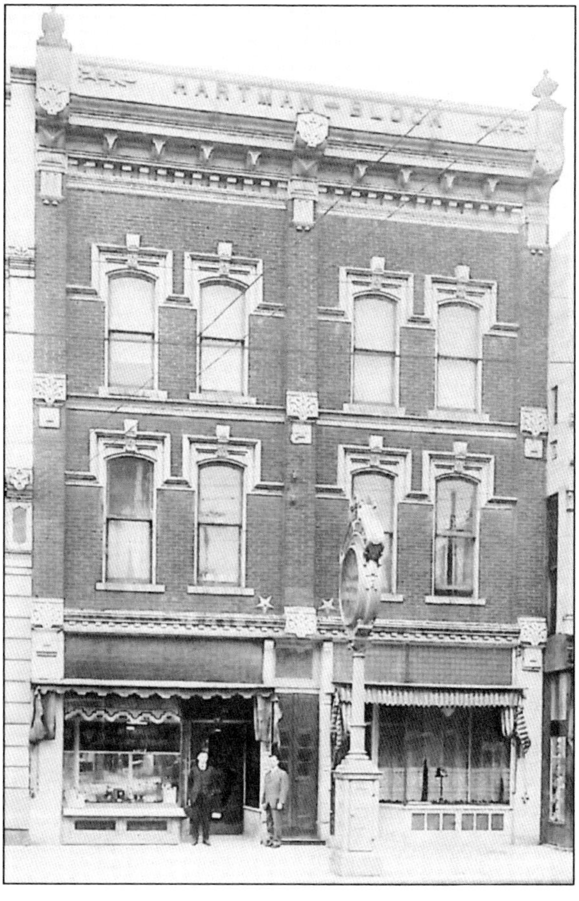

Placed in front of the Hartman Jewelry Store at the heart of downtown Wapakoneta, the landmark clock helped city residents keep time since its installation in 1906 and into the 1960s. The faithful, eight-day, weighted Seth Thomas clock needed to be wound only once per week by turning a large crank. Just as the red-and-white-striped barber pole is the sign for a barbershop, a clock was the sign for a jewelry store in days gone by.

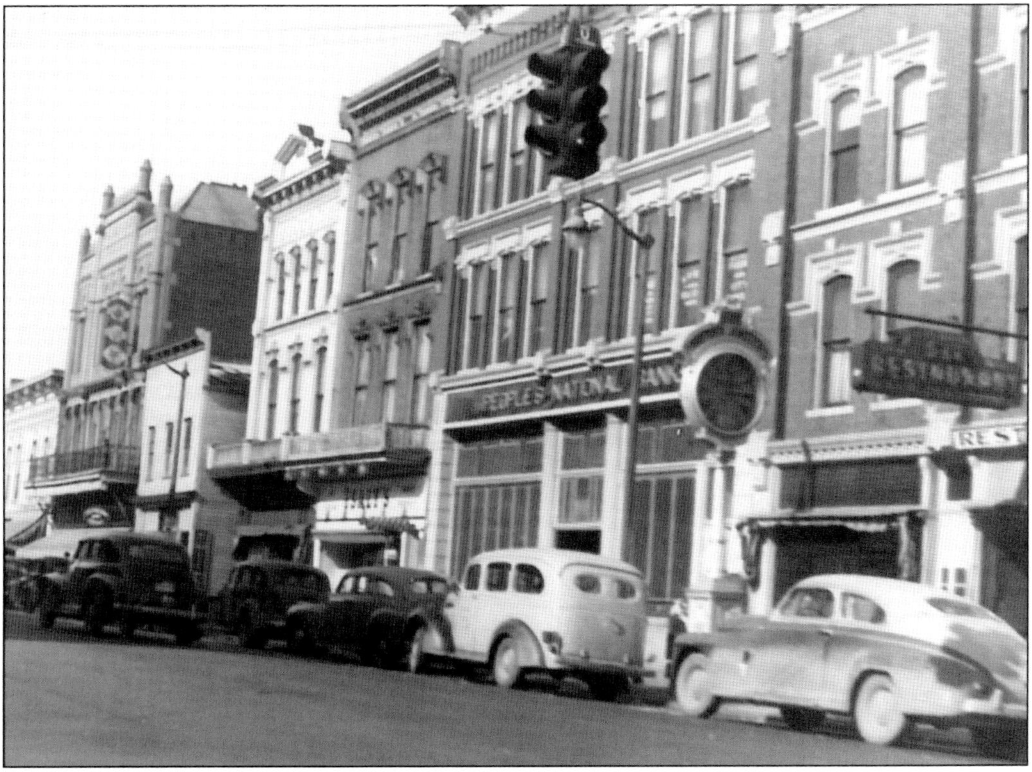

Henry Hartman established the Hartman Jewelry Store in 1876, but many town residents remember his son, Clem, as the optometrist and jeweler for over 50 years. The clock was removed after it was hit by a Pepsi truck, and later the Hartman Jewelry Store was razed to expand the People's Bank. Islay's Restaurant is located beside the Franke Building at 16 West Auglaize Street. (Courtesy of Dennis Hague.)

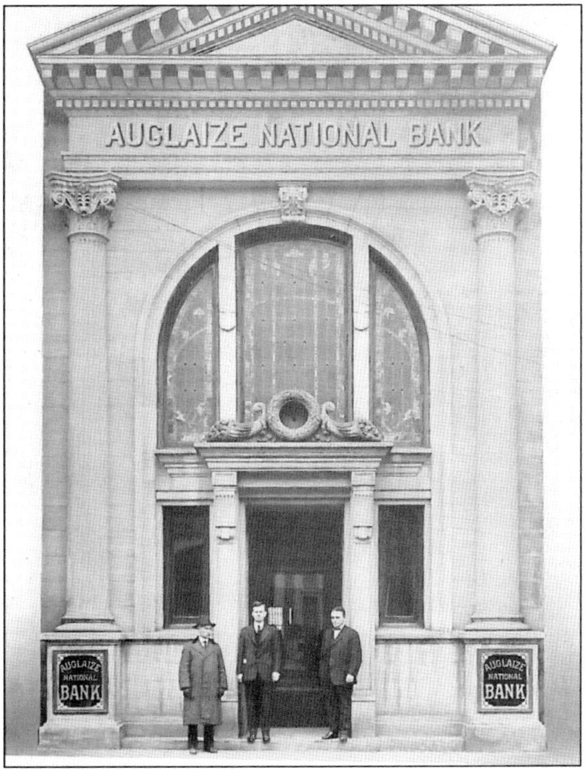

Built in 1911, the Auglaize National Bank design is attributed to architect Andrew DeCurtins, whose family of regional architects also designed and decorated Catholic churches, including the 1911 St. Joseph's Catholic Church in Wapakoneta. This East Auglaize Street building later became the Welfare Finance Company and is now a private residence.

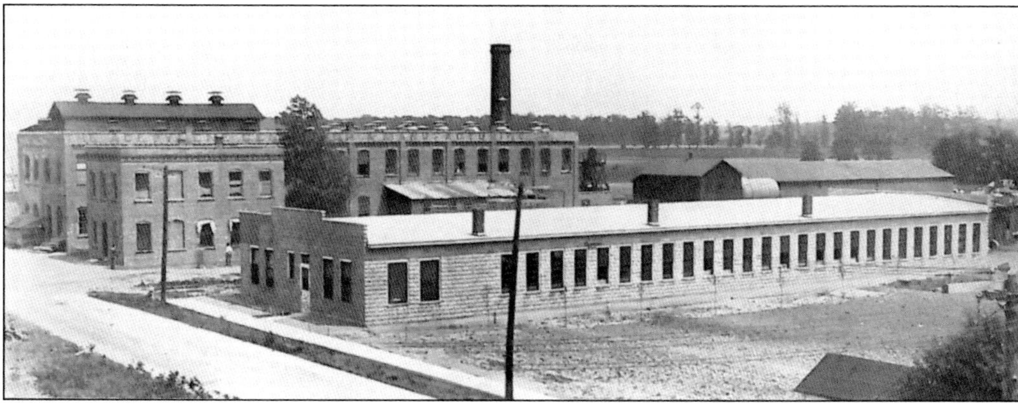

The John C. Turner Corporation, located in the former Abner Manufacturing building on Krein Avenue, made gun mounts for B17 and B24 military aircraft during World War II. Local serviceman Maj. James Shaw wrote from "somewhere in England" that he noticed a Turner stamp on a gun mount. Writing home, Shaw noted it was a small world and encouraged workers to keep up the good work in the war effort.

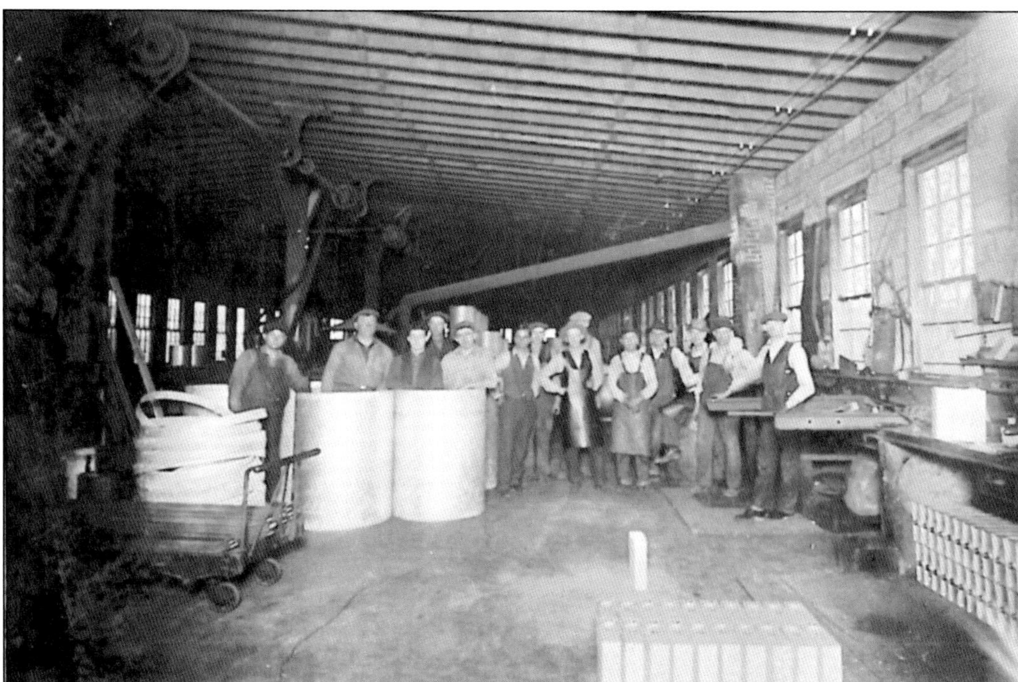

The John C. Turner Corporation, originally established in Dayton in 1915, was recruited to move its manufacturing operation to Wapakoneta in 1933 as a way to stimulate the local economy during the Depression. The Turner Corporation began to produce toys from leftover auto industry steel in the mid–1920s. Turner Toys are a very desirable collectable of the many "made in Wapakoneta" items. (Courtesy of Herbert Lunz.)

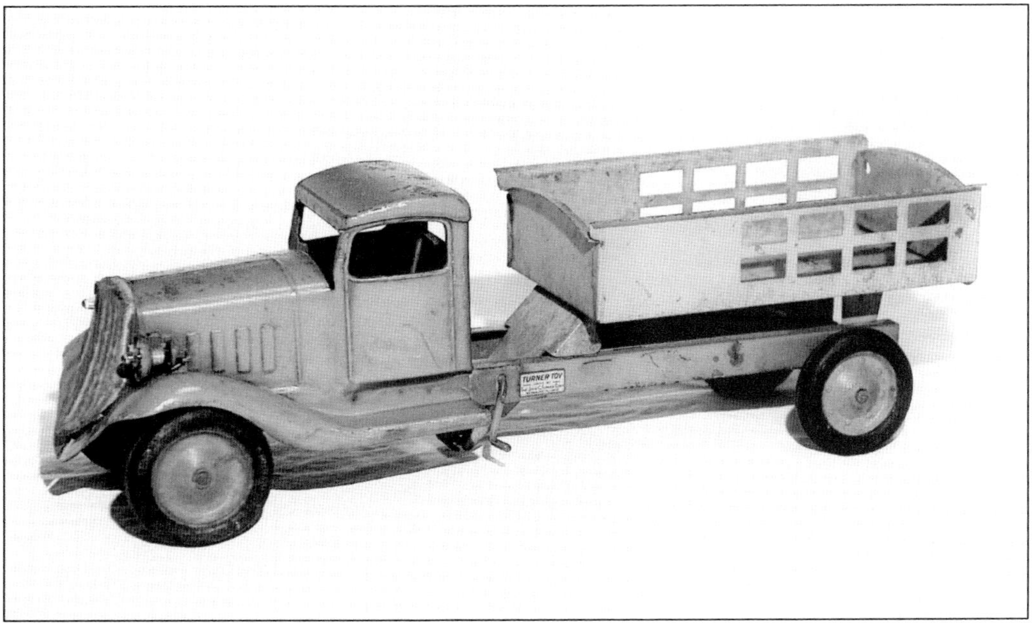

Items produced at the Turner Toy factory included this Ford-style truck, power shovels, doll sulkies, and airplanes. One story relates that children would rummage through the factory scrap pile for discards and hand them through the windows to the workers. The workmen would "fix them up a bit," and once returned, even the discards were most loved. (Courtesy of Steve Schuler; photograph by John Zwez.)

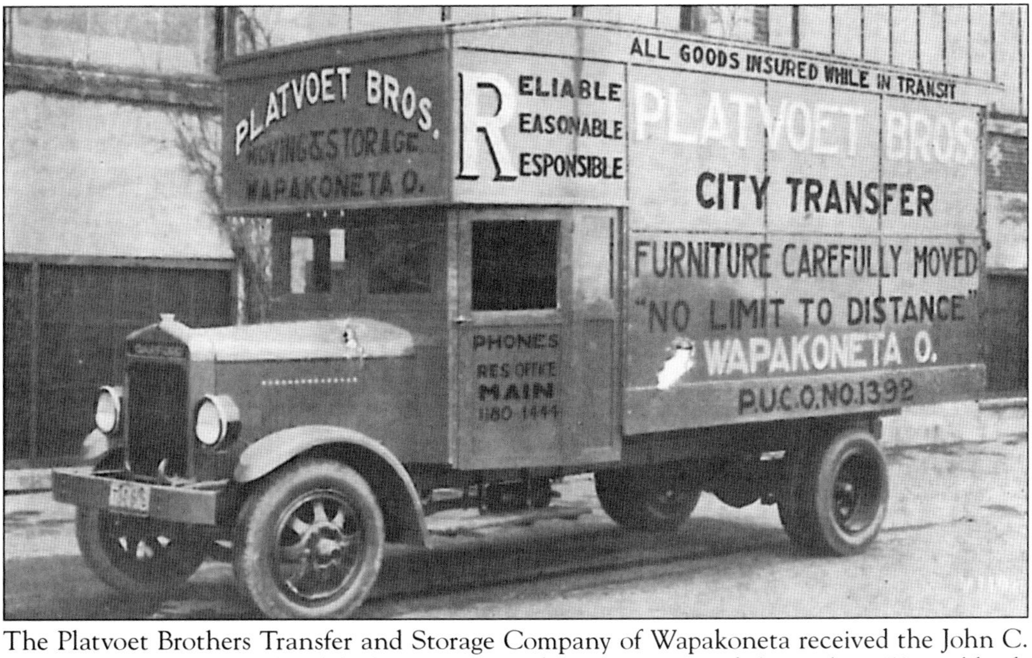

The Platvoet Brothers Transfer and Storage Company of Wapakoneta received the John C. Turner moving contract (paid for by city sponsors). It was estimated that at least 50 truckloads of equipment would be brought from Dayton to Wapakoneta, including 28 huge presses. If all the trucks were the size of the one pictured here, no wonder it took so many loads in the move. (Courtesy of Wapakoneta City Schools.)

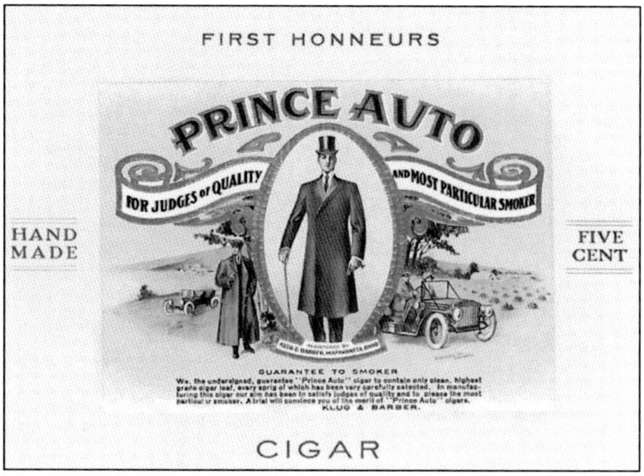

Klug and Barber Cigar Company, one of several small Wapakoneta cigar companies, went out of business as a result of the 1913 regional flood. Producing Prince Auto cigars, the company purchased an advertisement in the 1912 Wapakoneta High School Retrospective yearbook, placing a full-color box-lid label in the advertising space. At that time, an open cigar box was the only point-of-purchase advertisement display. (Courtesy of Wapakoneta City Schools.)

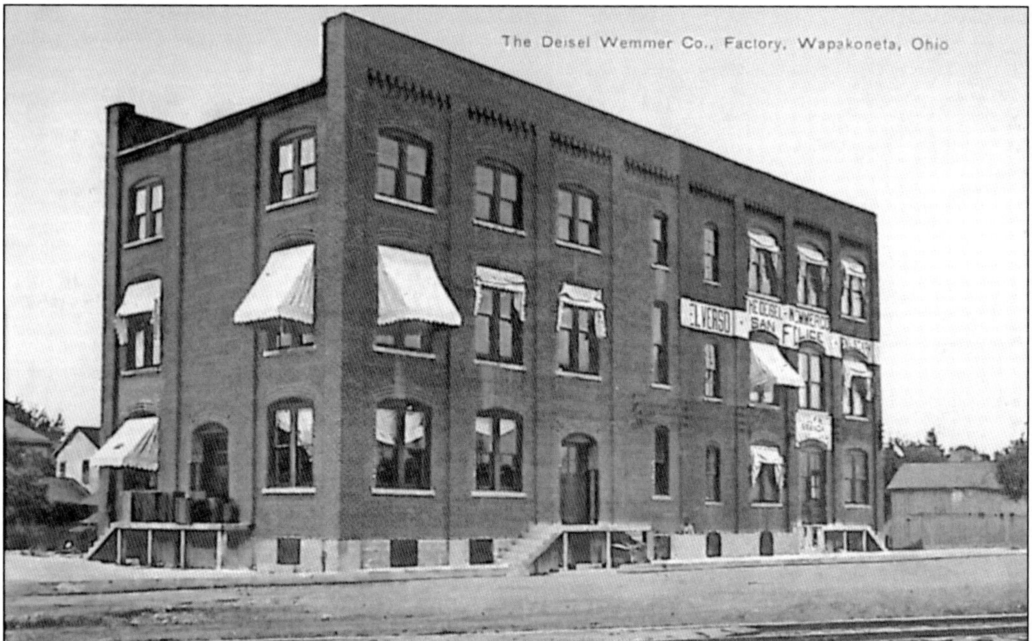

The Deisel-Wemmer Cigar Company (later known as DWG Cigar) began in the early 1880s as a two-person operation in the home of Henry Deisel of Lima, Ohio. The hand-rolled cigars were so popular by the early 1900s, many plants were scattered throughout northwestern Ohio. The Wapakoneta factory, No. 10, at Mechanic and Park Streets closed in 1934 and remained unused until destroyed by fire in 1987. (Courtesy of Janet Schuler.)

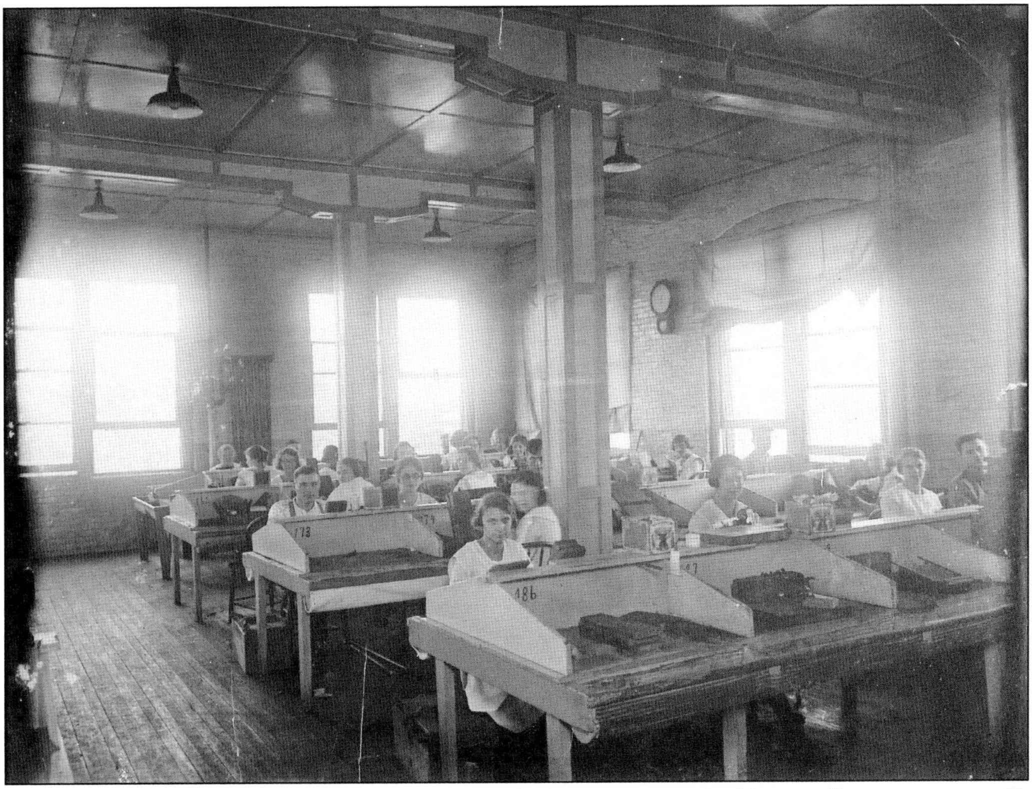

Workers inside the Deisel-Wemmer Cigar Factory had stations at worktables to roll cigars using small, hand-operated machines. The cigar boxes bearing the moose head at the top of the workstations were for placing the finished cigars. Large windows providing natural light helped illuminate the workstations. In 1911, there were 300 people employed at the Wapakoneta factory. (Courtesy of Norma Rickert.)

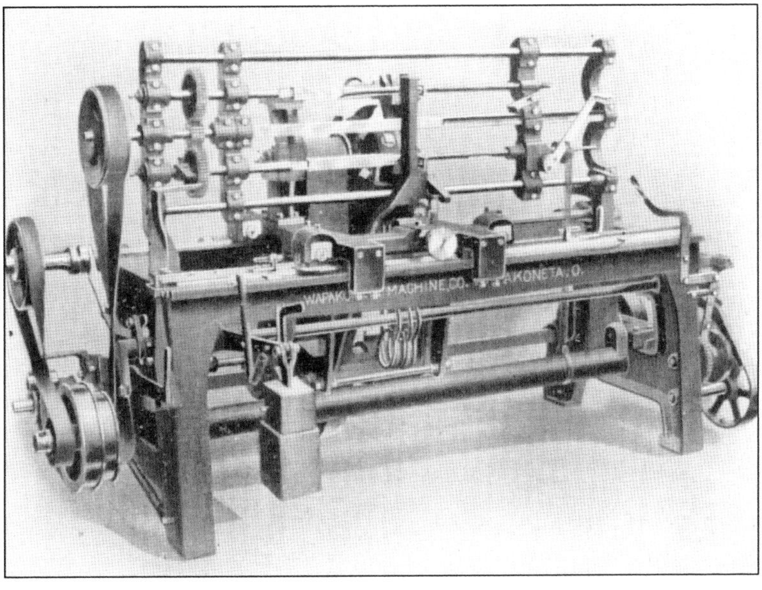

R. J. Schemmel and Carl D. Fischer organized the Wapakoneta Machine Company in 1891. The company specialized in engineered-for-the-job machine knives for woodworking. As the company gained an international presence, it was known for specialized knives used for metal shearing. (Courtesy of Wapakoneta City Schools.)

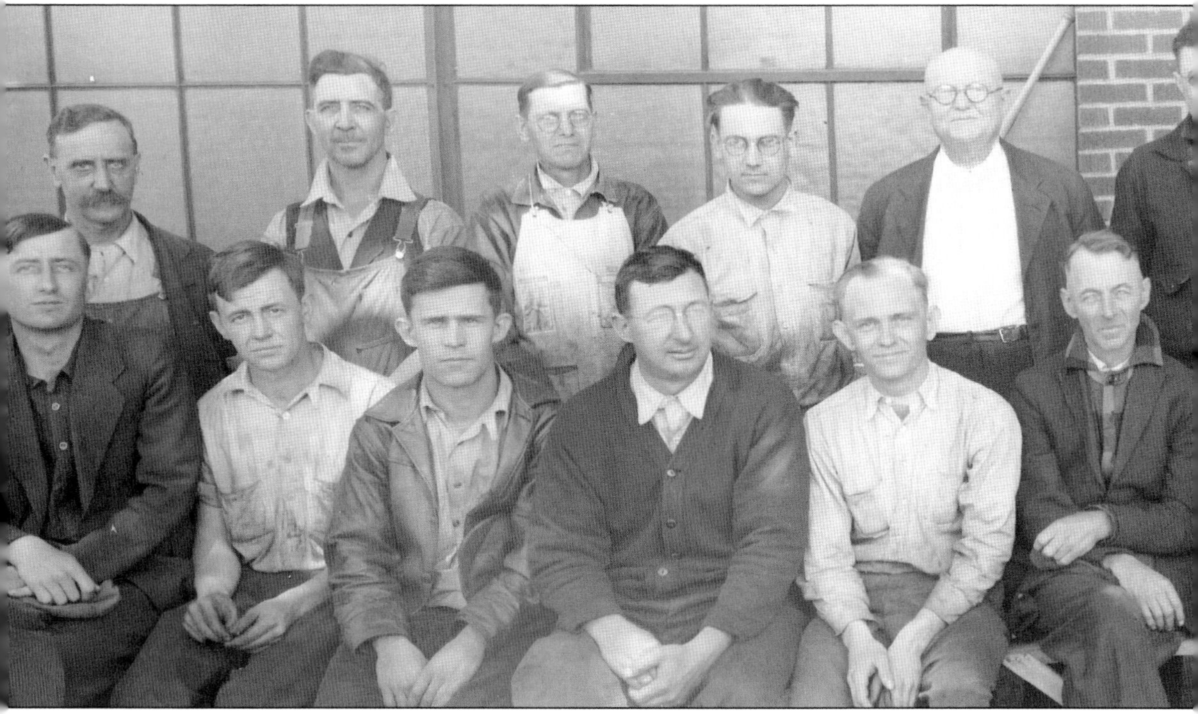

German immigrant Carl Daniel Fischer, founder of the Wapakoneta Machine Company, began producing spokes and wheels in 1871. Known to be an energetic and industrious man, Fischer started several businesses. This employee photograph taken in May 1930 includes, from left to right, (first row) Virgil Miller, Ralph Fischer, Irvin Elsass, Grover Miller, Fred Fischer, Harry Swink,

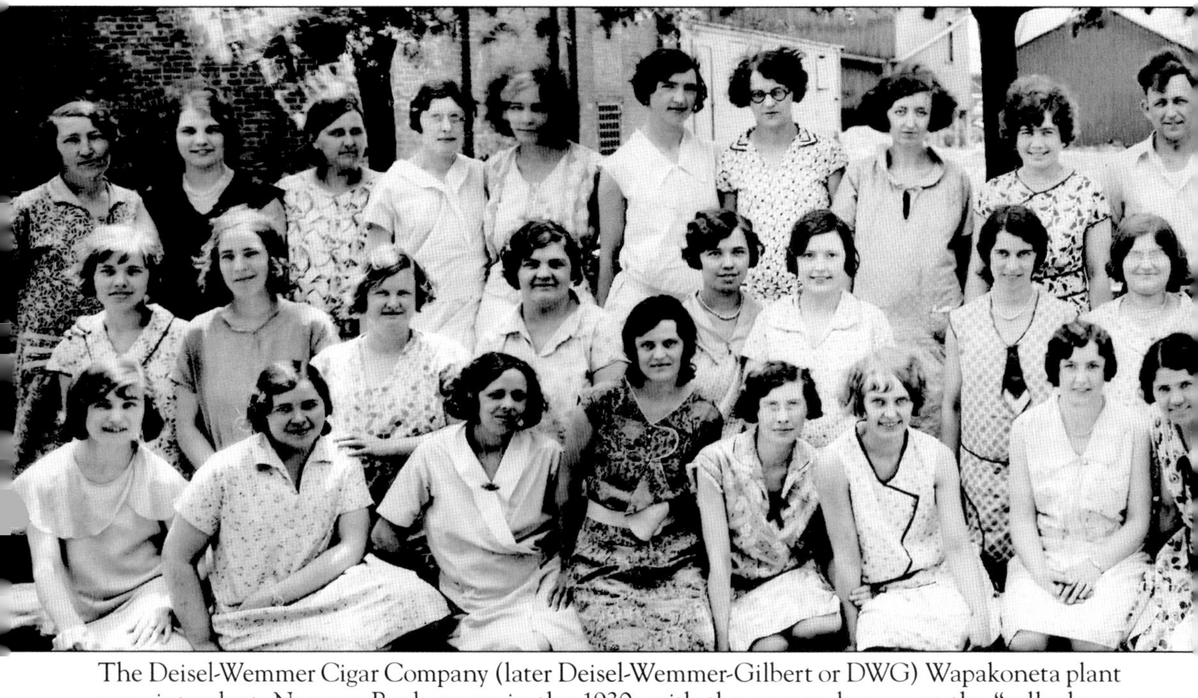

The Deisel-Wemmer Cigar Company (later Deisel-Wemmer-Gilbert or DWG) Wapakoneta plant superintendent, Norman Ruck, poses in the 1930s with the women known as the "cellophane

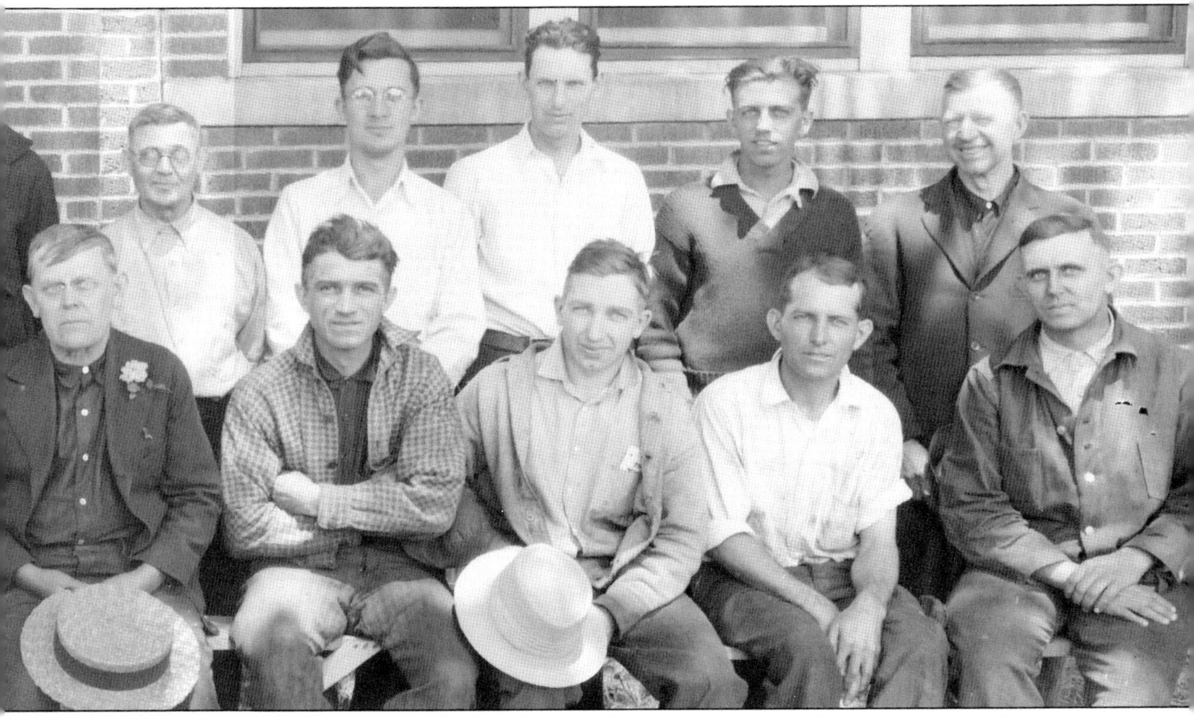

George Zint, Otto Rickert, Robert Brewer, Russell Koons, and Abe Coil; (second row) Mike Meyer, Sherman Coil, Ellis "Elby" Smallwood, Russ Wolfe, John Fischer, Paul Fischer, Ira McCune, Calvin Elsass, Clark Kridler, Merle Coil, and John Seitz. (Courtesy of Norma Rickert.)

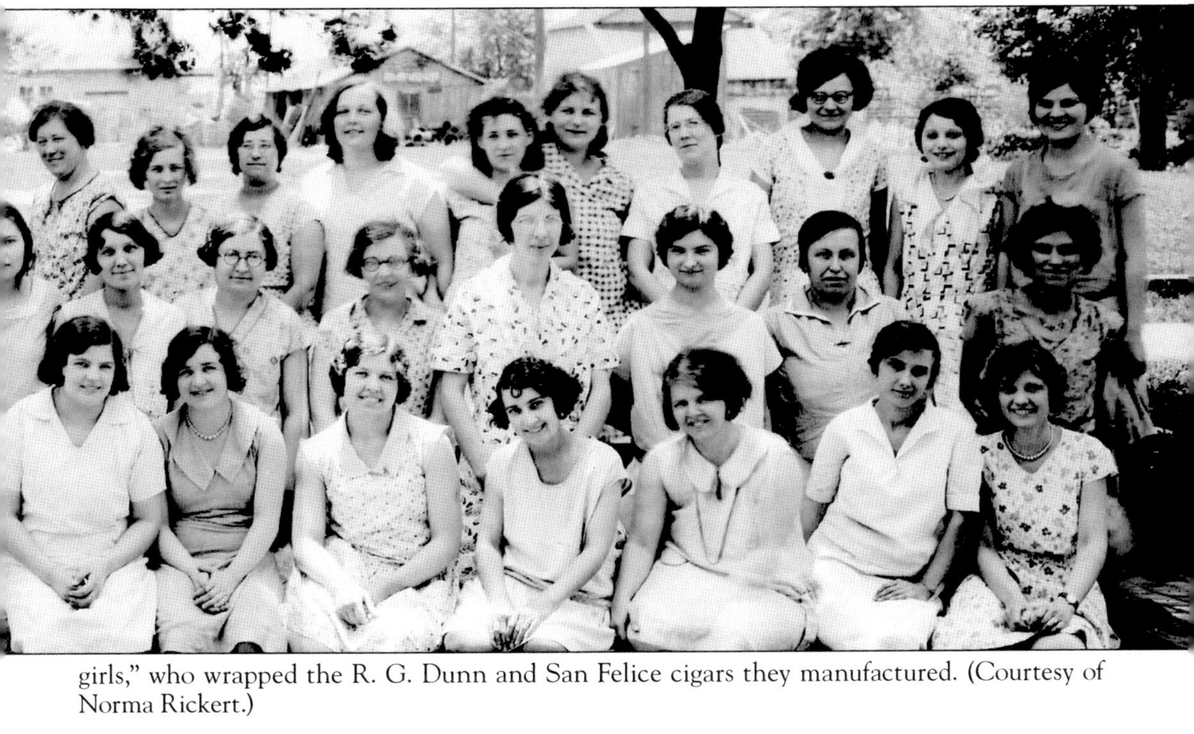

girls," who wrapped the R. G. Dunn and San Felice cigars they manufactured. (Courtesy of Norma Rickert.)

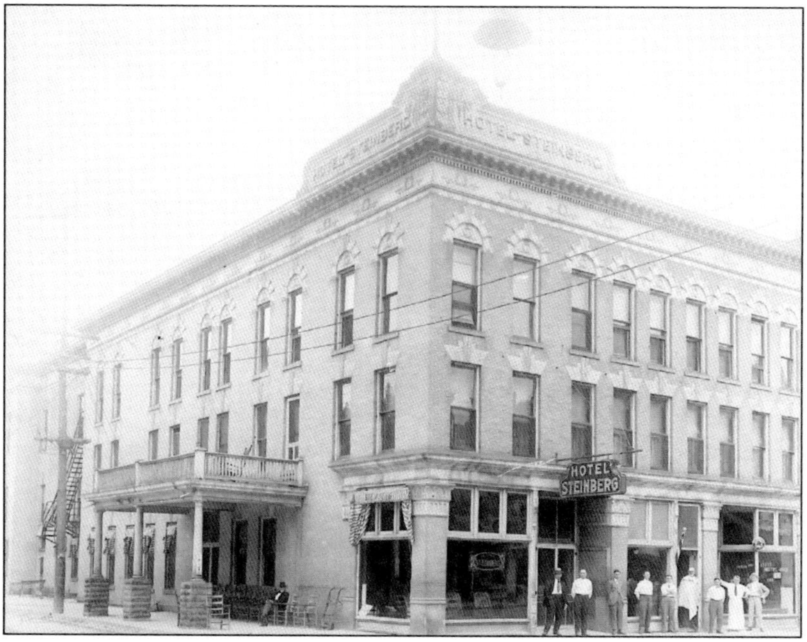

The Hotel Steinberg was built by Adolf Steinberg in 1898 at the corner of Perry and West Auglaize Streets. Later renamed the Hotel Koneta by new owners, this grand establishment was a popular destination for travelers and local special events. (Courtesy of Gail and Steve Walter.)

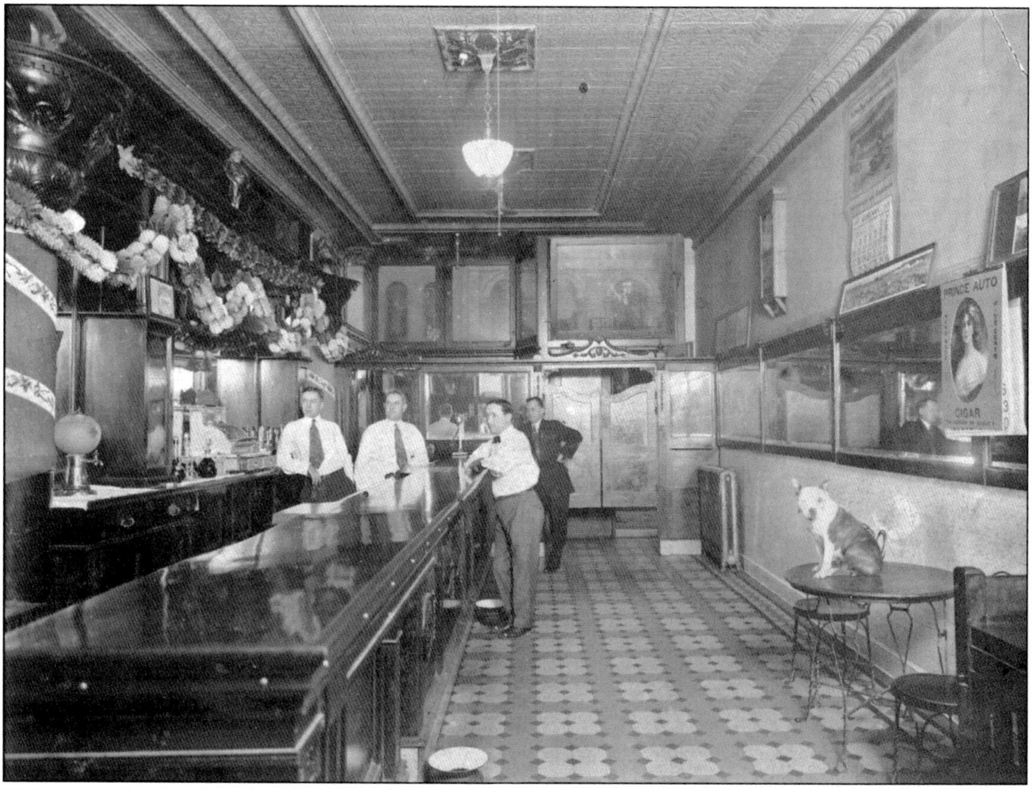

Taken inside the Hotel Steinberg, the staff is ready to serve customers at The Tavern. Tavern employees are Earl C. Bechdolt, Red Hall, Ditmor Spees, and Cliff Cleaves. Mike, the dog, waits patiently under a 1915 calendar on the right wall. Prince Auto cigars, made locally, provided another calendar for the tavern not yet opened for the New Year. (Courtesy of Gail and Steve Walter.)

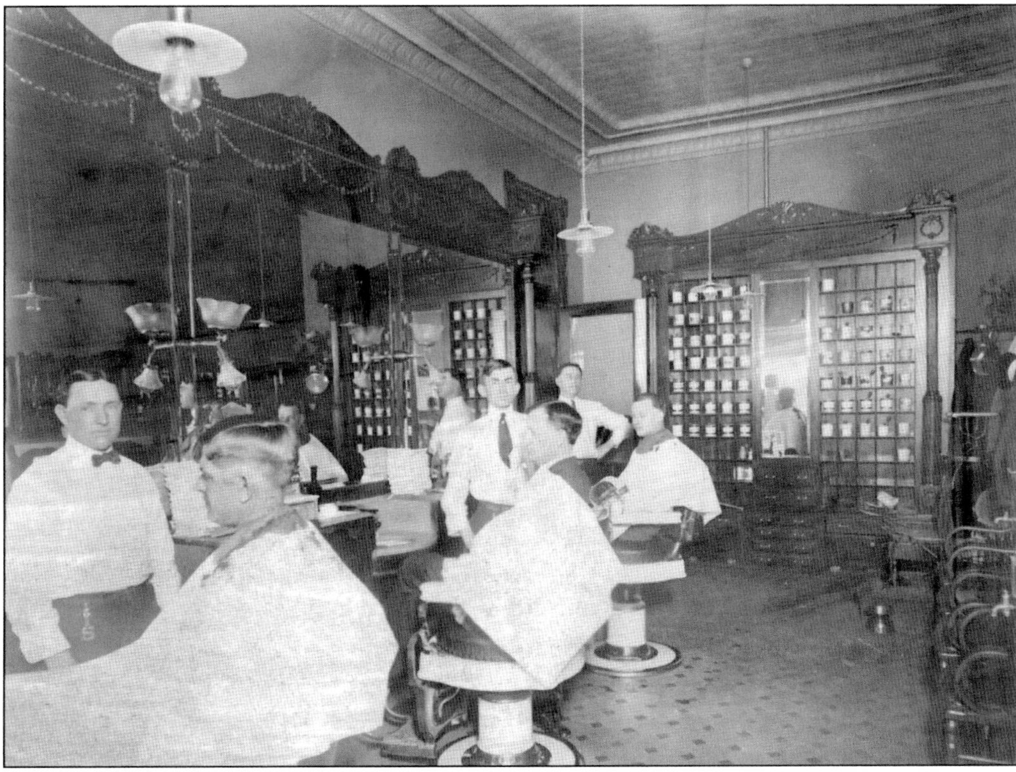

Barbers Ditmor Spees, Rollie Miller, and Lee Stanton are pictured at the barbershop located inside the fully appointed Hotel Steinberg in the early 1900s. Note the shaving mugs for the regular customers on the back wall and the shoe shine stand at the back right. Access to the barbershop was at the center door of the hotel or through the lobby. (Courtesy of Gail and Steve Walter.)

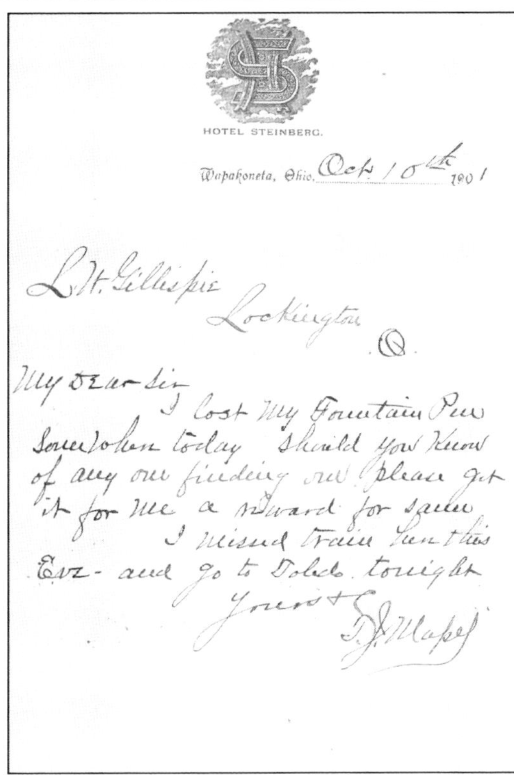

HOTEL STEINBERG.

Wapakoneta, Ohio, Oct. 10th 1901

L.H. Gillespie
Lockington
O.

My Dear Sir
I lost my Fountain Pen somewhen today should you know of any one finding one please get it for me a reward for same
I missed train here this Eve- and go to Toledo tonight
Yours &c
D.J. Mapes

Written on Hotel Steinberg stationary, this brief business note gives insight into the lives of the typical business traveler of 1901. Hopefully the pen was recovered. (Courtesy of Scott Knerr.)

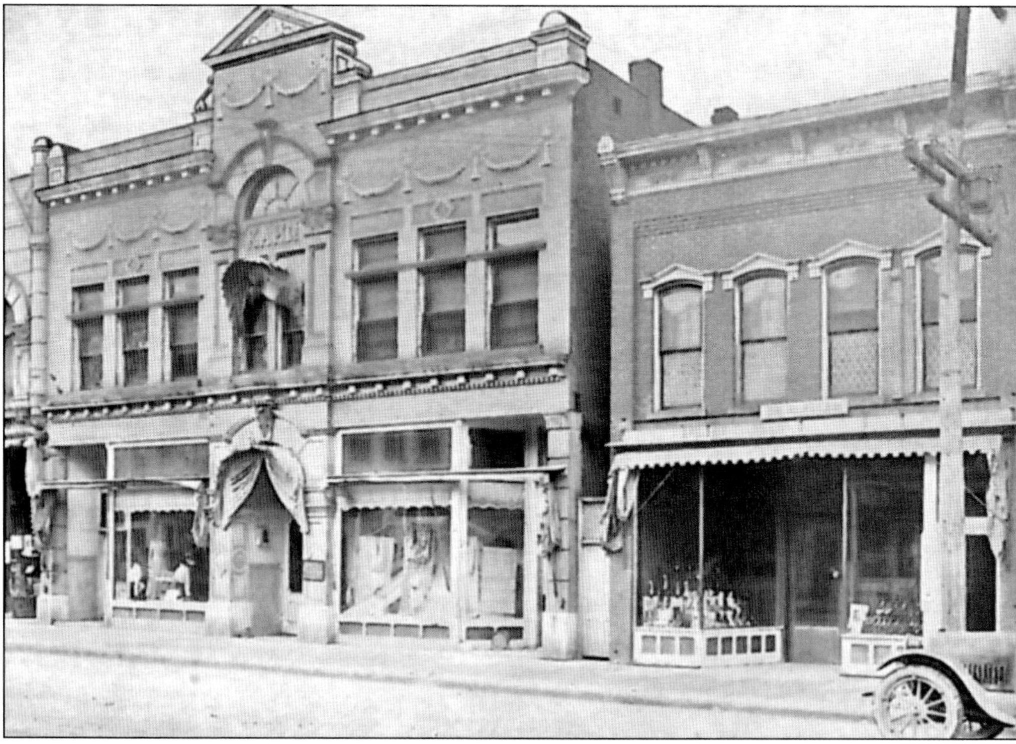

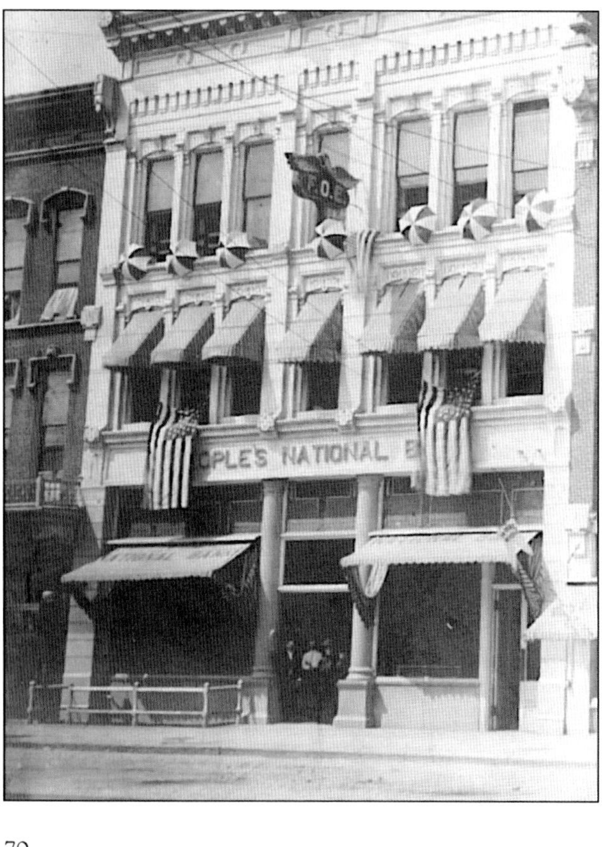

The Kahn Building at 30 East Auglaize Street is now the home of the Wapakoneta Chamber of Commerce, Wapakoneta Area Economic Development, and other organizations. Originally built in the 1890s, it was the enterprise of the Kahn Brothers Shoe and Dry Goods Store and later the Uhlman's Department Store.

The People's National Bank Building, located at 10 W. Auglaize Street, was photographed in 1913. This was the first home of the Fraternal Order of Eagles and, for many years, the location of a barbershop on the basement level. Once the location of the Fifth-Third Bank, the building now has a modern facade. Note the decorative umbrellas at the third-floor windows. (Courtesy of Vernon E. Doenges.)

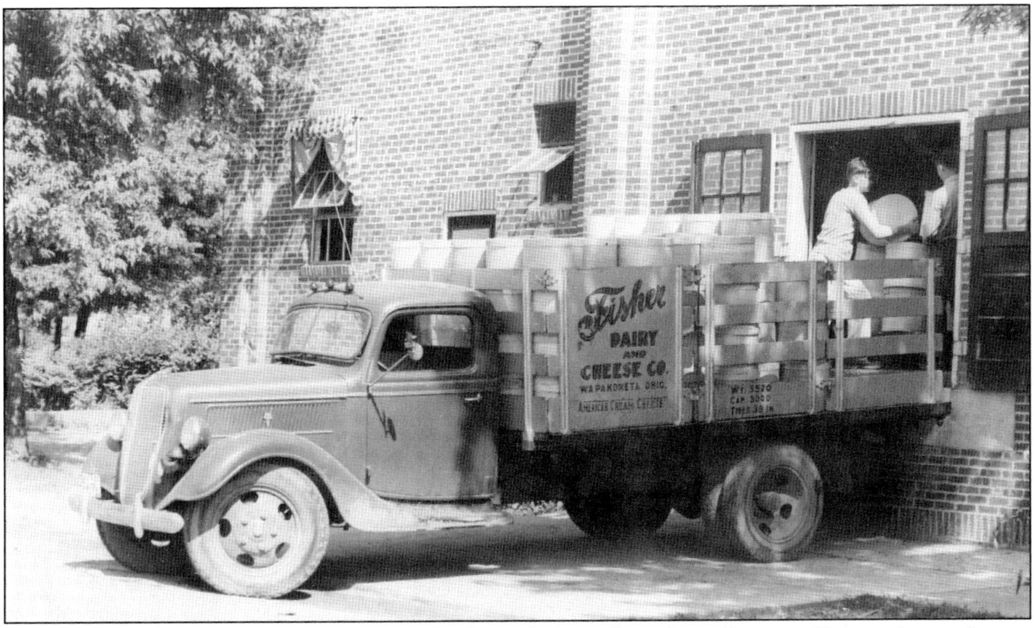

Fisher Purity Dairy began in 1912 when Charles Fisher purchased a milk route. Known for producing ice cream and cheese in the 1920s and operated by three generations, The Fisher Cheese Company grew to produce a variety of nationally distributed natural and processed cheeses. Before selling in 1976, it is estimated that 25 percent of Wapakoneta's population had at one time been associated with the company. (Courtesy of Joy Kantner.)

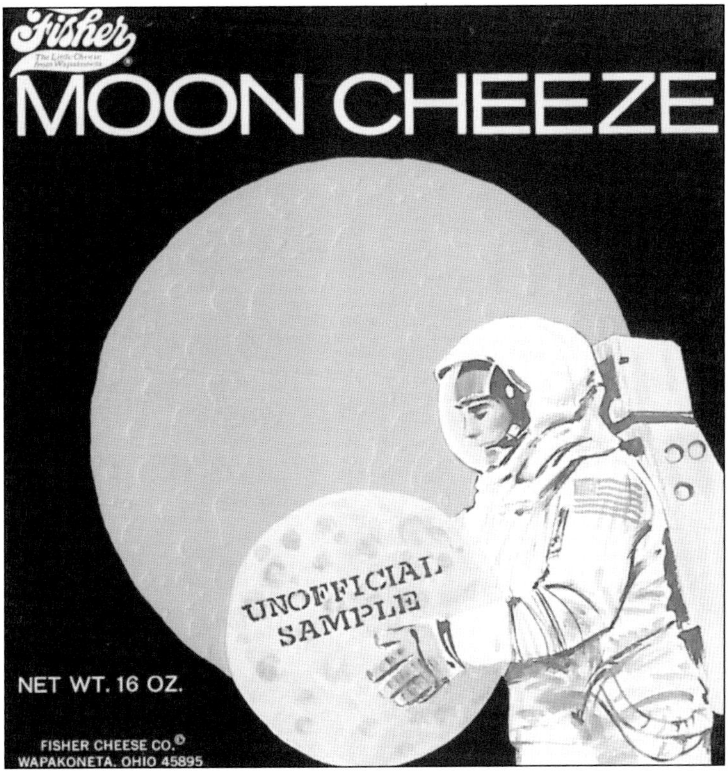

Many souvenirs and collectables honoring the *Apollo 11* lunar mission have been produced over the years, but among the favorites was the .75-inch Colby cheese slice (package pictured at right) known as Moon Cheeze. Wapakoneta's Fisher Cheese Company, makers of the well-known Chef's Delight Processed Cheese loaf, added Moon Cheeze to their product line after the 1969 *Apollo 11* mission. (Courtesy of Annabelle Zwiebel.)

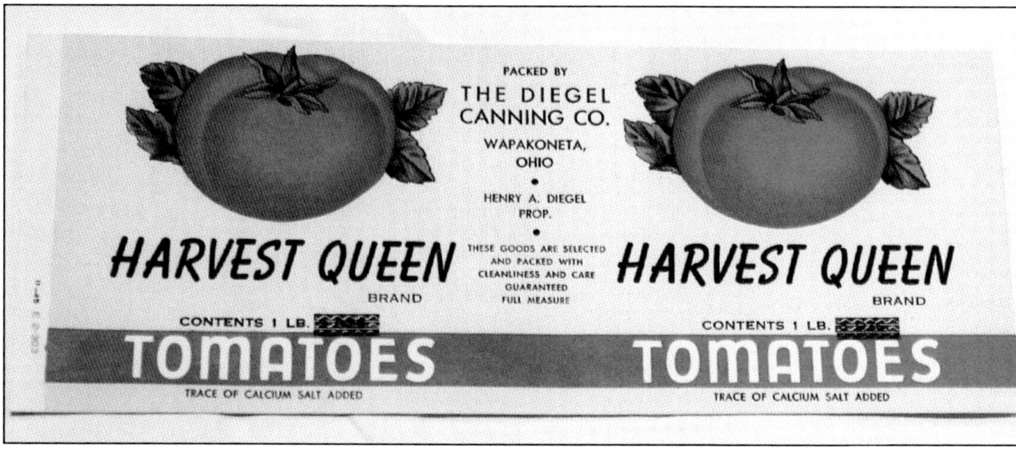

Canning Factory Road gets its name from the Diegel Canning Company that began in 1908 on the farm of Henry Diegel. At the height of the late summer production, two train carloads of processed juice left Wapakoneta for other packing plants in the region. Local farmers contracted to deliver tomatoes for canning, and many local residents worked hard to process great numbers of tomatoes and tomato products.

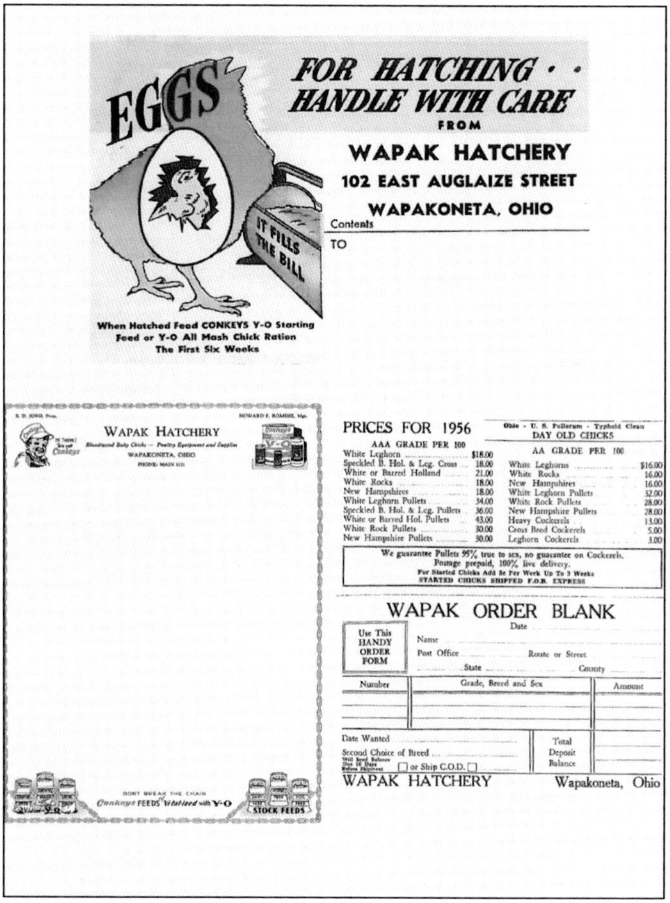

Wapak Hatchery, located at 102 East Auglaize Street, sent boxes of newly hatched baby chicks in the mail to many locations around the state. Rural Free Delivery drivers usually delivered chicks with the daily mail in early spring. Neuhauser Hatcheries, established in 1929, was located at 119 East Auglaize Street. One of the largest hatcheries in this part of Ohio, Neuhauser used electrically heated incubators. (Courtesy of Annabelle Zwiebel.)

Four

Recreations and Celebrations

In the early years of the 20th century, baseball fever in Wapakoneta reached an all-time high, fueled by the discovery of two Wapakoneta Reds team members by the Cincinnati Reds. Theodore "Whitey" Guese played for the Cincinnati Red Stockings in 1901, about the same time George "Long Bob" Ewing was recruited and went on to play several years for the Cincinnati team.

In addition to baseball, Wapakoneta had a variety of sports events as well as local music productions. These formed the basis of lower cost entertainment in the early years of the 20th century. Wapakoneta also had a series of opera houses and movie theaters for high quality productions. Hundreds of special event photographs may exist; however, several were selected for this chapter to also provide a glimpse of the city buildings in the background. As the photographs are studied, the reader can get a sense of the changes in the town landscape as well as events and celebrations that were important to city residents in the century past.

It is interesting to note that the Auglaize County Fair was a highlight in the lives of county citizens by providing a variety of events and shows from its inception in the 1850s. Early in this century, the Western Ohio Railway, part of the interurban railway, deemed the fair such an important event that changes in their schedule were made to accommodate fairgoers by letting them off at the front gate.

It has been said that if an event was to be celebrated, Wapakoneta held a parade. Photographs in this chapter represent some of the great events celebrated in the city, including parades. Overall, city residents have had the benefit of sports, music, and fun in their lives, and those times are celebrated with this brief photograph history.

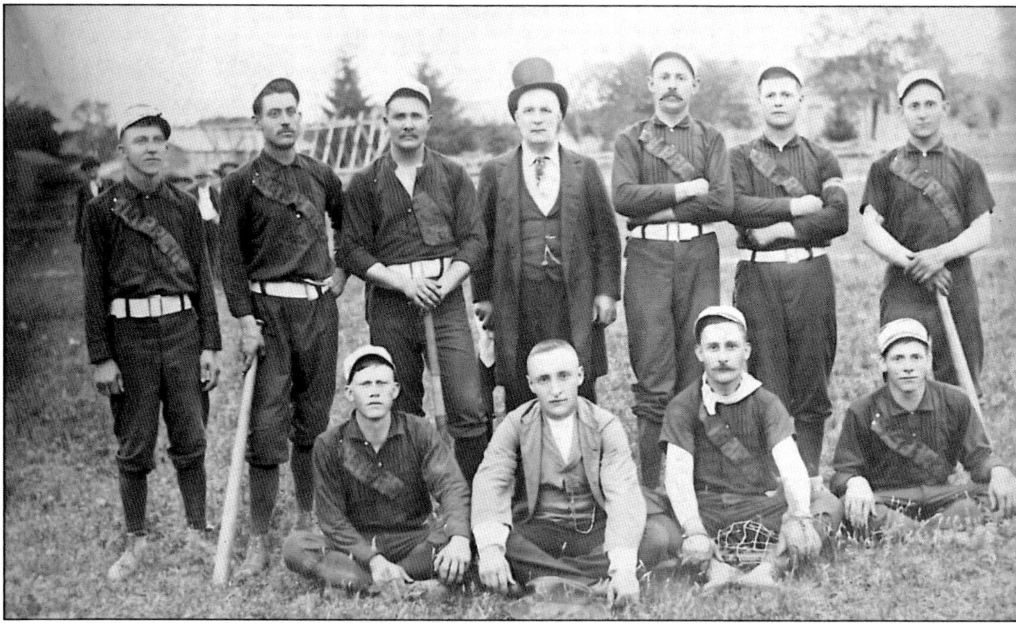

In 1885, Pres. Grover Cleveland was in office when the Old Wapakoneta Clippers played at the Winemiller Grounds, located on the east side of North Wood Street and County Road 25A. The players identified are, from left to right, (first row) Grover Winemiller, Charley Heinrich, John Heinrich, and George "Sizzy" Fisher; (second row) Mike Winemiller, Andy Bechdolt, Eddie Meyers, ? Heinrich, Philip Pitthan, Calvin Winemiller, and Marion Crawford. (Courtesy of Vernon E. Doenges.)

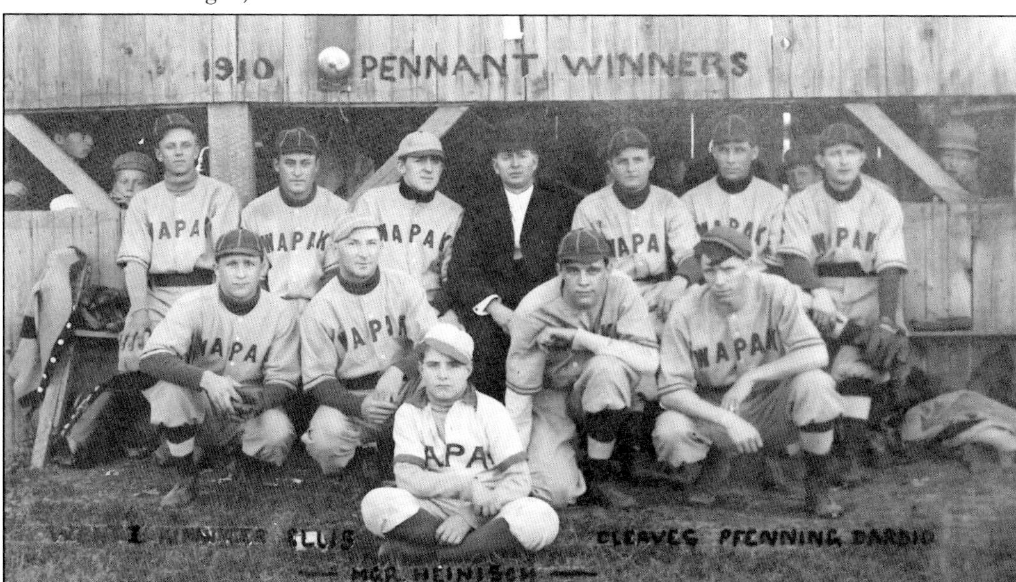

Wapakoneta was baseball crazy in the early part of the 20th century. It was playing for the Wapak Reds that Bob Ewing was spotted at a game in Sidney, leading to his Cincinnati Reds career. The Wapak Reds pennant winners are pictured at Kolter Park in 1910. Pictured here are, from left to right, (first row) Zaenglein, Eichler, unidentified batboy, Boll, and Linthicum; (second row) Wentz, Kinninger, Ellis, Manager Heinison, Cleaves, Pfenning, and Dardio. (Courtesy of Linda Knerr.)

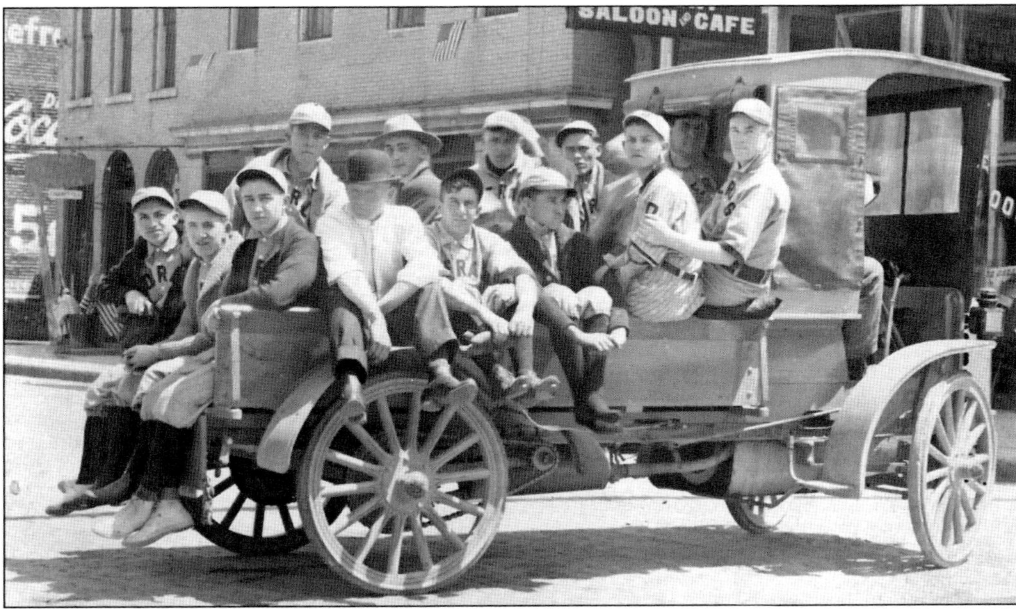

A group photograph of young ball players was taken in front of Yount's Café at 103 East Auglaize Street. The names on the back of this photograph are Lawrence Zwiebel, Fred Bubp, Frank Wenner, Herb Frinzal, Red Spees, Red Gibbs, Carl Trau, Wilbur Nichols, H. Hanks, Bernard Burns, Willie Anderson, Henry Stuart, and Ralph Bechdolt. (Courtesy of Linda Knerr and Vernon E. Doenges)

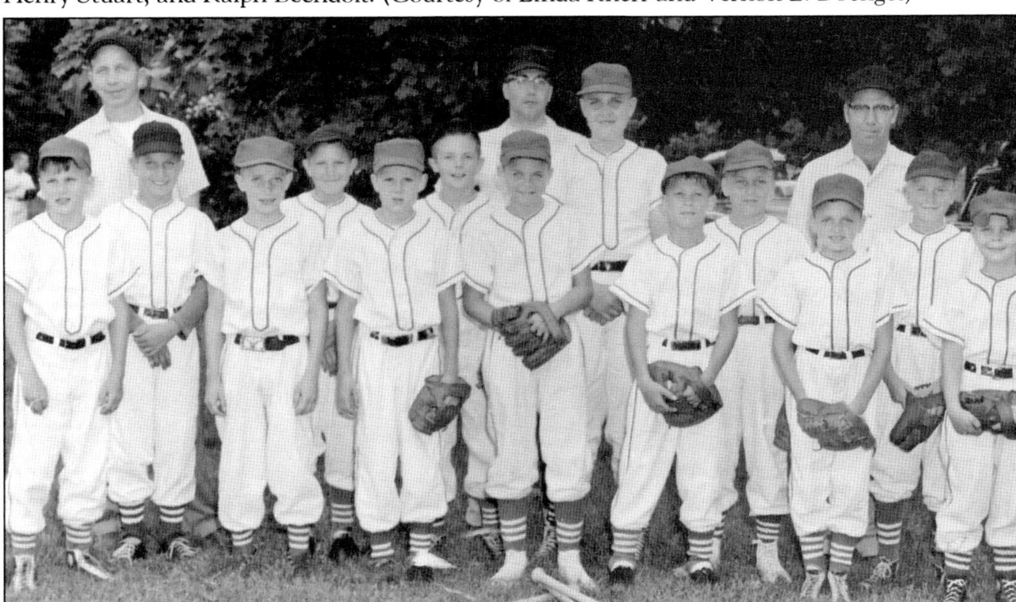

Taken in June 1957, this Wapakoneta City Recreation Department Little League team keeps the baseball spirit alive. The little league players in the staggered row are, from left to right, Dan Bobb, Bob Knoch, Bruce Kolter, Jim Elshire, Bob Wenning, Mike Harshbarger, Neal Malatesta, Steve Davis, Wayne Kiefer, Philip Snyder, Mike Schaub, Wayne Elsass, and Freddie Pepple. The coaches in the back are, from left to right, Mac Elshire, Gene Knoch, and Emery "Bus" Knoch. (Courtesy of Jim Elshire.)

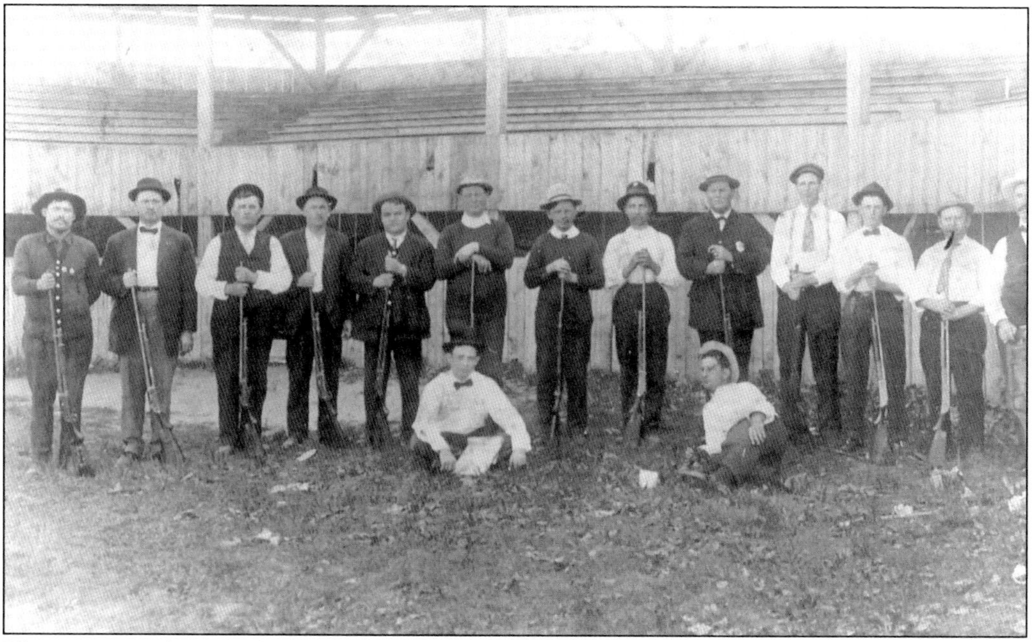

This rare 1910 photograph provides a look at the grandstand at Kolter Park, home of the Wapakoneta Gun Club. Kolter Park was used primarily for team sports but was also known for the trapshooting (clay pigeons) field. Located north of the Kolter and Koch Brewery, access to the park was east off Water Street, north of the bridge. (Courtesy of Fred Zint.)

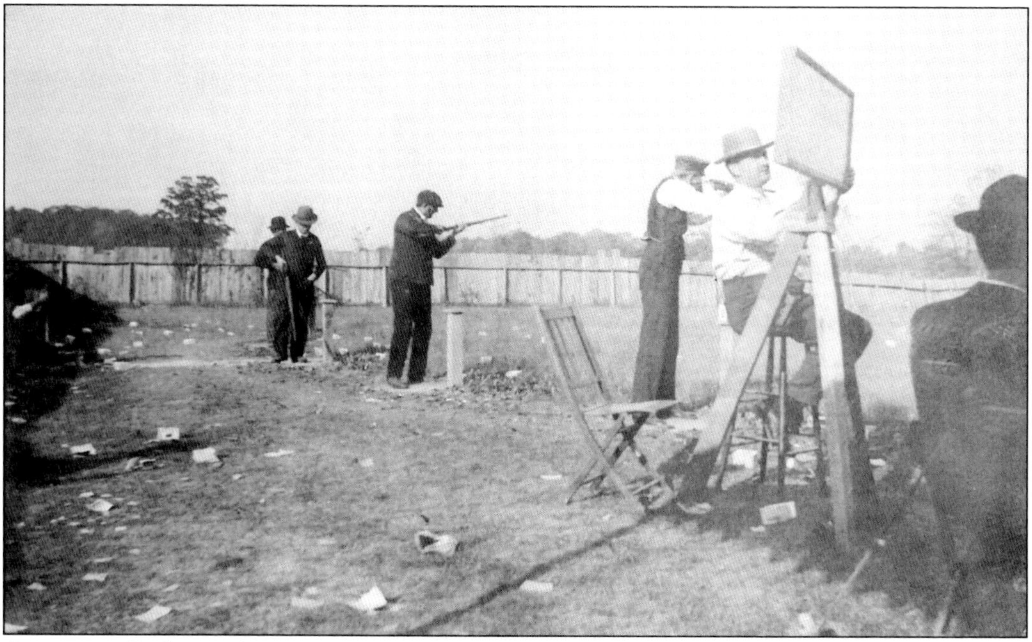

Cincinnati Reds member Long Bob or "Old Wapak" Ewing (fourth from the left) is one of the shooters at the Kolter Park trapshooting range. Frances Bowsher, hardware store owner and well-known sponsor of the sport, is the scorekeeper. Theodore "Whitey" Guese, a local boy who played one year with the Cincinnati Reds, is visible at the photograph's edge in shadow. (Courtesy of Jim Bowsher.)

Taken at the American Legion, this 1908 sophomore basketball team includes Harry Kahn, kneeling front and center. The American Legion Building later became the "Rec" or "Wigwam." Graduating in 1910, Harry became manager and coach of the Wapak Reds, a semipro basketball team. Always a promoter of local sports, Kahn was front and center in the promotion of Wapakoneta and Auglaize County. (Courtesy of Scott Knerr.)

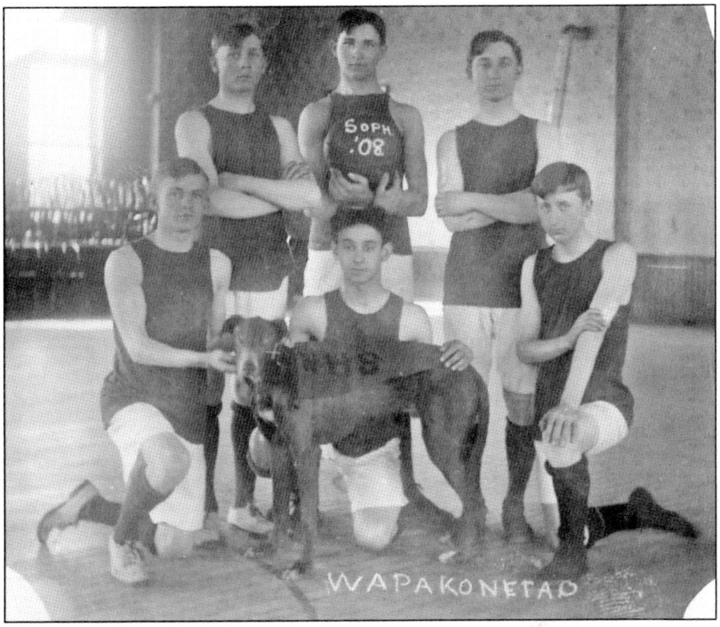

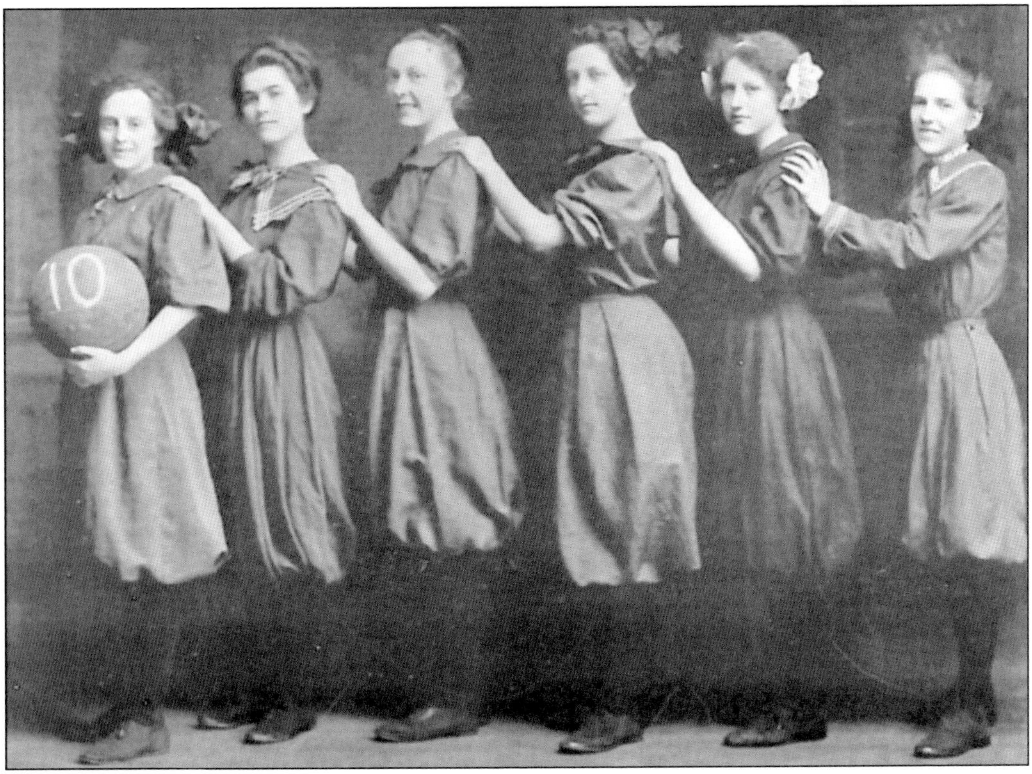

This Blume High School basketball team is sporting the latest fashion. Interscholastic sports swept the nation during this time, providing great social change from the Victorian attitudes regarding women, the development of teamwork for both boys and girls, and entertainment for local audiences. The team pictured includes, from left to right, Pansy Lorton, Fentrus Shaw, Ruby Wintzer, Eva Gossard, Luetta Schilling, and Mildred Faber. (Courtesy of Wapakoneta City Schools.)

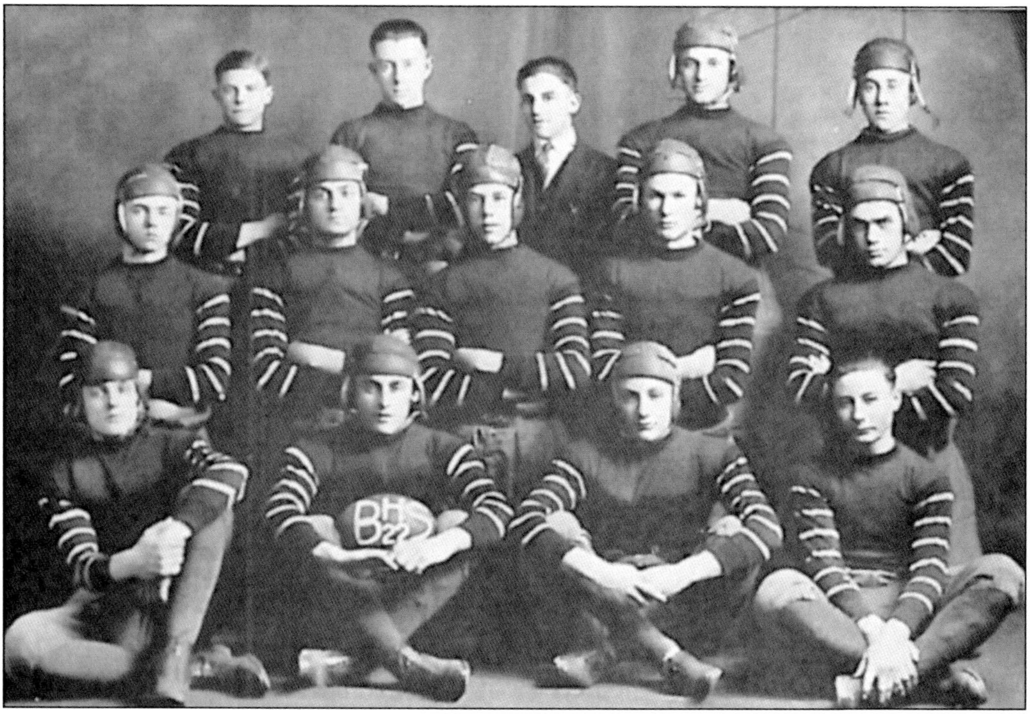

The Blume High School Retrospect of 1922 records the first football team for the school. The season was held in fall 1921 with Richard Ruppert as quarterback. Team members pictured here are John Shockey, Horace Fenton, Marvin Ebinger, Harold Bailey, Howard Zerkel, Reinhold Erickson, Robert Runkle, Frederick Klipfel, William Lechner, Orville Killian, Guilford Archer, Ralph Idle, Robert Gross, Kurt Mueller, Richard Slonaker. (Courtesy of Wapakoneta City Schools.)

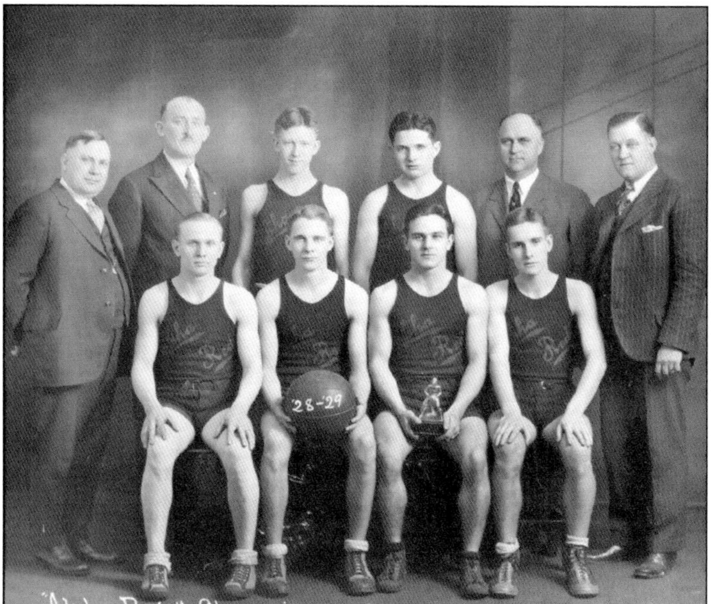

The Alpha Café sponsored the city basketball championship team of 1928–1929. The partnership of Alpha owners Schwepe and Miller ended in 1934 at the death of Schwepe, who died in an Indian Lake boating accident. Team members, sponsors, and coaches are, from left to right, (first row) Rollie Neidemire, Howard "Nutz" Brunn, Lefty Marshal, and Morris Smith; (second row) Hap Vossler, Harry Schwepe, Bernard "Ham" Lucas, Ed Laut, Joe Miller, and Degan Siferd. (Courtesy of Tony Steinke.)

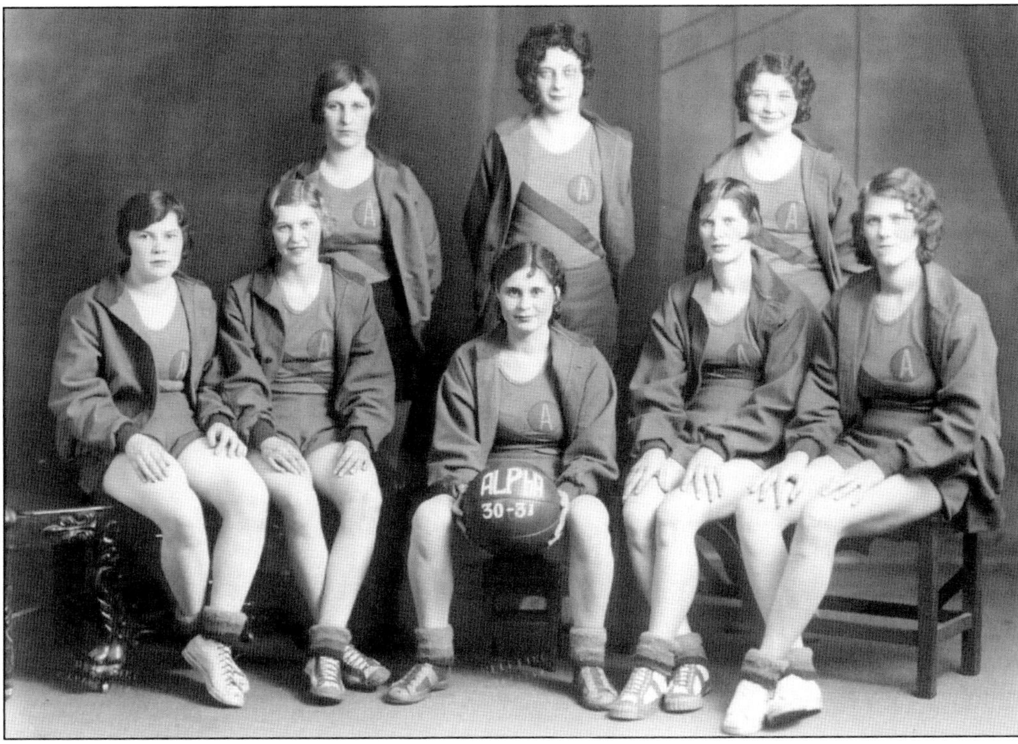

The Alpha Café also sponsored a women's adult league basketball team. In the days before television, sporting events served as one of the main inexpensive forms of entertainment for local residents. Pictured here are, from left to right, (first row) L. Schuler, Letha Dill, Lavera Gilbert, Beulah Stelzer, and Marsele Phillips; (second row) Evelyn Wingardner, Florence Runkle, and Doris Baughman. (Courtesy of Tony Steinke.)

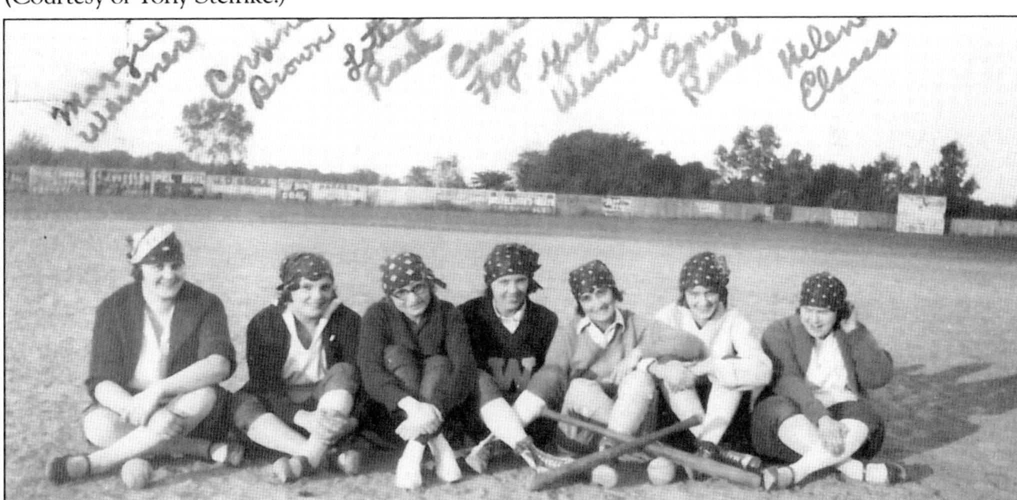

Pictured here are, from left to right, Maggie Weisner, Corrine Brown, Lottie Ruck, Carrie Fogt, Grayce Weimert, Agnes Ruck, and Helen Elsass, representing the many fun times enjoyed by generations of city residents at Kolter Park. These ladies played for the Deisel–Wemmer Cigar Factory softball team. The fence around the ballpark sported advertising, and through it, access could be made to the trapshooting area. (Courtesy of Norma Rickert.)

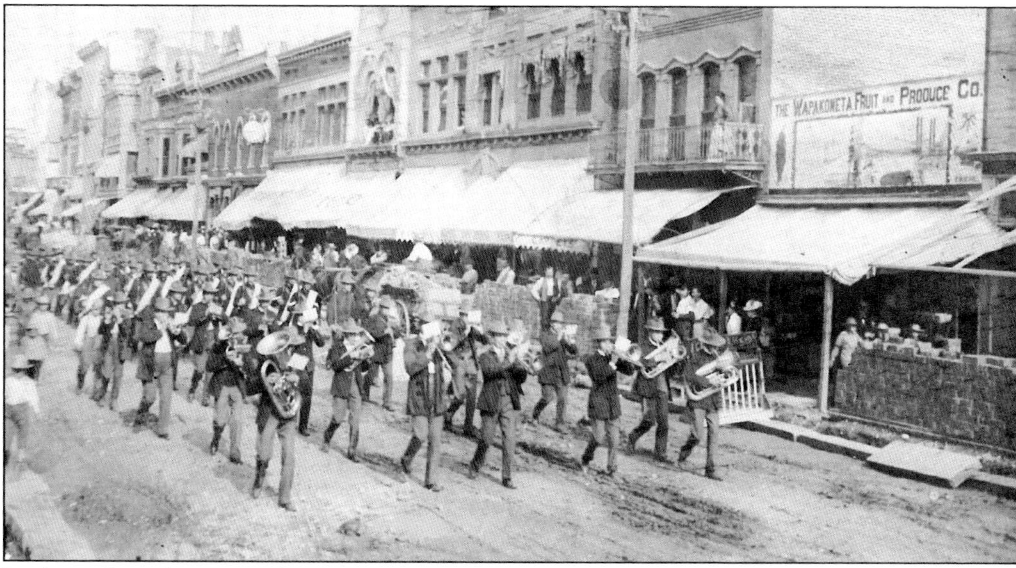

In the early 20th century, bricks to pave the street are stacked on the side, but in the mean time, the parade must go on! Taken at a transitional time in the city, Auglaize Street shows evidence of great activity. (Courtesy of Vernon E. Doenges.)

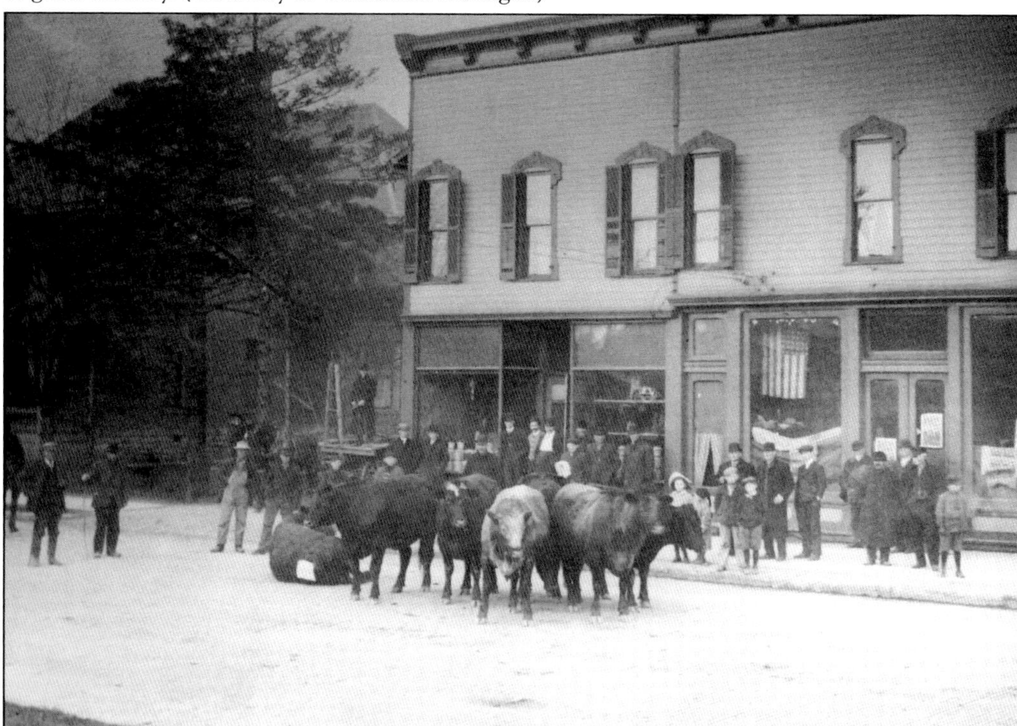

A parade of a different kind, this photograph also shows the new brick surface of East Auglaize Street as cows are herded past the Shafer Block at 205 East Auglaize Street. Werner and Kah Meat Market, located on the left side, operated a butchering facility located behind this retail store. Note the wagon and standing driver in the alley at the left of the Shafer building. (Courtesy of Linda Knerr.)

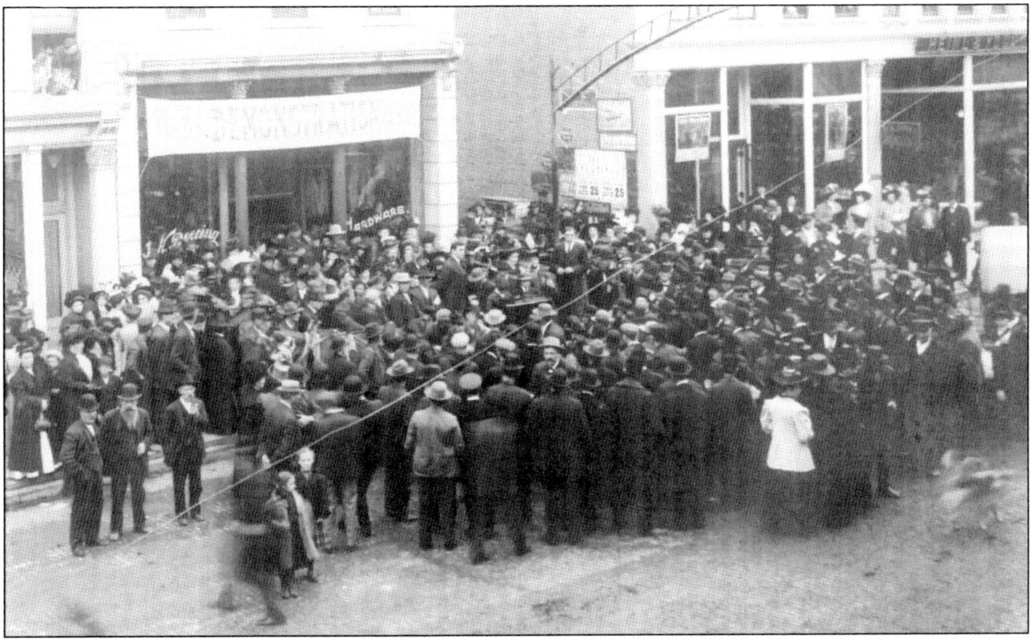

A large crowd has shown up for the demonstration at Doering Hardware at 19 East Auglaize Street. Whatever the item of interest may be, it has the gentlemen's attention. The horse-drawn wagon is nearly hidden by the many onlookers. (Courtesy of Jim Bowsher.)

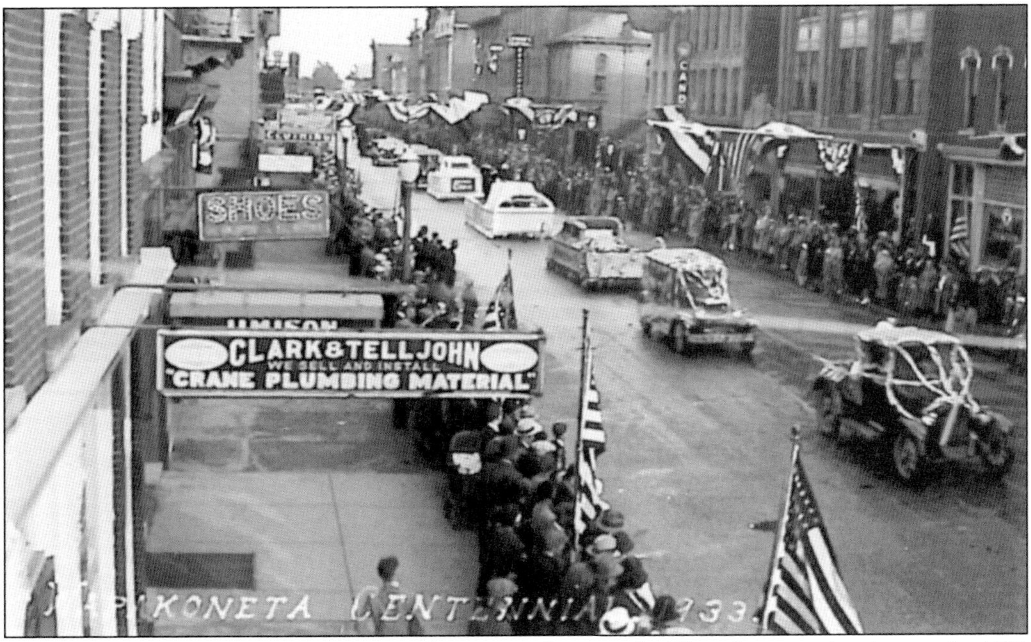

Wapakoneta has often celebrated special events with a parade. This photograph taken at the 1933 Wapakoneta City Centennial celebration was no exception. That year, many townspeople and civic groups produced a variety of floats and marching units. Note the candy store sign at the Hotel Steinberg, also known as the Hotel Koneta, on the right. (Courtesy of Vernon E. Doenges.)

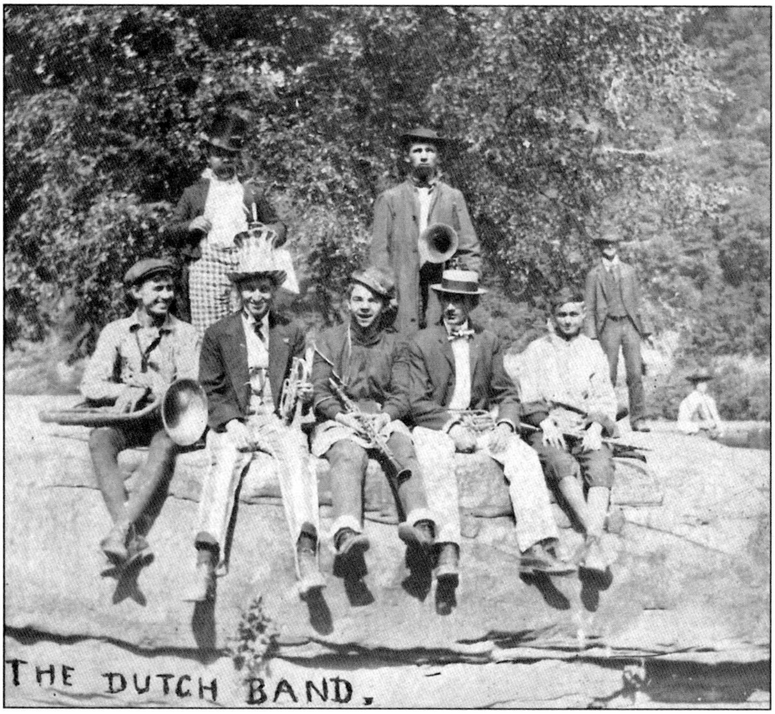

Proud of their "Dutch" or German heritage, The Dutch Band gathers for a photograph in 1904. Frank Schemmel, grandson of German immigrants, is the tuba player at the front left. (Courtesy of Eloise Maxson Archer.)

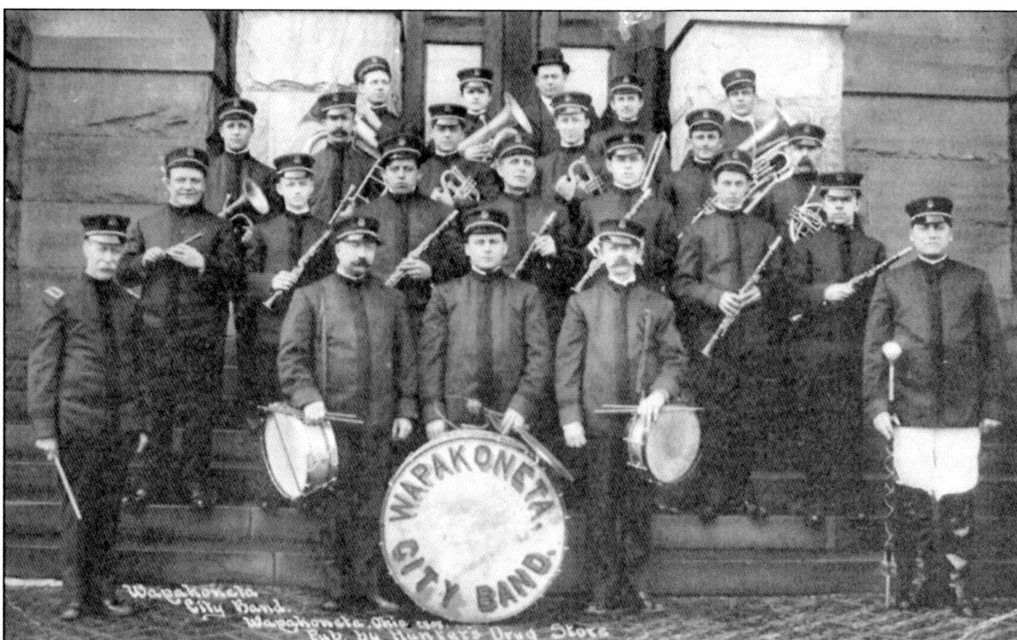

The 1909 Wapakoneta City Band members gather at the courthouse. Pictured here are F. M. Williams, Lawrence Weimert, Edward Nester, Otto Kimbel, Vernon B. Arnold, Clarence Zaenglein, Chas. Heitzwebbel, Fred Nester, Chas. Zaenglein, Frank Maurer, Dennis Gessler, John Lear, Harry Hanold, Raymond Vossler, August Wintzer, Edmund Klein, Gussie Gessler, Ray Barber, Frank Schemmel, Louis Dobie, Christ Vossler, Harry Nagel, and Edward Zink. (Courtesy of Vernon E. Doenges.)

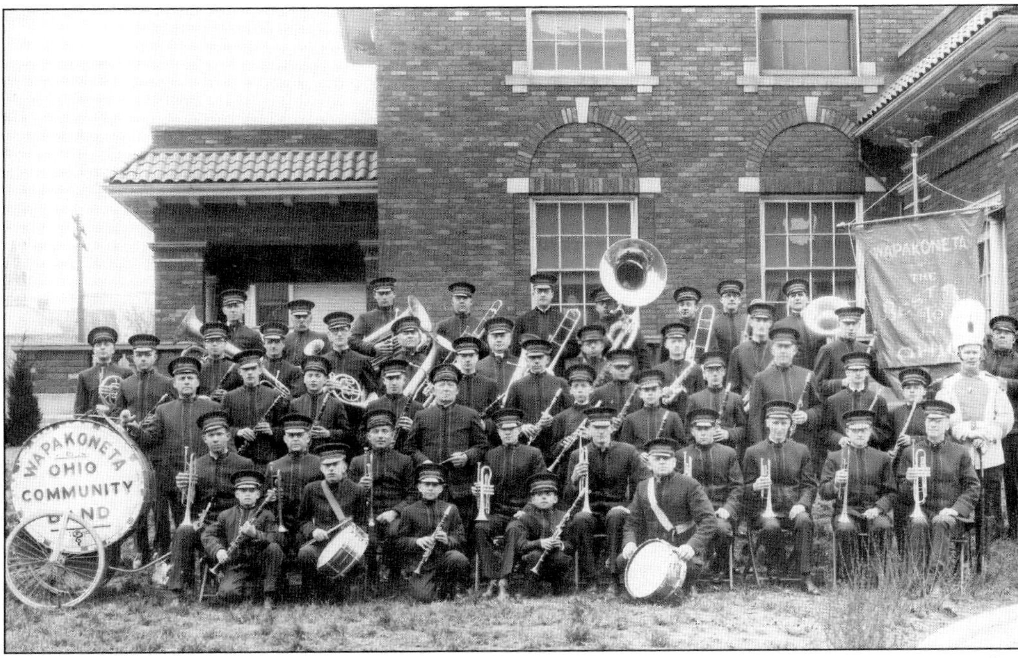

This 1920s Wapakoneta Community Band grew from a 1909 version and sports a new name. One constant was Frank Schemmel, identified as the first brass player in the back row. Taken at the Elks building built in 1924 on Perry Street, the Elks basement became the band's rehearsal hall. Note the drum conveyance in this drum and bugle corps. (Courtesy of Eloise Maxson Archer.)

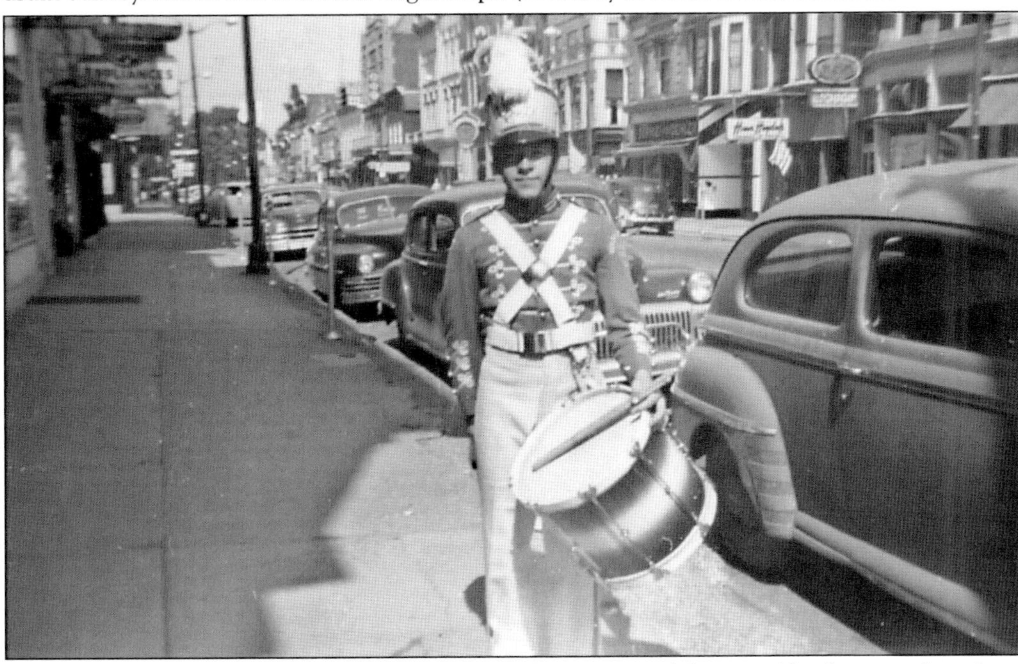

In 1953, Richard Stearns was a member of the Eagles-sponsored drum and bugle corps that played marching music for many years at parades and events. Corps members of all ages represented Wapakoneta throughout the region. Stearns poses on East Auglaize Street with the Alpha Café in the background (on the north side of the street). (Courtesy of Richard Stearns.)

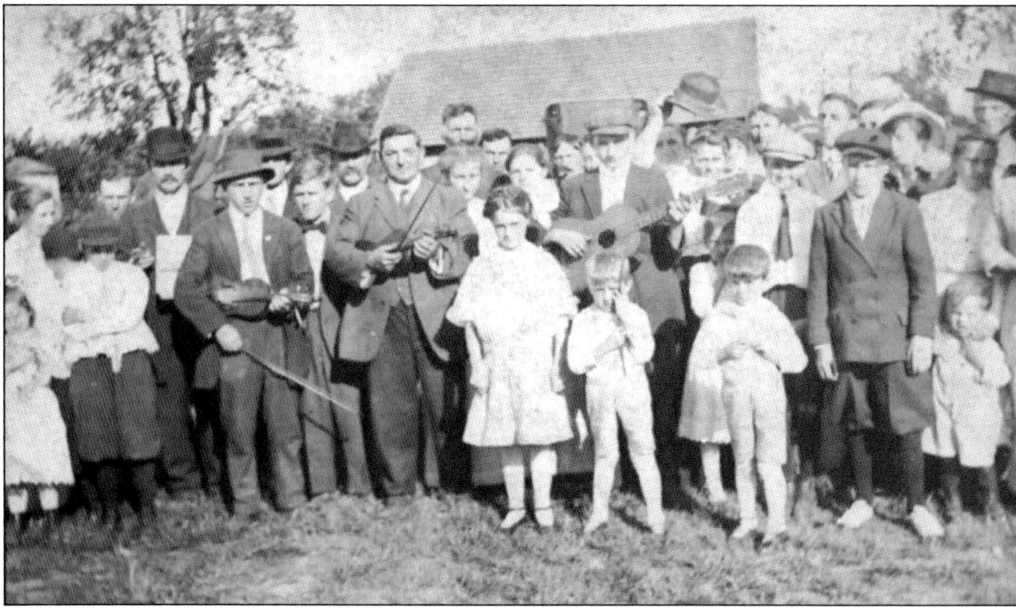

The annual Wheel Makers Beneficial Association picnic was held on August 26, 1923, at the fairgrounds, where over 150 wheel makers and their families gathered. A chicken dinner, cake walk, horseshoe pitching, and contests of all kinds were enjoyed while the Elmer "Belty" Hague Orchestra composed of Hague (right fiddler), Clem Hague (guitar), Richard "Bud" Hague, and Jim "Mulligan" Waltz (left) furnished the music. (Courtesy of Robert Hague.)

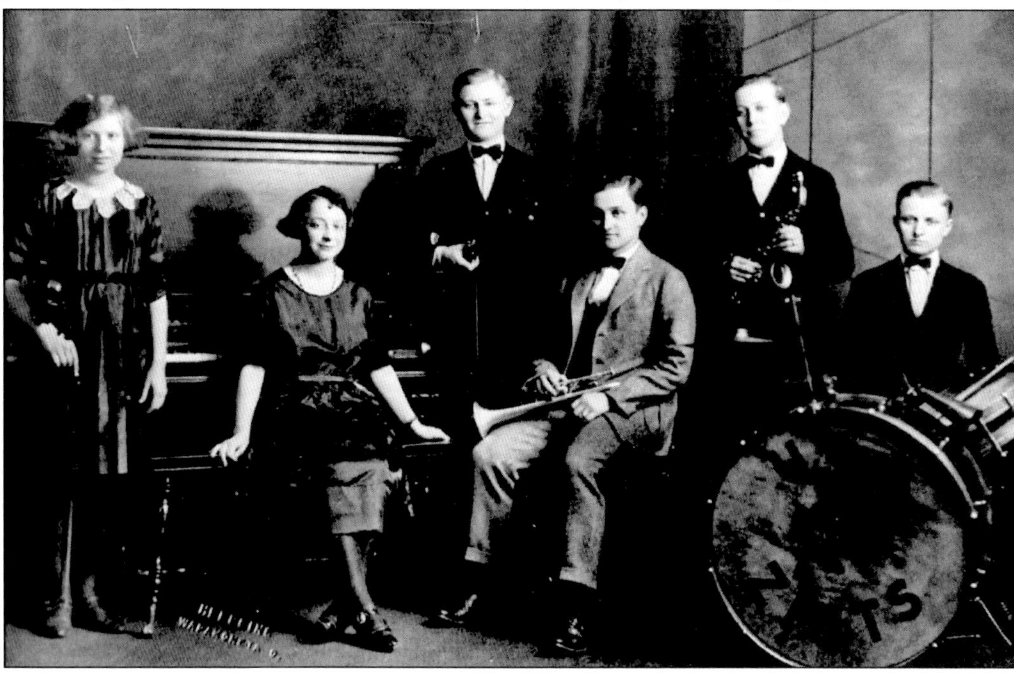

The Zint Family Orchestra, captured by the Helpling Studio in 1917, was composed of Lucile, Beulah, Frederick, Raymond, Kermit, and Arthur. The orchestra played at dances and special events throughout the region and specialized in the modern "dancing swing" of the era. Over the years, family members belonged to other popular bands in the area. (Courtesy of Fred Zint.)

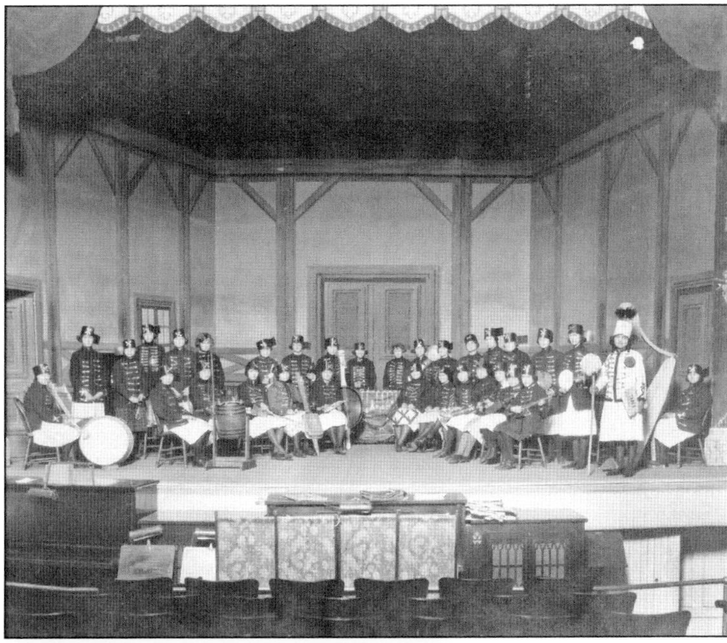

This Blume High School Kitchen Cabinet Band performed at the Brown Theater in November 1922. All of the instruments are kitchen items, including the Standard churn at the stage front. The Brown Theater served the community as an auditorium for school productions and graduations in addition to providing big name commercial stage productions and entertainers. (Courtesy of Eugene and Shirley Pohlable.)

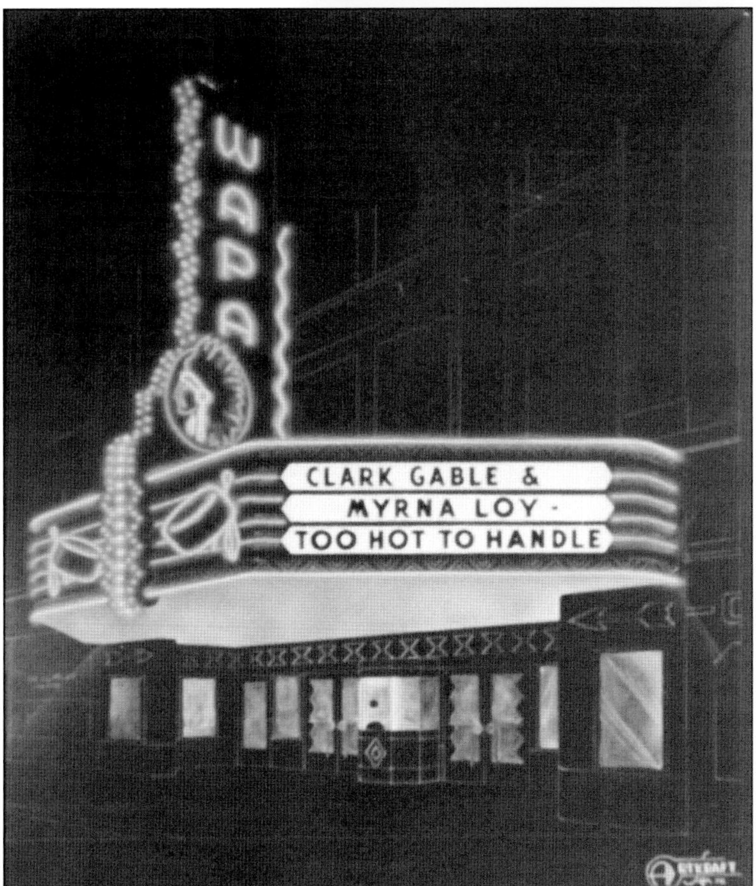

The Brown Theater, constructed in 1904, was a gift to the citizens of Wapakoneta by industrialist Michael Brown. During the 1930s, the stage area was converted for big screen movies when the demand for stage productions was in decline. According to an article in the *Wapakoneta Daily News* on October 1, 1953, former owner Emil George replaced the original tile pilars and canopy with a glass-front, "zephyr type" marquee with a lighted neon Native American motif. It was renamed the Wapa Theater in 1938. (Courtesy of Robert C. Wiesenmayer.)

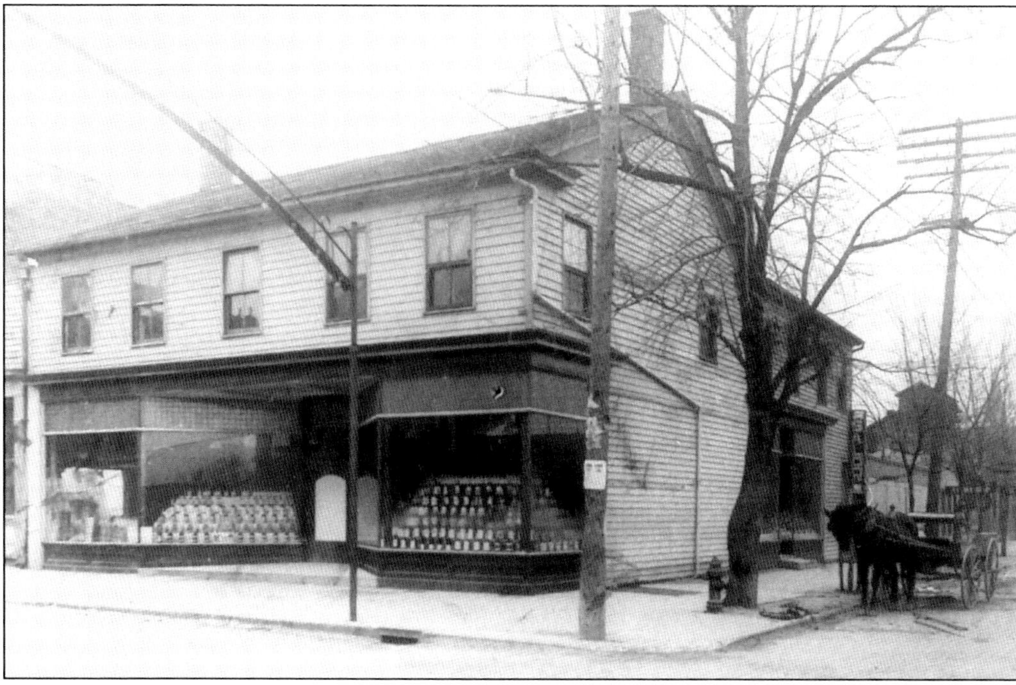

The Jacob C. Zint family lived above the restaurant and saloon in the early years of his business career when this photograph was taken, c. 1905. Later a new proprietor, Oscar Harris, would open the Corner Café, located at the southeast corner of Auglaize and Blackhoof Streets. (Courtesy of Fred Zint.)

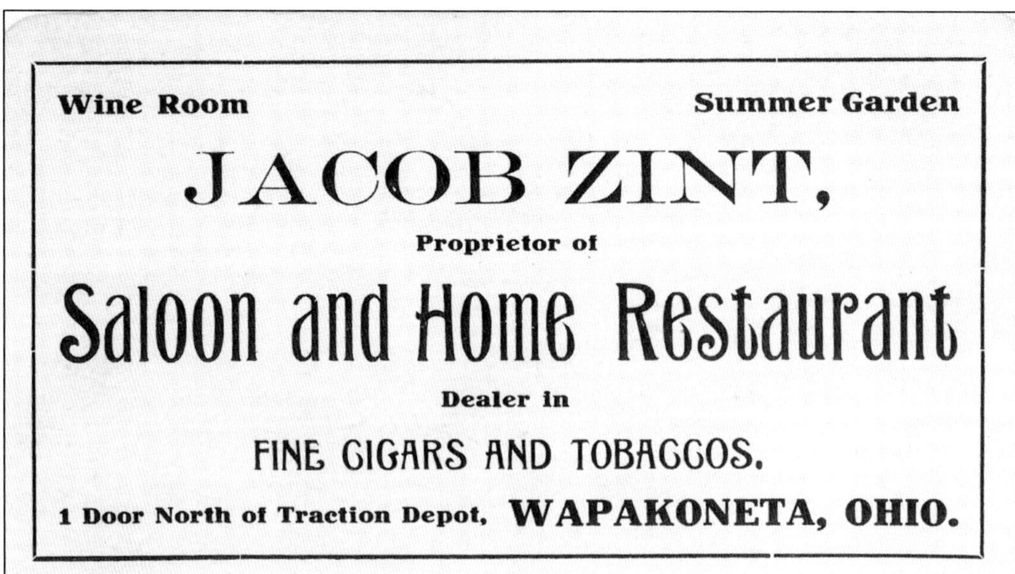

Zint's Saloon was close to the interurban depot, which helped secure the success of his establishment. The saloon entrance on Blackhoof Street, visible by the horse and buggy in the image at the top of the page, was also the location of a summer garden or *bier garten*. Ladies were not permitted in the saloon, but they were welcome to enjoy the summer garden. (Courtesy of Scott Knerr.)

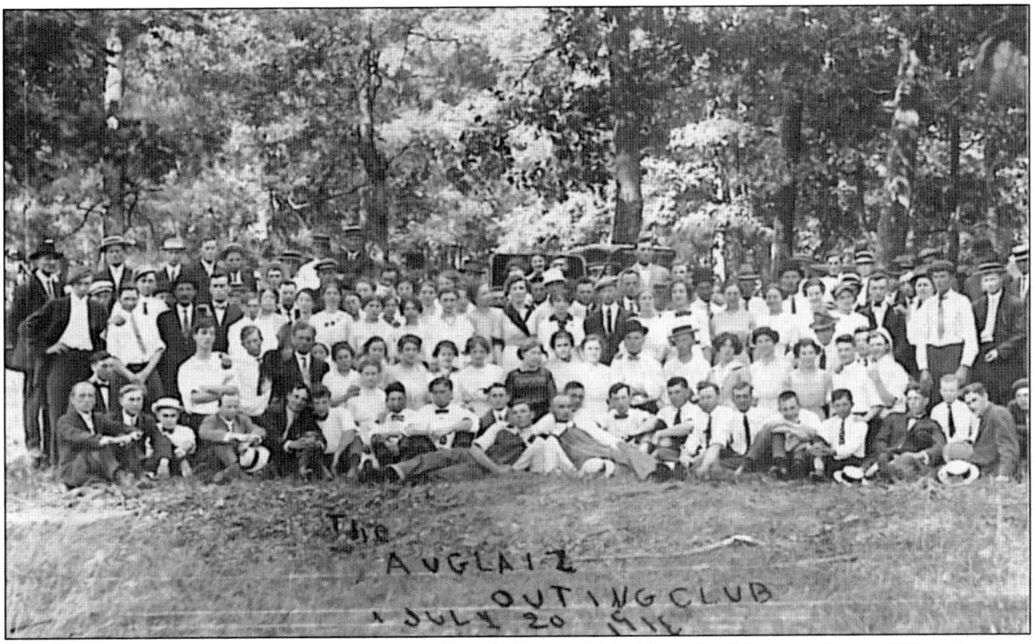

The Outing Country Club was a popular club in 1913. Exactly 56 years later, Wapakoneta residents would be celebrating Neil A. Armstrong's successful walk on the moon, but on this afternoon, everyone posed for a photograph on the banks of the Auglaize River. Later this Fox Ranch Road location would have a nightclub and tavern known as The Dale. (Courtesy of Vernon E. Doenges.)

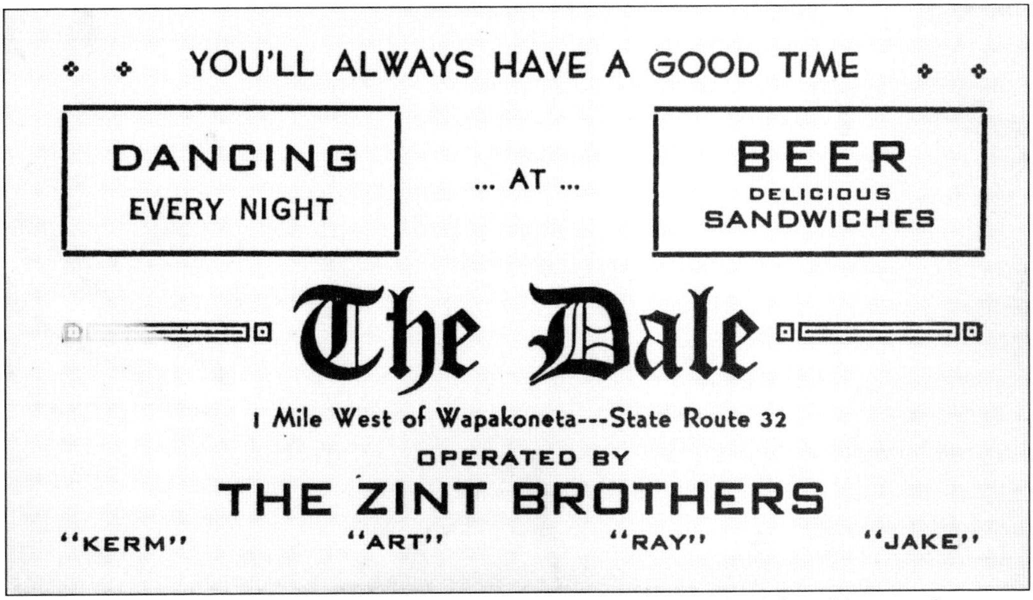

The Dale opened to a crowd of over 500 on July 7, 1934. The new nightclub and beer garden resort at the former Wapakoneta Country Club house was owned and operated by the Zint Brothers. (Courtesy of Scott Knerr.)

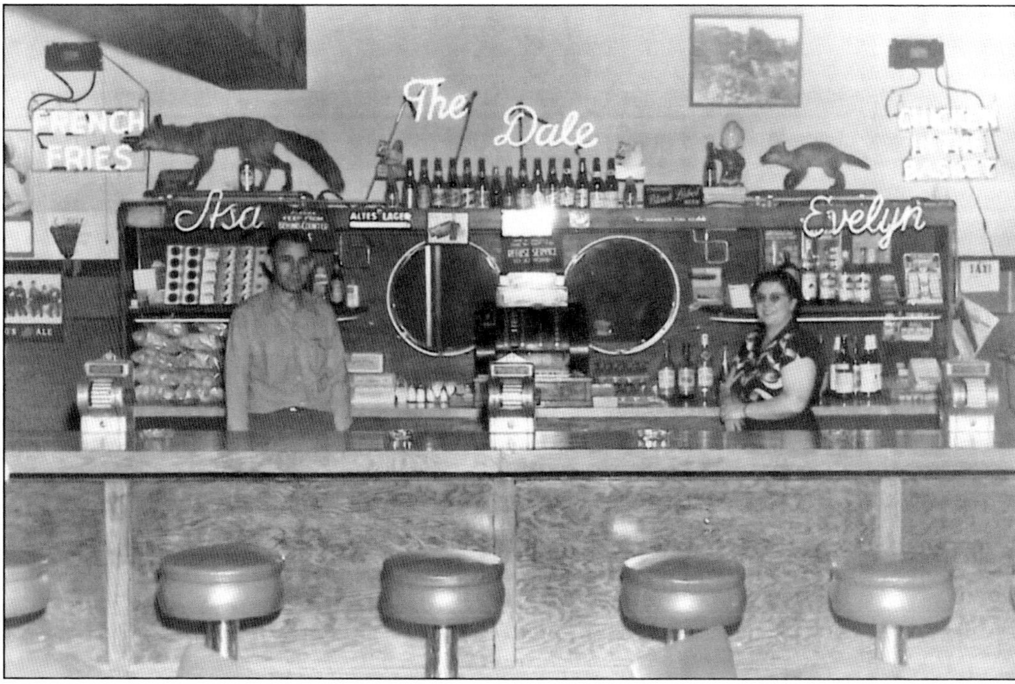

Many area citizens enjoyed meeting at The Dale. The owners of the tavern in the 1940s, Evelyn and Asa Houts (pictured), greeted everyone with a smile. Note the neon signs in the background and the preserved foxes on the back bar. Taxidermy decor was typical of many taverns in this time period. (Courtesy of Vernon E. Doenges.)

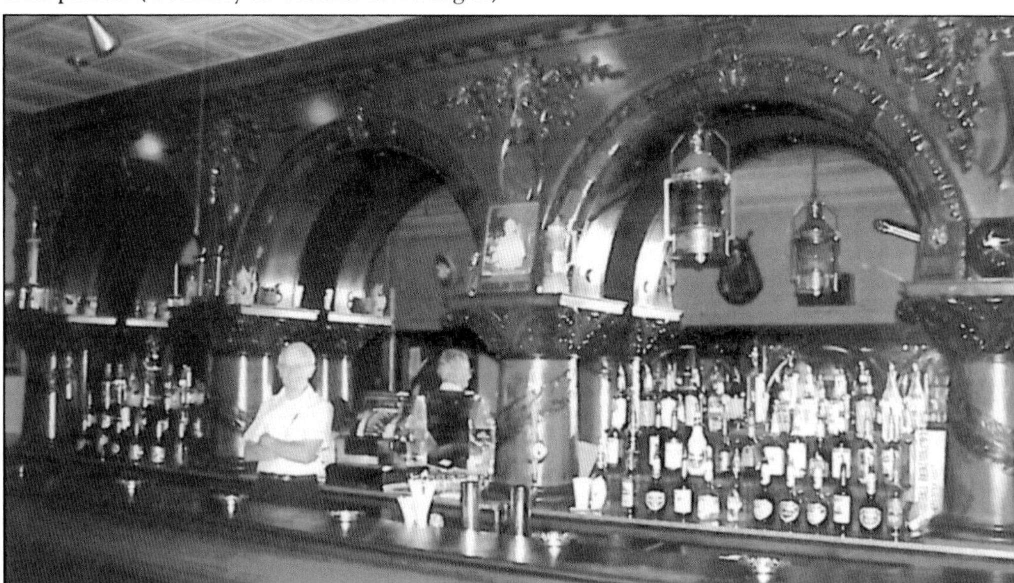

The Alpha Café is located in downtown Wapakoneta, previously owned and operated by Bill Gutman (pictured). Other previous owners include Harry Schwepe, Joe Miller, and Harry Brunn. The 1893 hand-carved white oak back bar, built by the Brunswick Balke Collender Company of Cincinnati, is original to the cafe. Once located across the street, the Alpha was moved to its present location in 1962. Tony Steinke is the current owner. (Courtesy of Tony Steinke.)

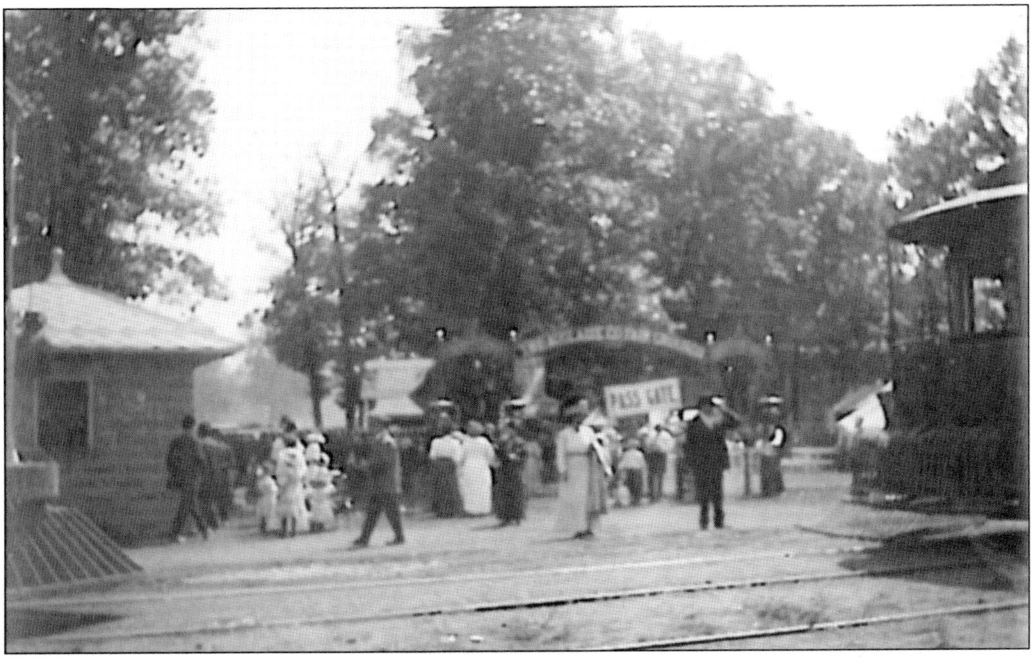

The Western Ohio Railway ran down West Auglaize Street towards St. Mary's, past the main gates of the Auglaize County Fairgrounds. During fairground events, the interurban would schedule stops for fairgoers. Looking much like it does today, the entrance of the Auglaize County Fairgrounds shows the original curved sign above the front gate. (Courtesy of Vernon E. Doenges.)

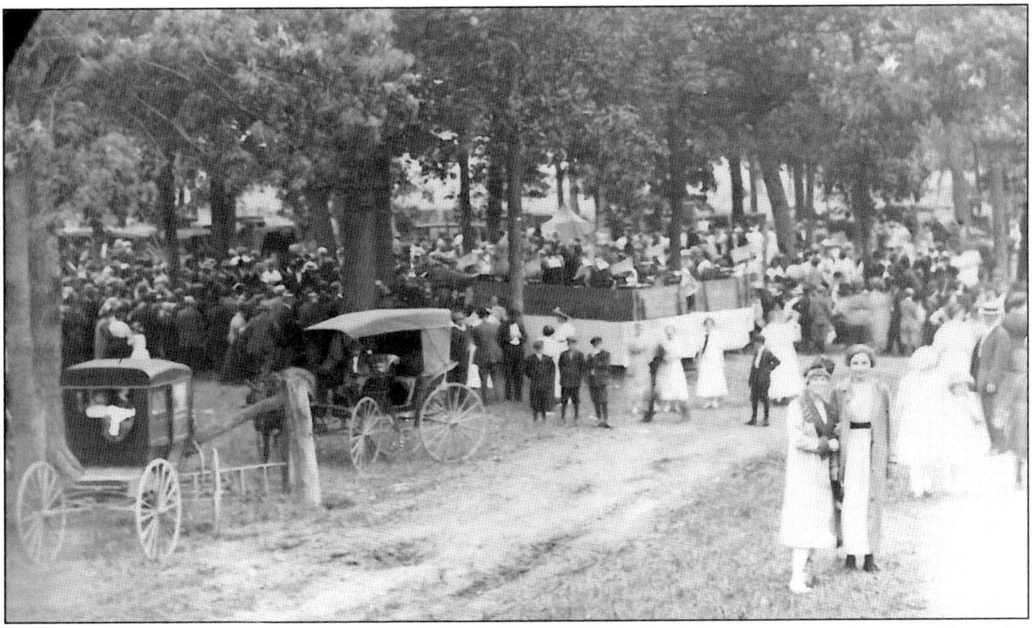

The Auglaize County Fairgrounds is within the city limits of Wapakoneta. Events held at the fairgrounds have been a place for people to gather for many generations. In years past, fairgoers would pack a picnic lunch and enjoy the day with friends and family. Large trees continue to grace the fairgrounds, providing a canopy of shade for reunions and special events. (Courtesy of Vernon E. Doenges.)

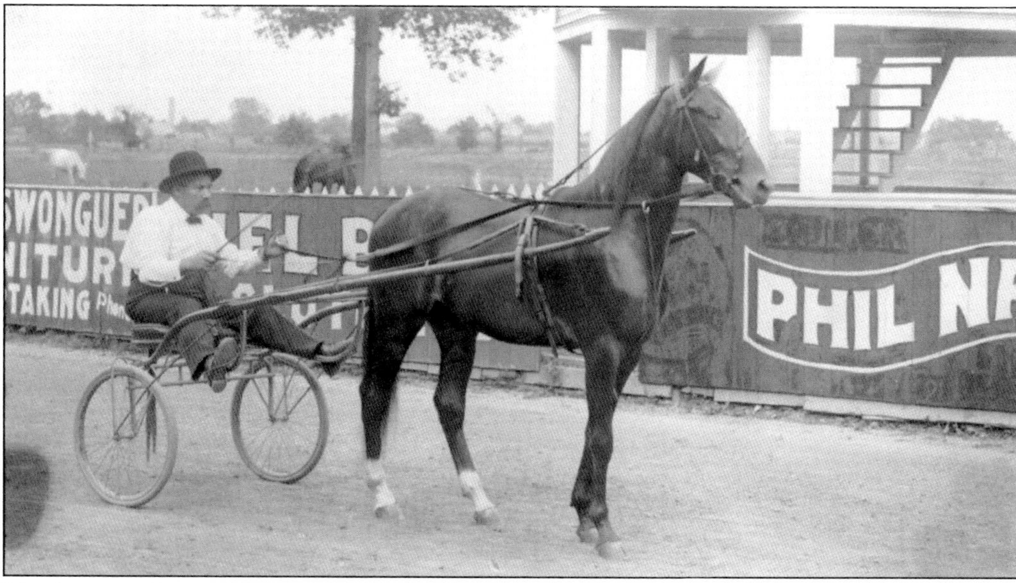

The history of horse racing at the Auglaize County Fair began in the earliest days of this Auglaize Agricultural Society event when the racetrack was first constructed in 1866. Here a sulky racer of long ago poses in front of the judging tower and press box on the inside of the racetrack. Racing continues to be an entertainment highlight at the county fair. (Courtesy of Auglaize County Historical Society.)

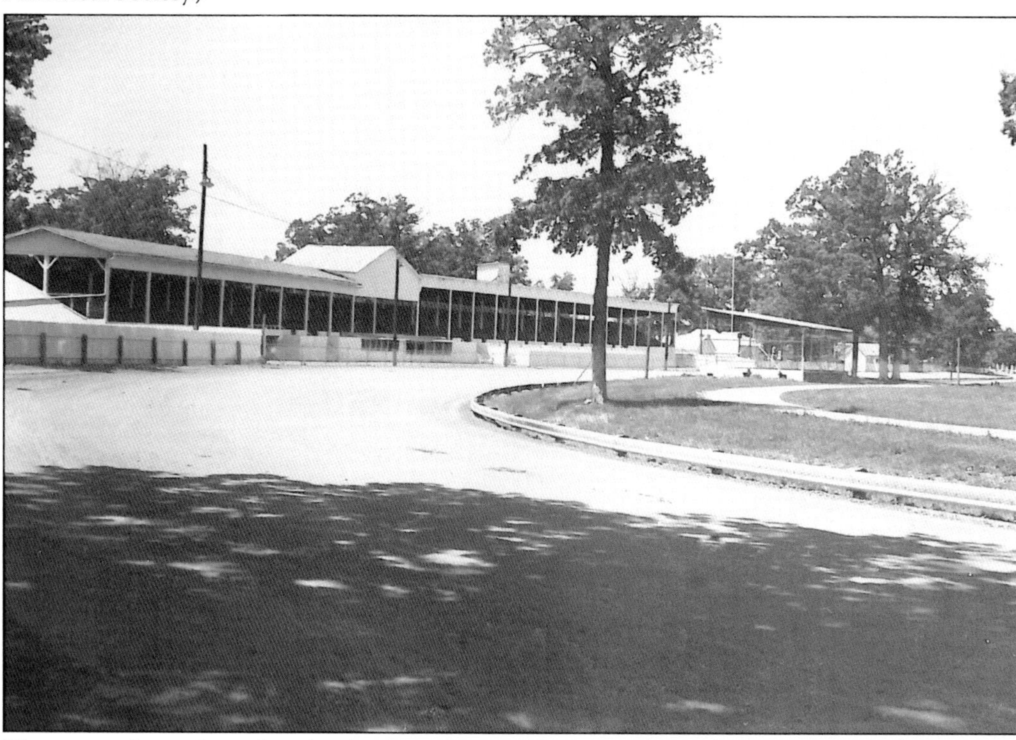

The original grandstand at the Auglaize County Fairgrounds was built in 1885 for $2,000. The covered grandstand served the community until 1977, when the two sections of the grandstand were removed for new construction in 1979. (Courtesy of Vernon E. Doenges.)

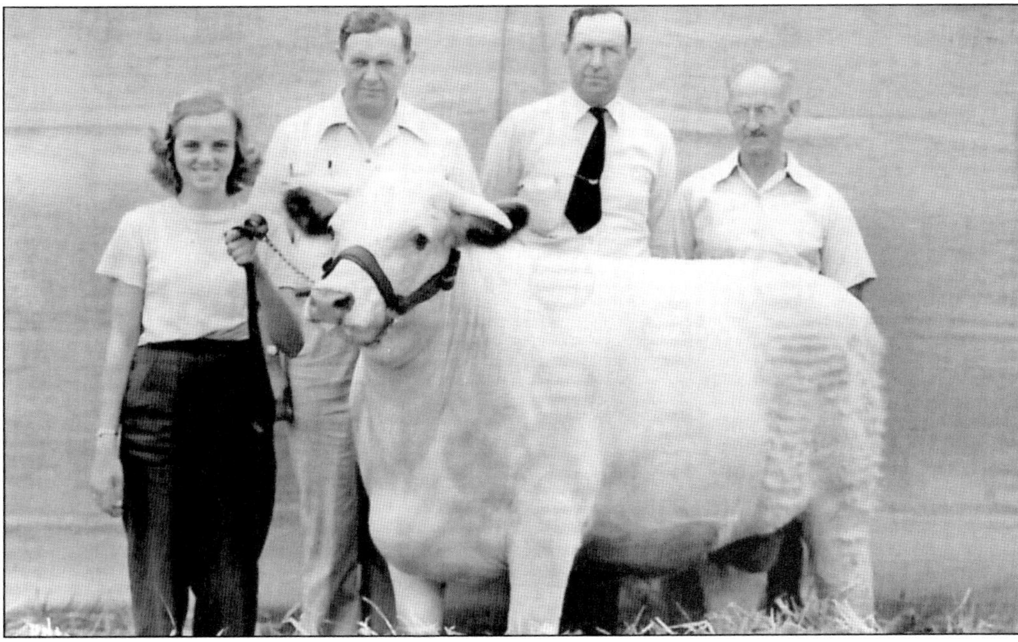

The Auglaize County Agricultural Society has encouraged junior fair members with an auction of prize-winning champions in the closing days of the fair. In the early 1950s, Marilyn Henkener (Hoge) is shown with her prize-winning shorthorn steer. Pictured here are, from left to right, Marilyn Henkener; Clarence Brown, Auglaize County agricultural agent; Ross Downing, auctioneer; and E. G. Hassler, New Knoxville High School vocational agriculture teacher. (Courtesy of Auglaize County Agricultural Society.)

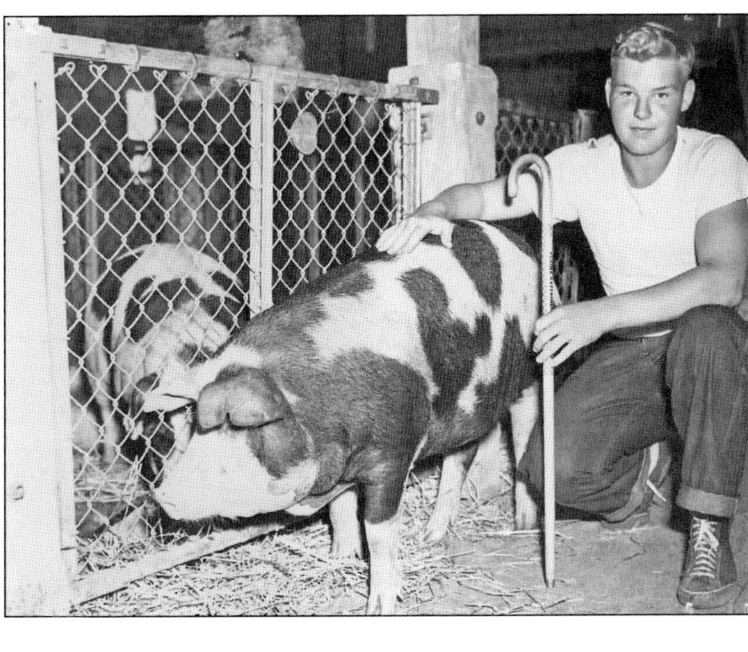

Jack Springer won the Grand Champion Breeding Gilt at the Auglaize County Fair in 1950. The 17-year-old's win with the spotted Poland China hog also garnered him a trip to the national Future Farmers of America Convention in Kansas City that fall. (Courtesy of Auglaize County Agricultural Society.)

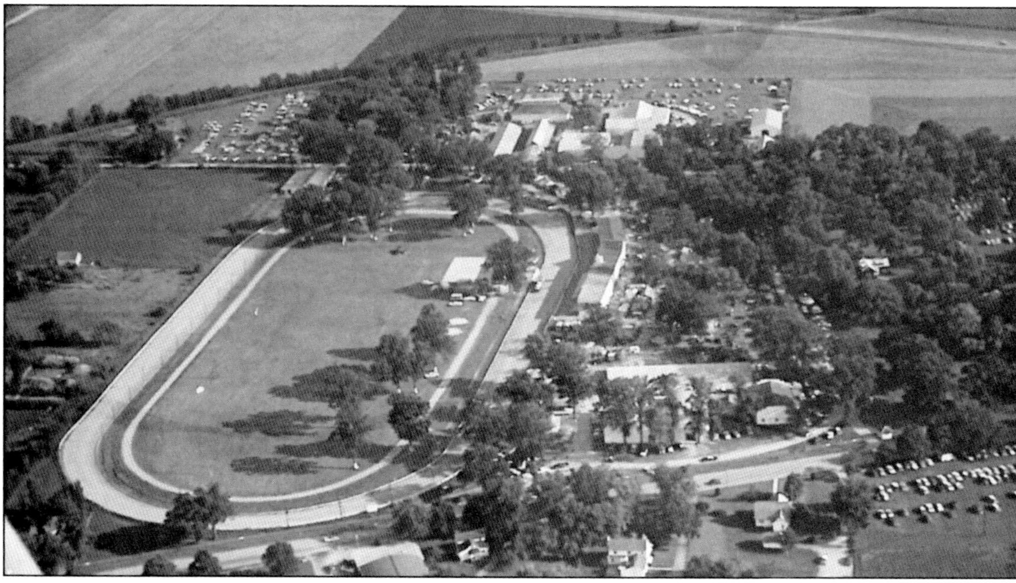

This aerial view of the fairgrounds was taken in 1961. West Auglaize Street is in the lower section of the photograph. Note the beautiful shade trees inside the track oval and the country fields to the south of the livestock barns. The grandstand is at the right of the racetrack. (Courtesy of Vernon E. Doenges.)

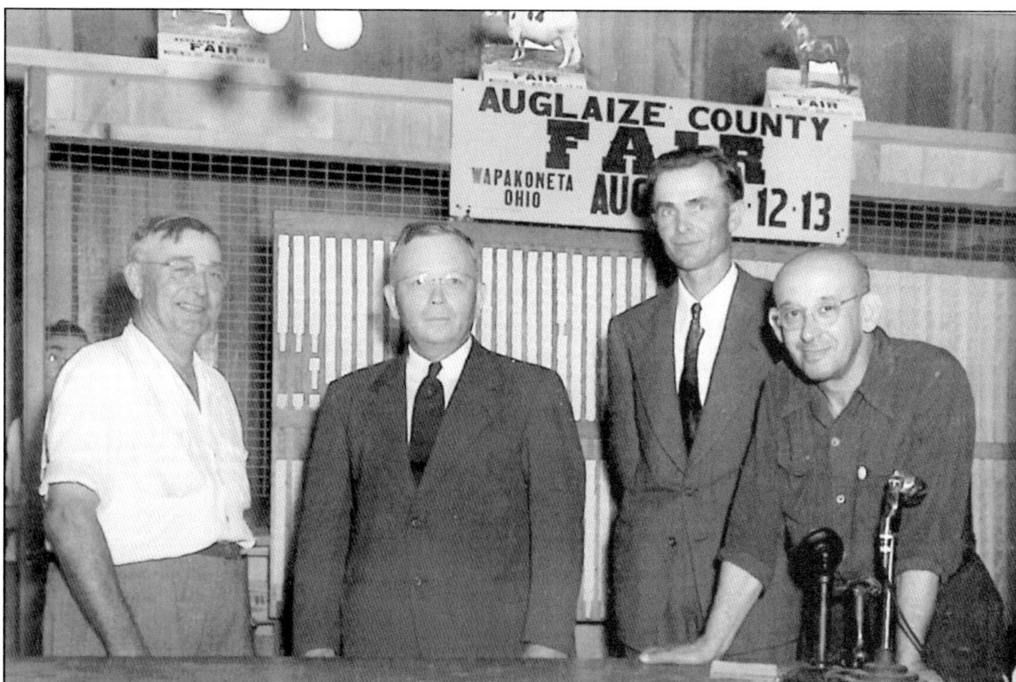

Auglaize County celebrated 100 years in 1948 with a variety of activities throughout the county. Those serving on the centennial committee are, from left to right, unidentified; Elmer Katterheinrich; Edison Schumann, general chairman; and Harry Kahn, executive secretary. Harry Kahn was also associated with the Auglaize County Agricultural Society for over 50 years, serving as secretary for 36. (Courtesy of Auglaize County Agricultural Society.)

Five

A Community Kaleidoscope

Although many of the images presented in this chapter may appear to be unrelated, as a group they represent the citizens who make up the town and surrounding area known as Wapakoneta. Relying on the ideals of immigrant work ethics, the determination of spirit, and the sense of pride in the 19th century, local citizens have worked hard to build a caring community.

Within these pages we celebrate the many fine people who have contributed to the growth of the city and community life. Although it is not possible to represent every organization, family, or businesses that made these contributions, the photographs included provide a feeling for the events and experiences that have shaped city growth and development.

One event included in this chapter is the regional flood of 1913, which also affected many other communities in the state. The memory of that time is still a consideration in river management today. The Helpling Photography Studio recorded many scenes of the Easter Sunday flood on March 23. As citizens dealt with the flood waters, newspaper articles reported stories of local interest, including one of a horse driven into the swirling waters and how local resident Frank Kohler saved the animal by cutting the harness to keep it from drowning. It was also reported that the men driving the buggy were "tipsy" and "got out of the buggy and into the arms of the law." Gentlemen travelers stranded at the Hotel Steinberg were sent 50 newspapers to ease the boredom of the flood.

Stories of local interest continue to fuel appreciation of our own family and community histories and celebrations. It is hoped that the reader will look at the photographs within these pages and add his or her own family histories to the images chosen.

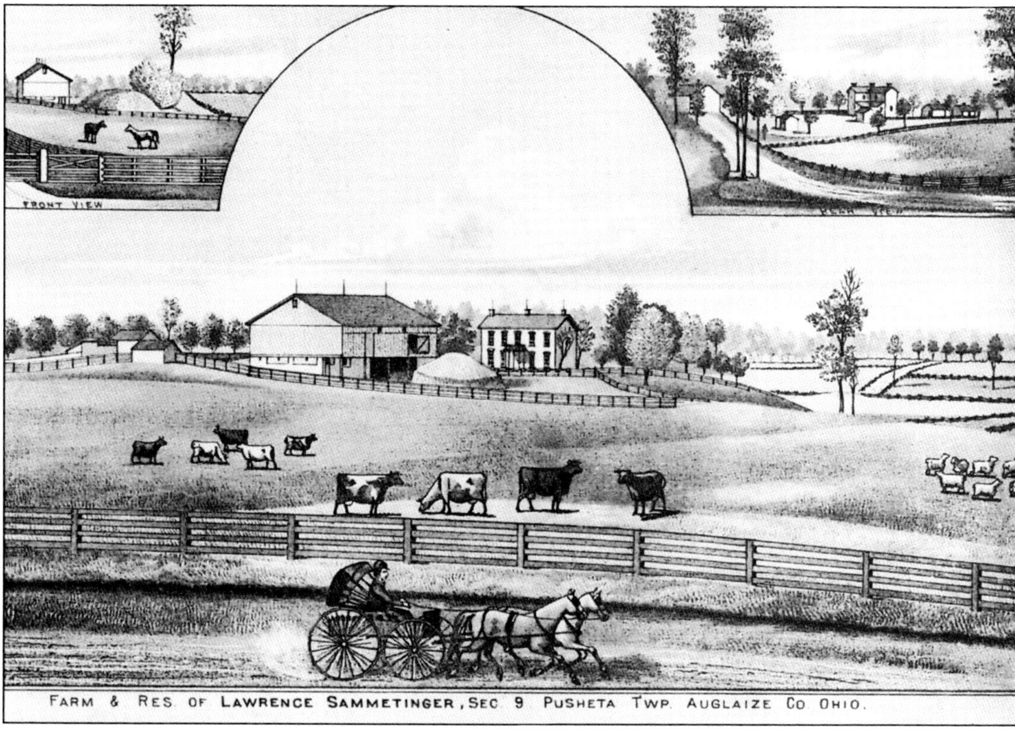

Lawrence Sammetinger, born in Bavaria in 1815, emigrated with his family to what is now Auglaize County in 1835, settling on Pusheta Road. First elected in 1863, Sammetinger served as county commissioner and justice of the peace for many years. Although published in the *1880 Atlas of Auglaize County*, the farm is recognizable today (south of Wapakoneta, near the southbound lane of I-75).

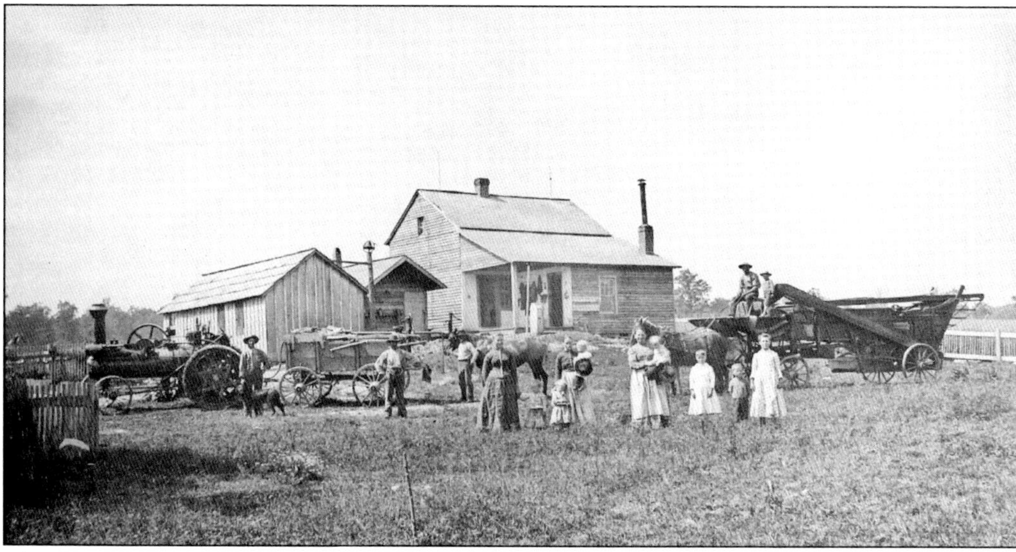

The Martin Sammetinger farm was established in 1872 on Pusheta Road. Pictured above is the original log house, which burned in 1916. Note the grain separator, which is pulled by a team of horses, and the steam-engine tractor at the left. The Martin Sammetinger family, pictured in front, sold this farm in 1891. (Courtesy of Dona Zwiebel.)

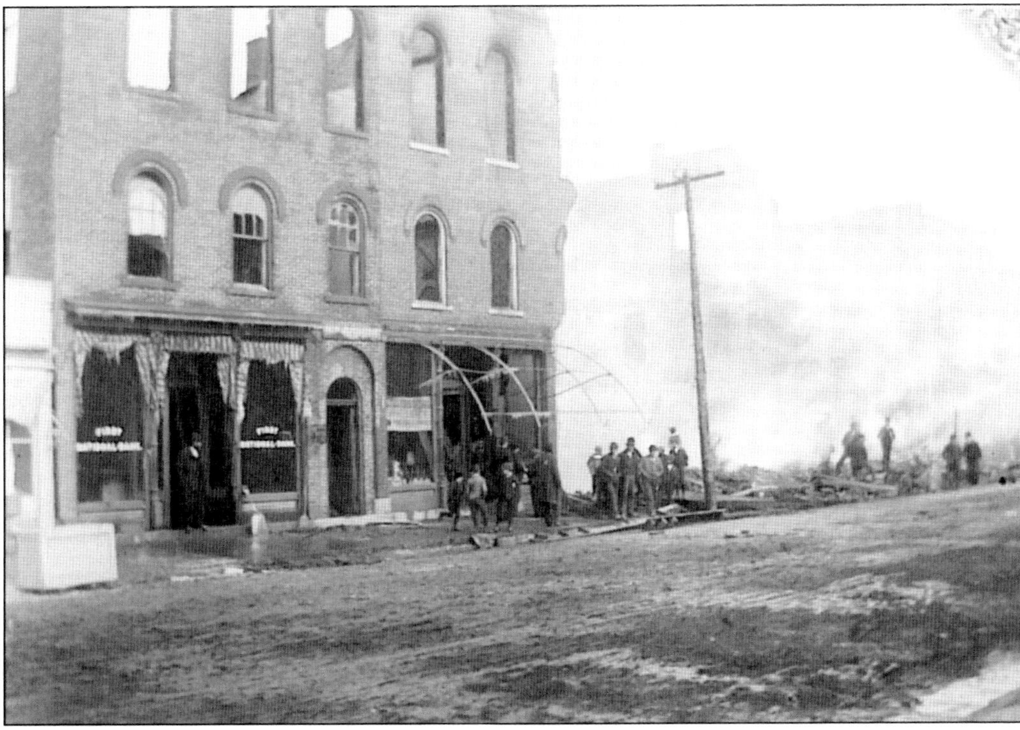

One of the most devastating fires to occur in Wapakoneta began on February 10, 1894. The fire destroyed 15 businesses and organizations in the Mechanic Block, shown above. Among those burned out were First National Bank, Hamer Masonic Lodge, Knights of Honor, J. L. Bargain Store, Buckeye Cigar Company, Fisher Clothing Company, Kahn Brothers, Lee and Snoderly Liquor Store, and G. D. Broughton, photographer. The Mechanic Block is now one of the buildings in Wapakoneta's National Historic Commercial District. (Courtesy of Karen Nuss Kohler.)

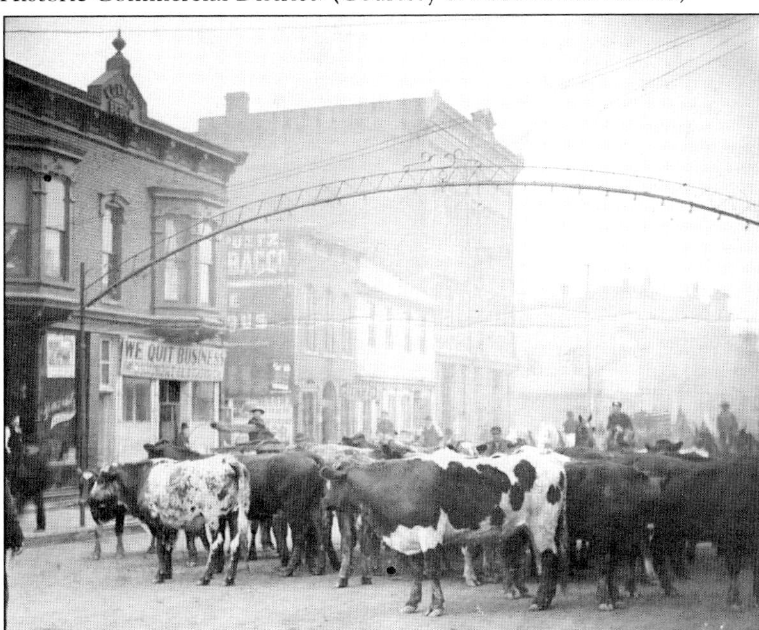

Cows on the main thoroughfare were once a regular occurrence due to the loading pens near this Auglaize Street railway crossing. The photograph was taken looking west from the crossing. Note the arch of incandescent lights over the street and buckboard to the left. Farmers are at the rear on horseback, driving the cows to the railway. (Courtesy of Vernon E. Doenges.)

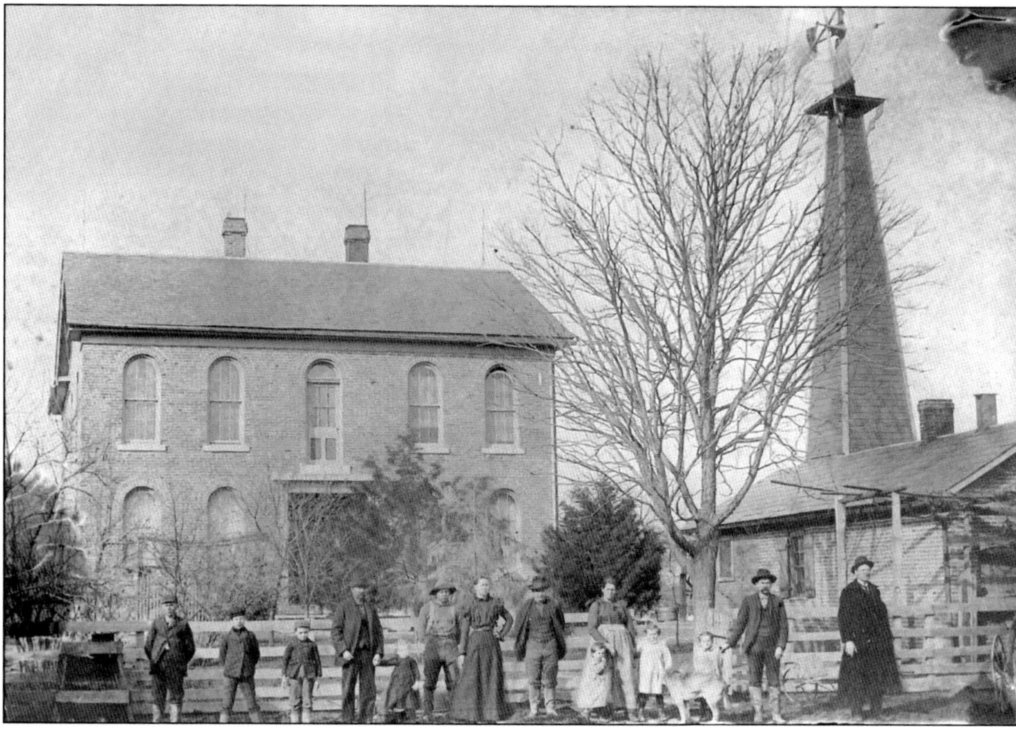
Typical of the many brick homes that once dotted the countryside, the Albert Knatz homestead on Kolter Road is the scene of this family's photographic record. Note that the unusual windmill housing resembles an oil derrick. (Courtesy of Peg Schlenker Prater.)

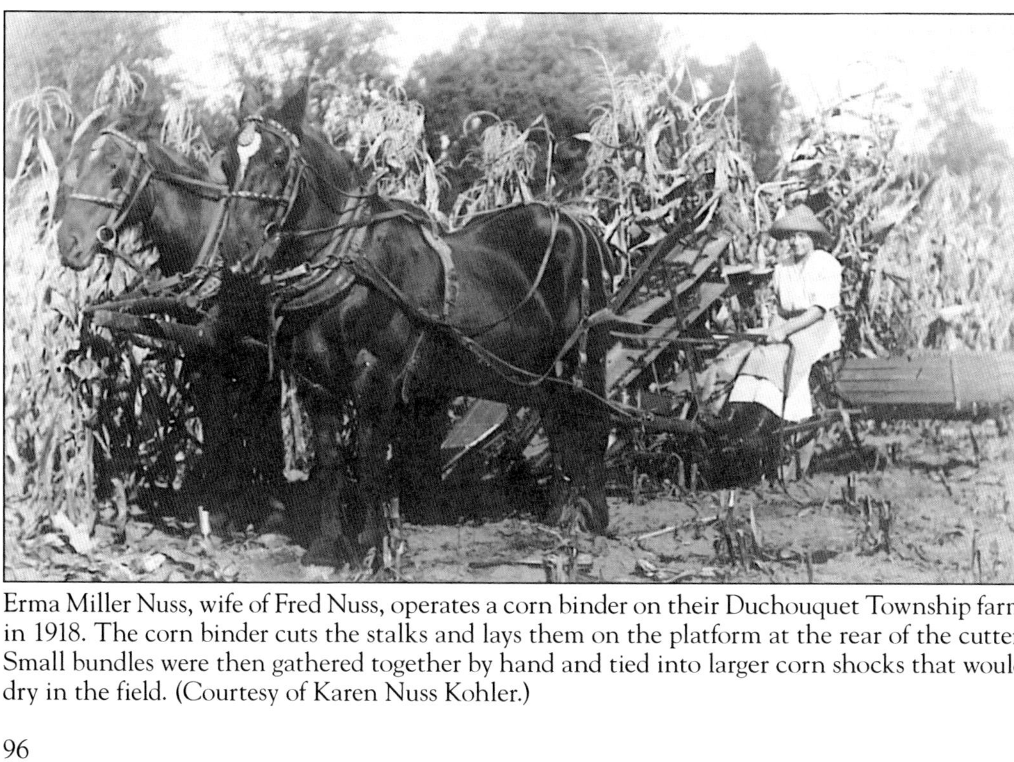
Erma Miller Nuss, wife of Fred Nuss, operates a corn binder on their Duchouquet Township farm in 1918. The corn binder cuts the stalks and lays them on the platform at the rear of the cutter. Small bundles were then gathered together by hand and tied into larger corn shocks that would dry in the field. (Courtesy of Karen Nuss Kohler.)

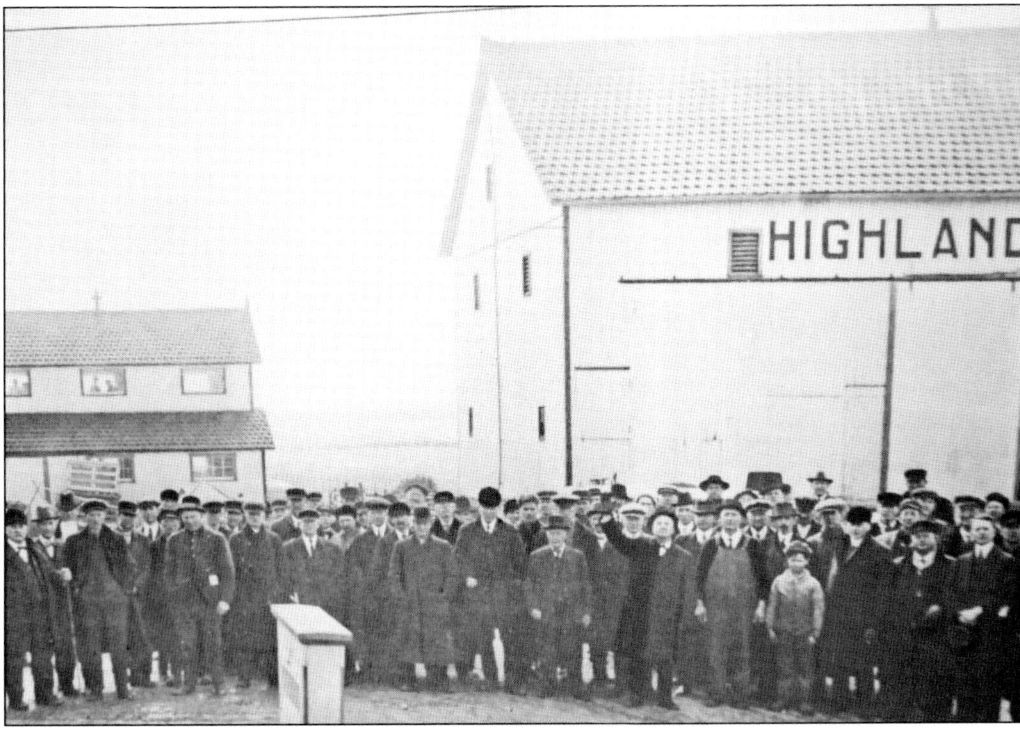

Featured in the *1917 Atlas of Auglaize County*, this sale of big-type Poland China hogs was on the F. O. Brown farm on Middle Pike Road. The small barn behind the crowd had a small arena where livestock sales were held regularly. Imagine dressing in suits and ties for a livestock sale in today's social climate.

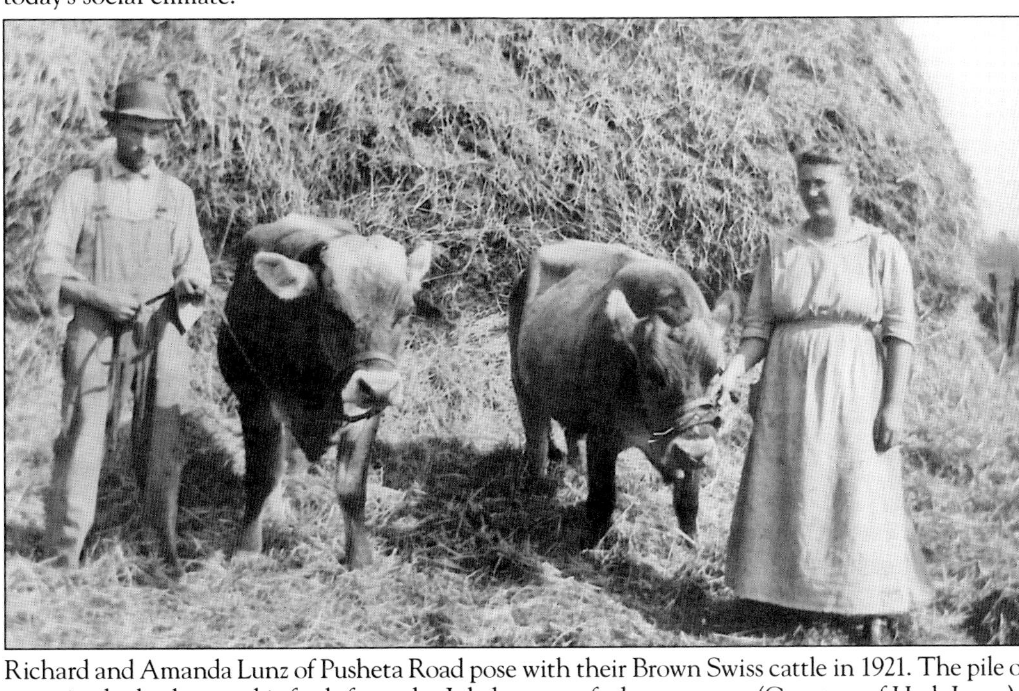

Richard and Amanda Lunz of Pusheta Road pose with their Brown Swiss cattle in 1921. The pile of straw in the background is fresh from the July harvest of wheat or oats. (Courtesy of Herb Lunz.)

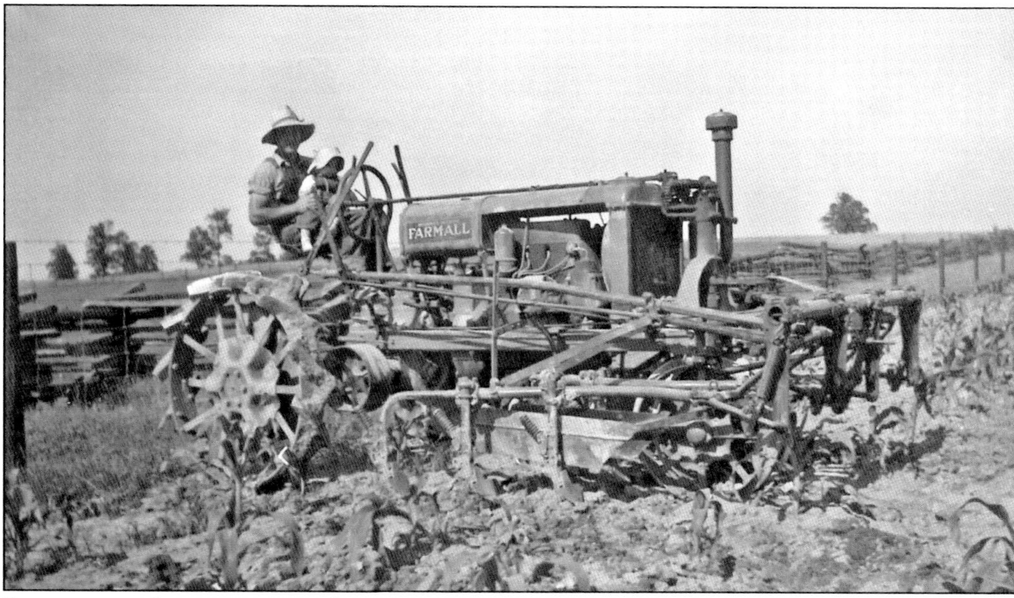

Farming was the occupation of many area residents from the time of settlement to the present. Tractors made fieldwork easier, and greater acreage was tillable with more modern equipment. Note the split rail fence in the background, once a common occurrence on many local farms. (Courtesy of Peg Zwiebel Schlenker.)

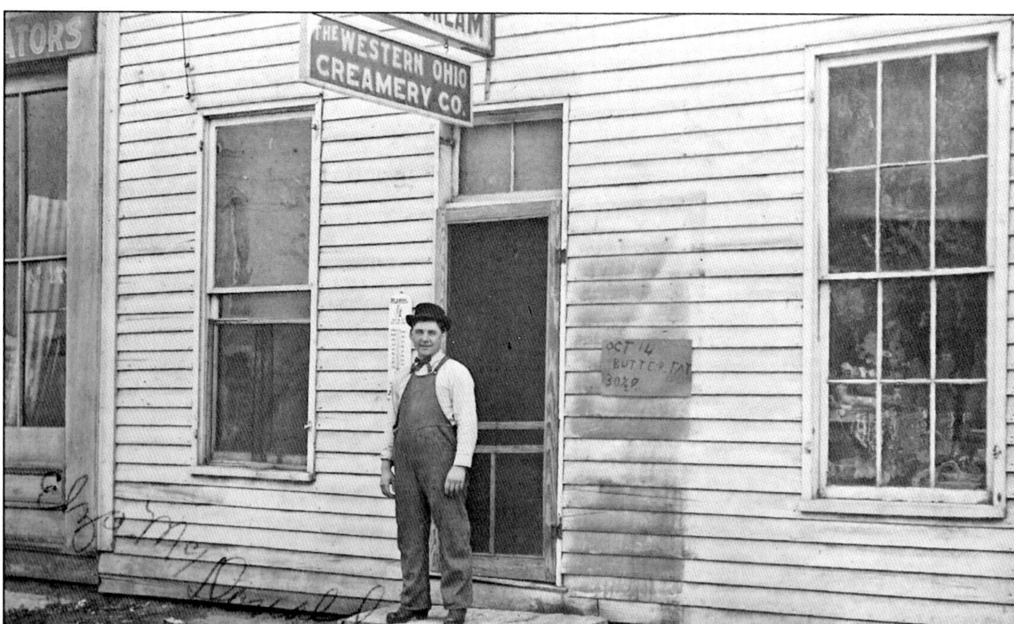

The Western Ohio Creamery Company, located at 4 Willipie Street, was listed in the 1915 Wapakoneta City directory. This photograph recorded Elza McDonald in October 1913, when butterfat was 30.5¢ per gallon. (Courtesy of Scott Knerr.)

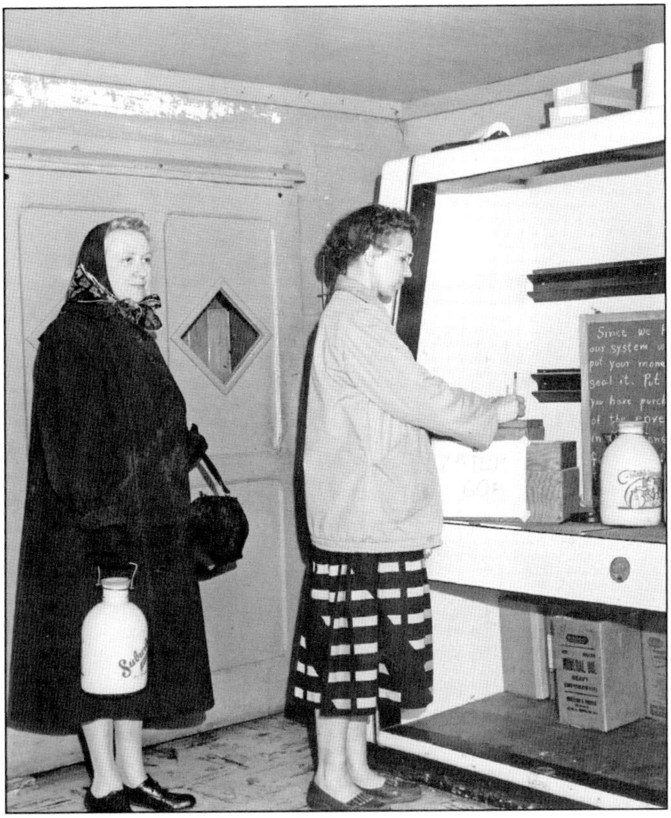

The John H. Schlenker farm sold milk by the gallon from its dairy operation on Glynwood Road. Neighbors and townspeople, using the honor system, put money in a brown envelope and dropped it in a collection box. On this particular day, milk was 60¢ a gallon. (Courtesy of Peggy Schlenker Prater.)

In the 1950s, the John H. Schlenker farm was a working dairy farm, specializing in Holstein cattle. Pastureland in the photograph is now the Grandview Estates subdivision. (Courtesy of Peggy Schlenker Prater.)

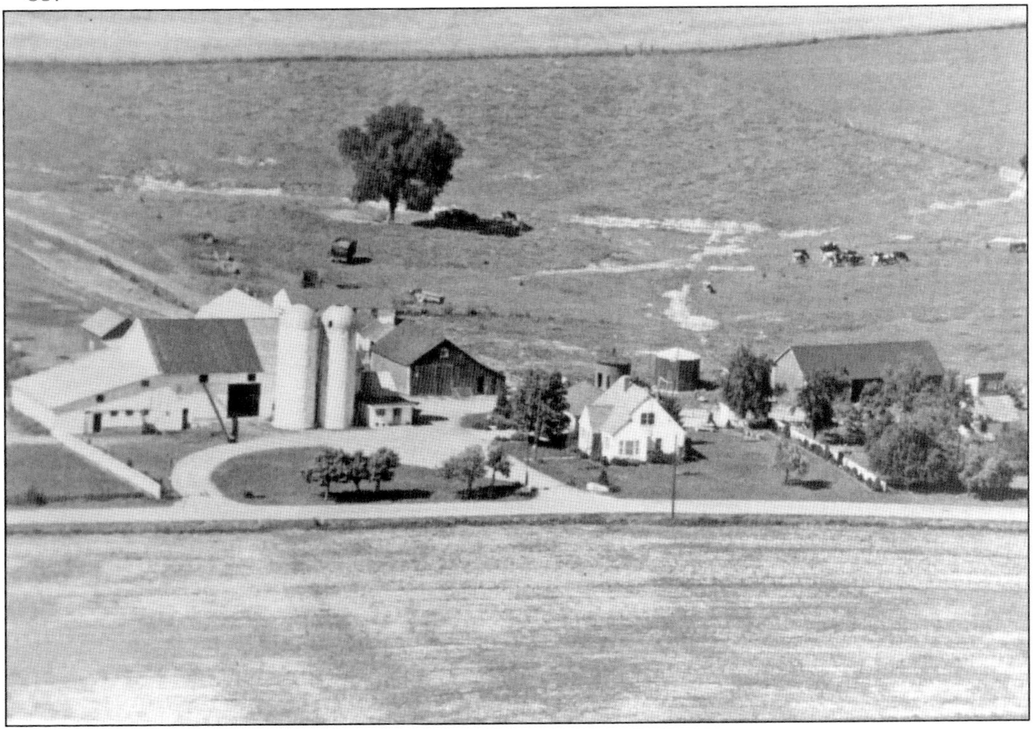

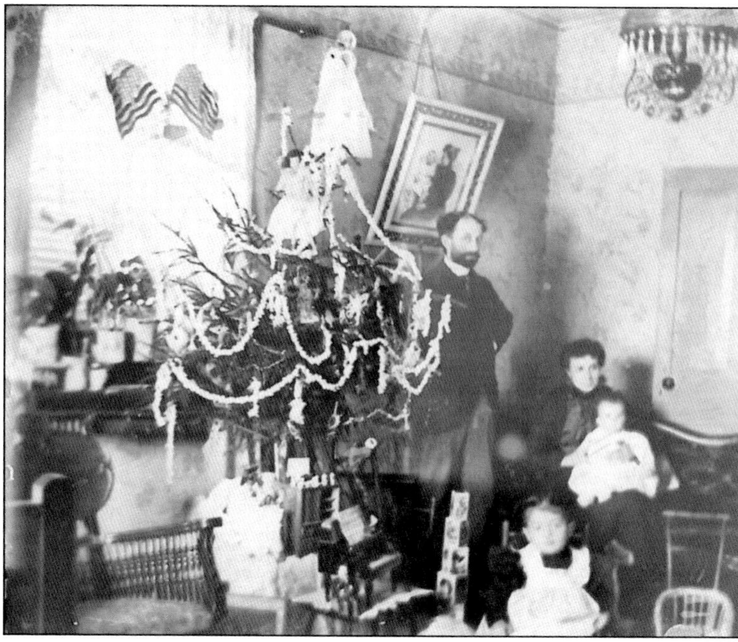

Celebrating Christmas with a well-decorated tree, Bert T. and Catherine (Katie) O'Neil Blume pose with their daughters, Naomi (foreground) and Helen, about 1900. Note the toy piano, blocks for the baby, and a doll carriage. (Courtesy of Bob and Nancy VanSkiver.)

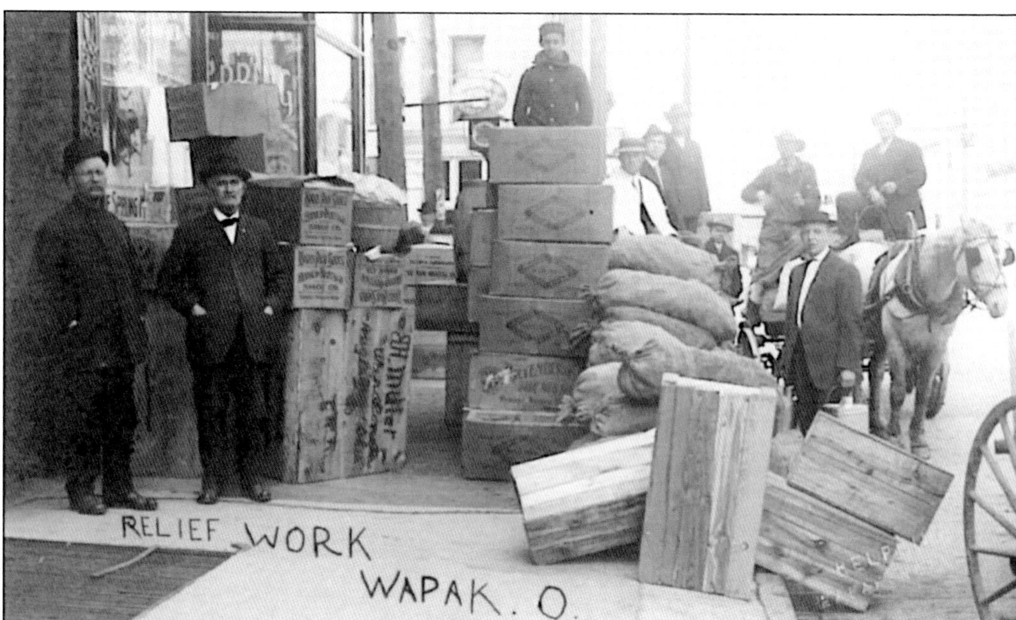

Harry Kahn (as a boy at top of boxes), son of Leon and Hattie Steinberg Kahn, is already involved with civic affairs. Later, as a personable member of the community, Kahn ran a shoe store and served as secretary of the Auglaize County Fair for 36 years. Called "Mr. Wapakoneta" by many, Kahn was an avid promoter of the city, youth, and business. (Courtesy of Vernon E. Doenges.)

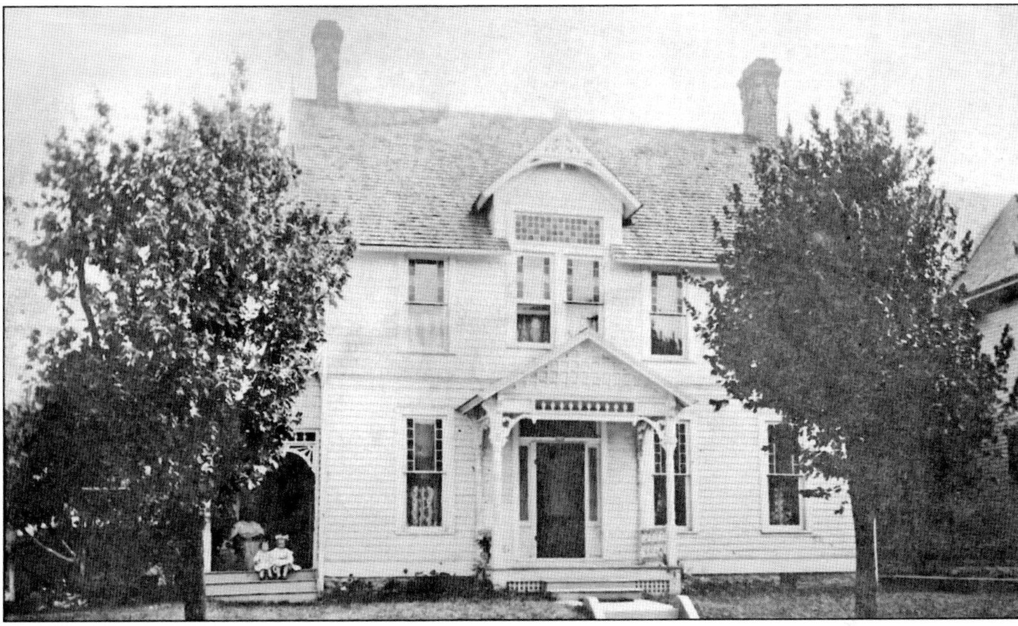

Homes built in the late 1800s are the framework of residential areas surrounding the downtown business district of Wapakoneta. The 307 West Pearl Street home of William L. and Jeanette Hasting includes daughters Cecil and Gladys on the side porch. Hasting was an oil pumper on the family farm near Two Mile, a postal worker, and a concrete and bridge contractor. (Courtesy of Eugene and Shirley Pohlable.)

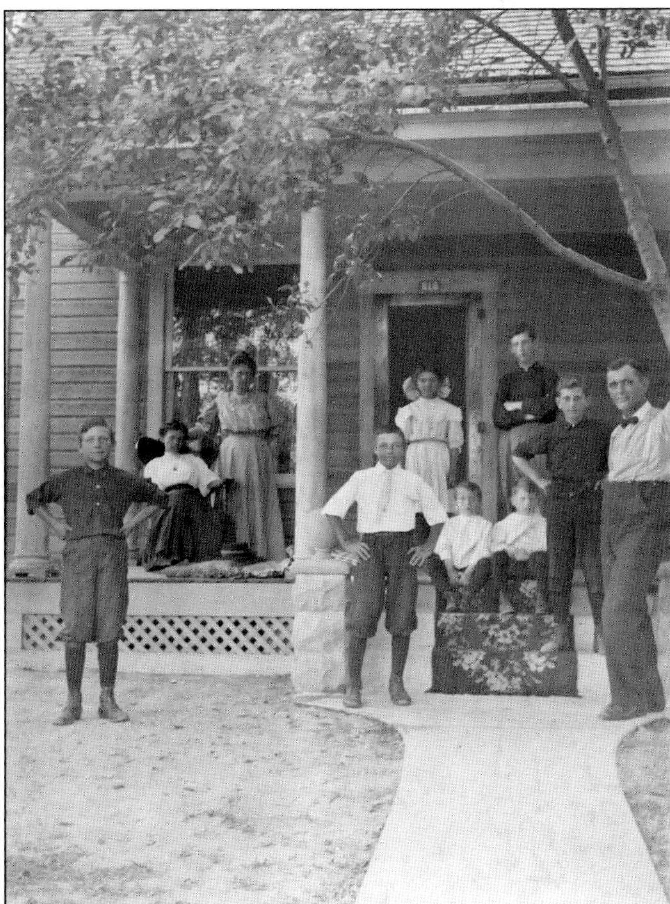

The Ed Ruck Family of 816 East Bellefontaine Street gathers for a picture around 1910. At this time, flash cameras were most often available for professionals. Family photographs were usually taken by traveling photographers. (Courtesy of Norma Rickert.)

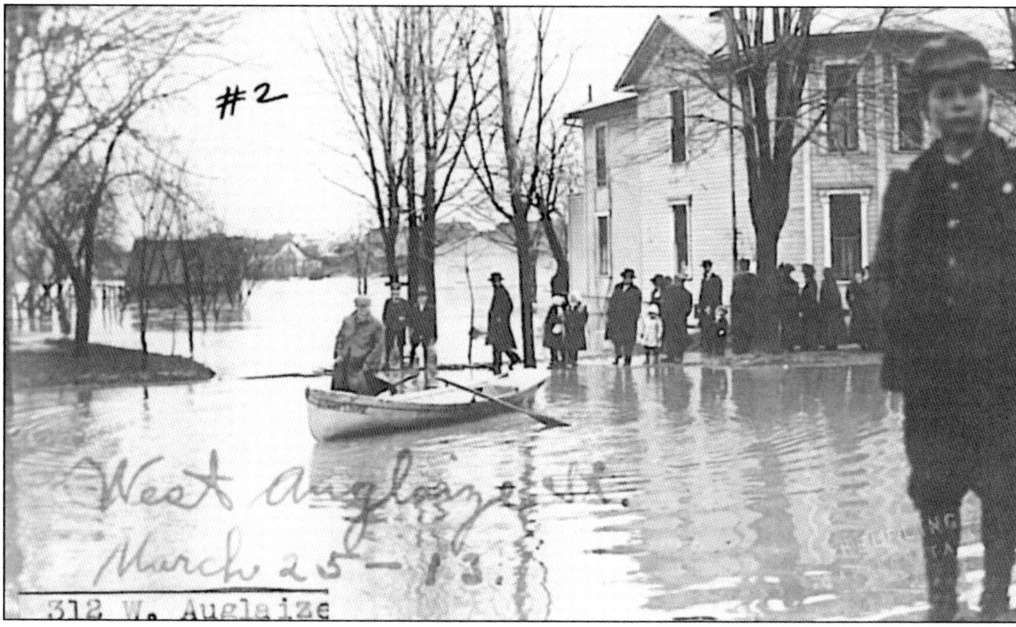

The biggest flood Wapakoneta ever experienced was Easter Sunday, March 23, 1913. Dr. E. F. Heffner, Bill Timmermeister, and Art South rowed down West Auglaize in a boat, negotiating waters 4 feet deep. When they got to Hamilton Road, waters were so rapid that they had to turn back. Above, flood victims were evacuated by boat on March 25, 1913, at 312 West Auglaize Street. (Courtesy of Vernon E. Doenges.)

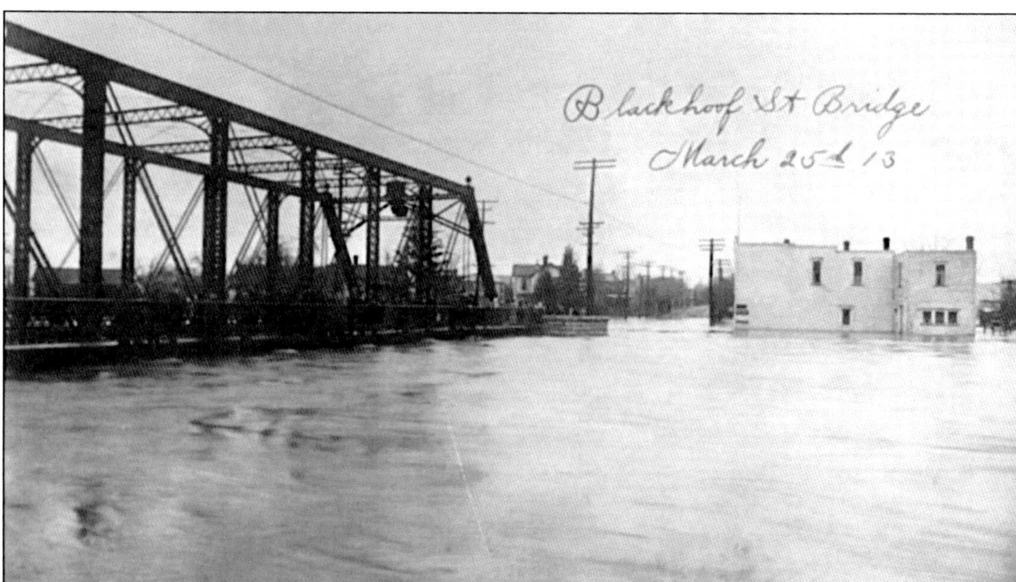

Looking north, the Blackhoof Street Bridge over the Auglaize River was well past its banks in the 1913 flood when this photograph recorded the flood damage. Newspapers reported macadam or asphalt was washed from pavement and foundations from sidewalks. The *Wapakoneta Daily News* wrote that "rumors spread faster than the waters" in this small town, but they also reported that kitchen utensils and a calf were floating down the Auglaize River. (Courtesy Vernon E. Doenges.)

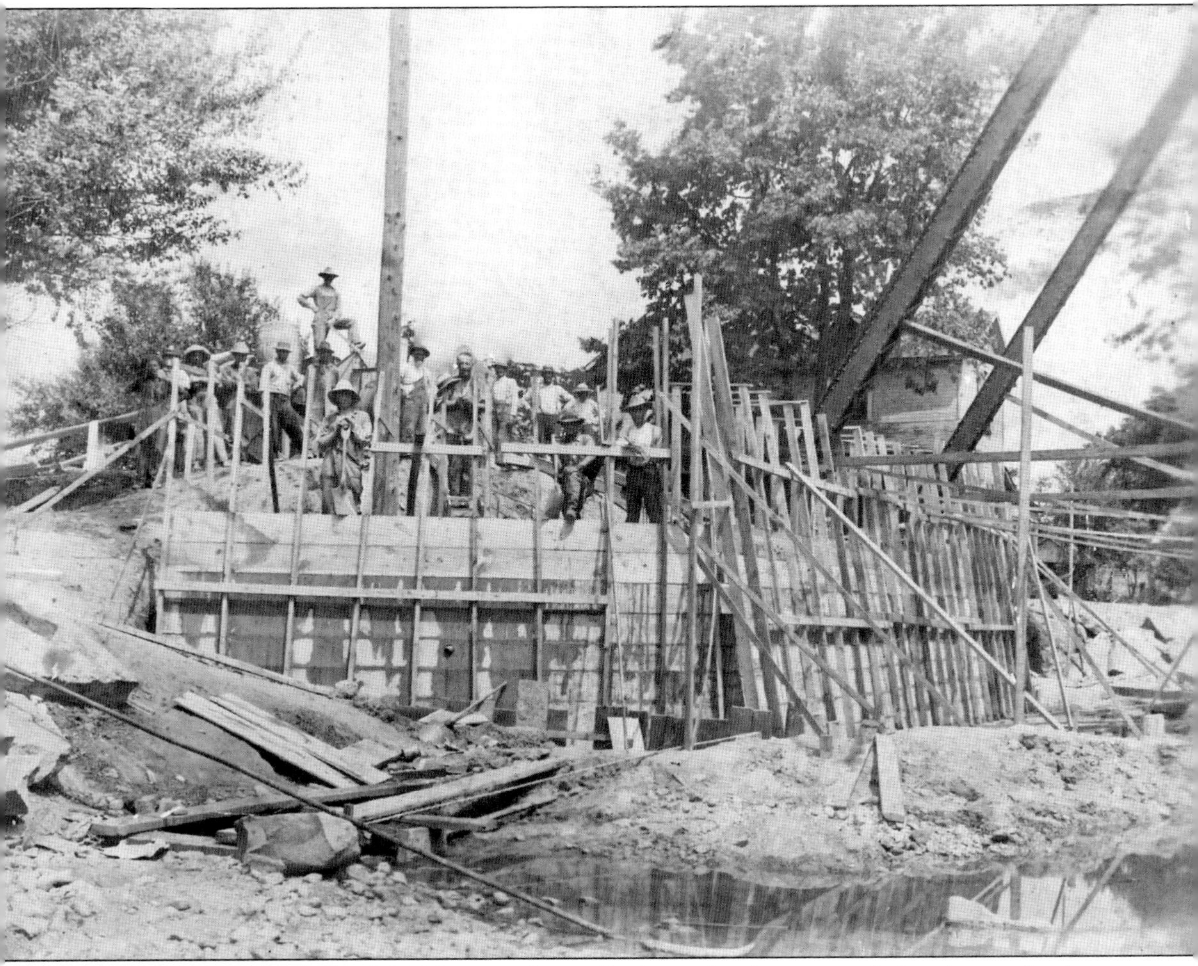

After the 1913 flood, the 1890 Harrison Street Bridge embankment needed major repair, since the west abutment of the bridge settled while retaining the raging waters. William L. Hasting, a cement contractor, made notes on the back of this photograph. Bridge reconstruction included six and a half train car loads of stone, 3 car loads of lake sand, 200 barrels of cement, and 2 tons of reinforcement. The bridge remained in use until replaced in 1966 by a larger bridge. Once again replaced in 2009, the new structure is reminiscent of the steel truss bridges that were built in the 1860s and 1870s.(Courtesy of Eugene and Shirley Pohlable.)

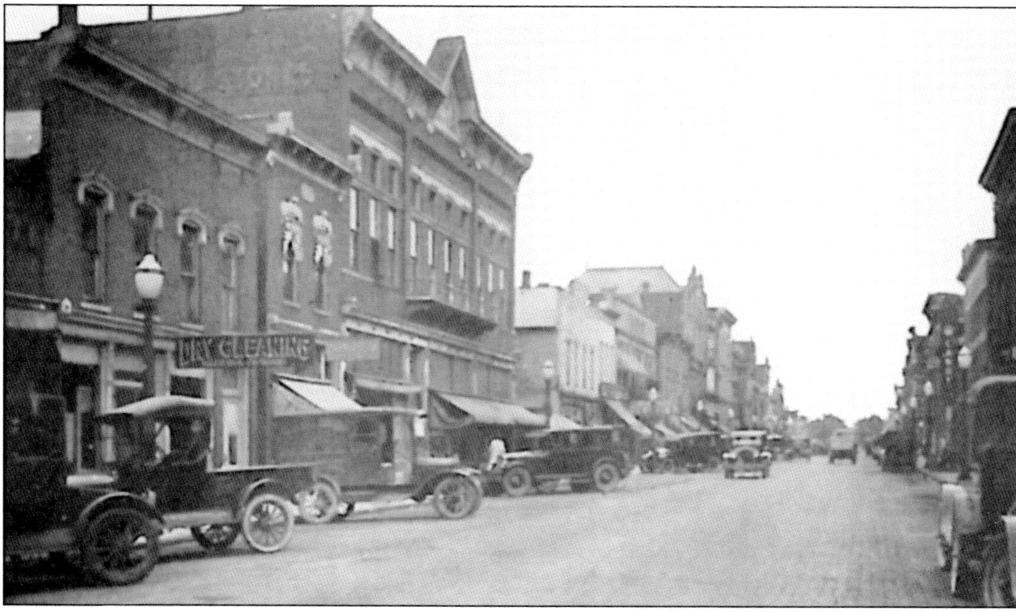

The large building in the left foreground is the former Timmermeister and Rogers Dry Goods Store and Opera House built in 1885. The second floor opera house is up a large central iron-tread staircase. Once the Brown Theater was built in 1904, this opera house became obsolete, since the new theater was built to accommodate moveable stage sets and provide dressing rooms for the production staff. (Courtesy of Norma Rickert.)

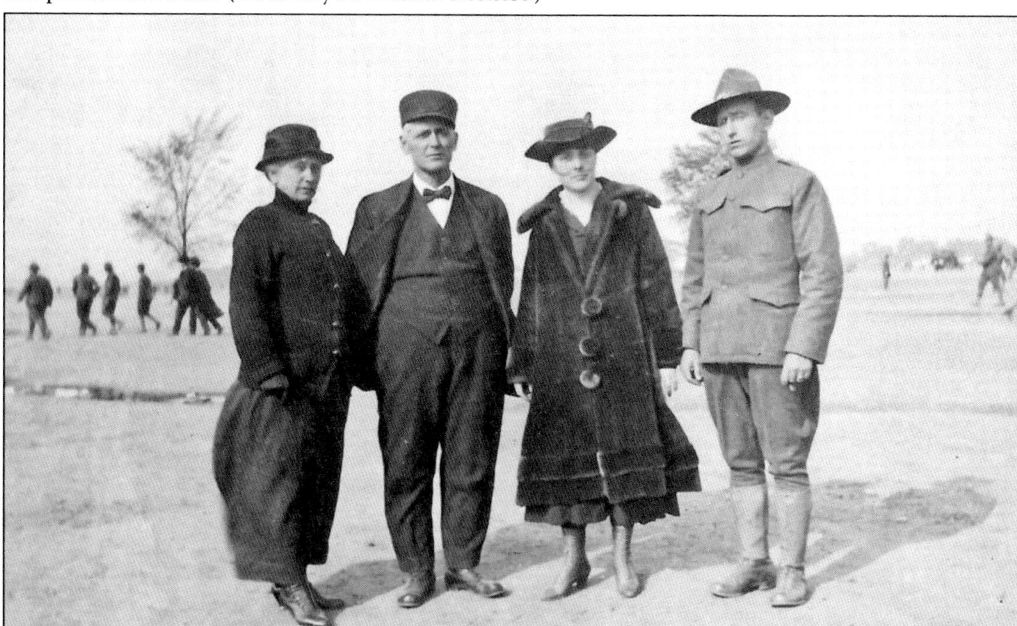

Called to arms when the United States entered World War I, many young town citizens became soldiers and nurses, lending their talents to the war effort. Ralph Ruck (far right) is seen with his wife, Cornelia, and parents, Flora and Ed Ruck, when they visited his military training camp. Note the ladies' hats; the flat-topped, conductor-style cap; and the classic World War I Army uniform. (Courtesy of Norma Rickert.)

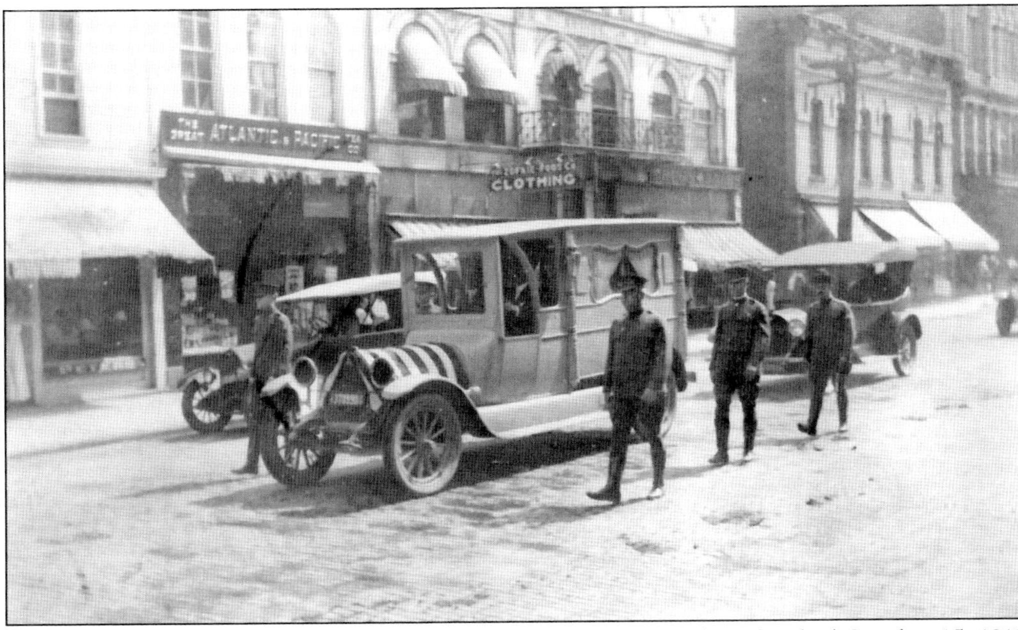

The funeral procession of Wapakoneta soldier Andrew C. Reineke, who died October 15, 1918, in France, passes through town on Auglaize Street. He is buried in St. Joseph's Cemetery. The hearse is draped with the American flag. (Courtesy of Linda Knerr.)

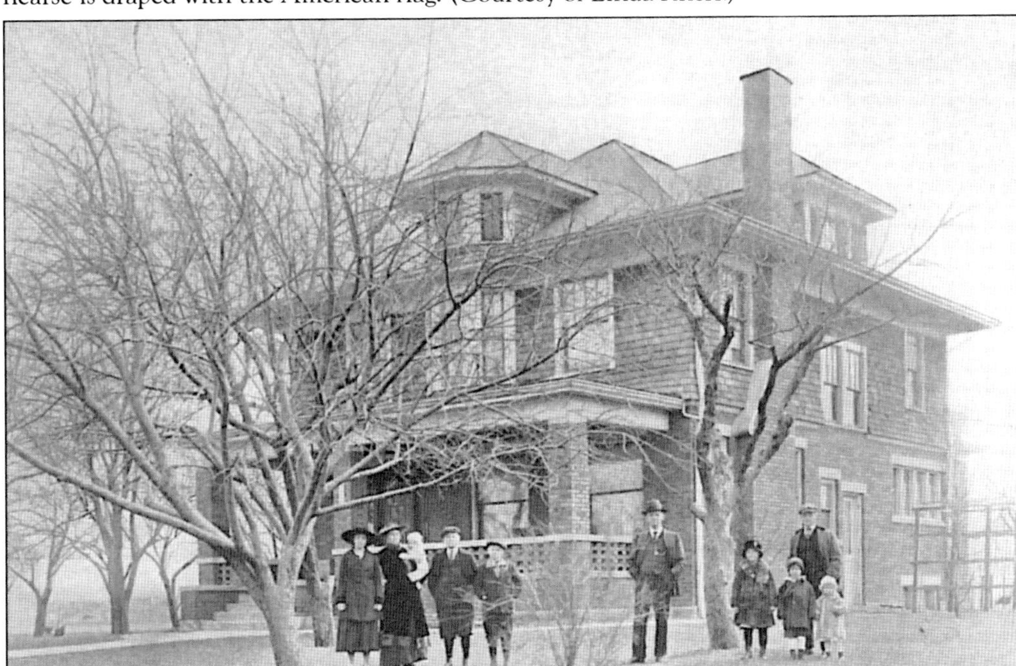

The Jacob C. and Katherine Schmidt Zint family, at their new home on West Pearl Street, was featured in the *1917 Atlas of Auglaize County*. Many residents recall a small wooden observatory built by Jacob Zint Jr. atop the family garage at this address. Jacob Jr. also built scientific instruments from scratch and one, a seismograph, recorded the official intensity of a 1930s earthquake centered in Anna, Ohio.

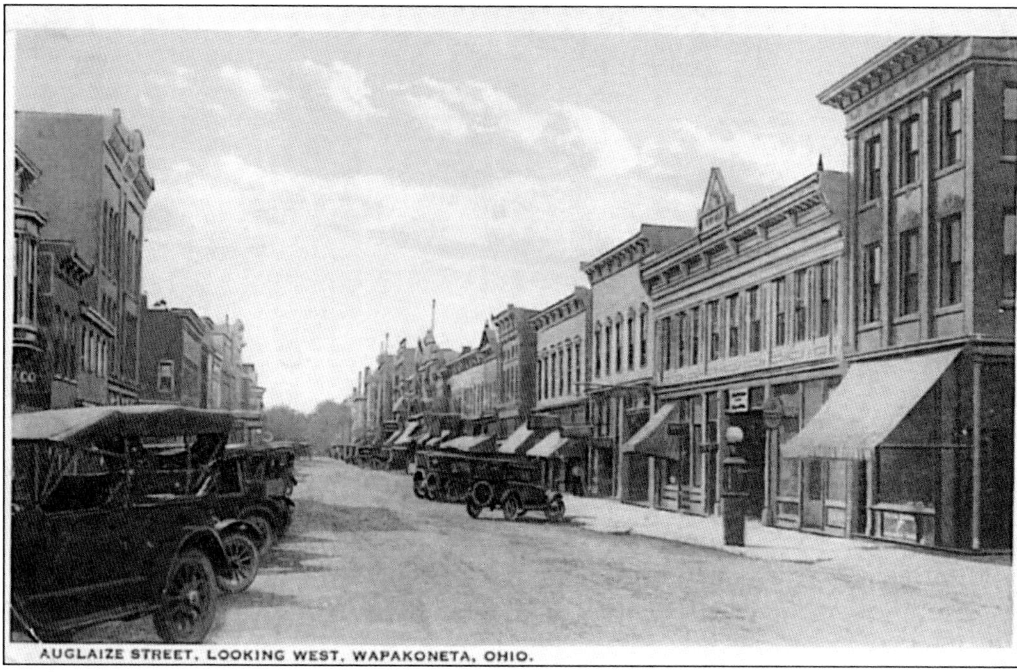

Auglaize Street in the 1920s featured a brick-paved thoroughfare and an at-the-ready gas pump at 119 East Auglaize Street for the many new cars in the city. The trees at the far end of the business district enhanced the residential portion of West Auglaize Street. The first two buildings on the right, no longer standing, once housed Wahrer's Garage and the Neuhauser Hatchery. (Courtesy of Vernon E. Doenges.)

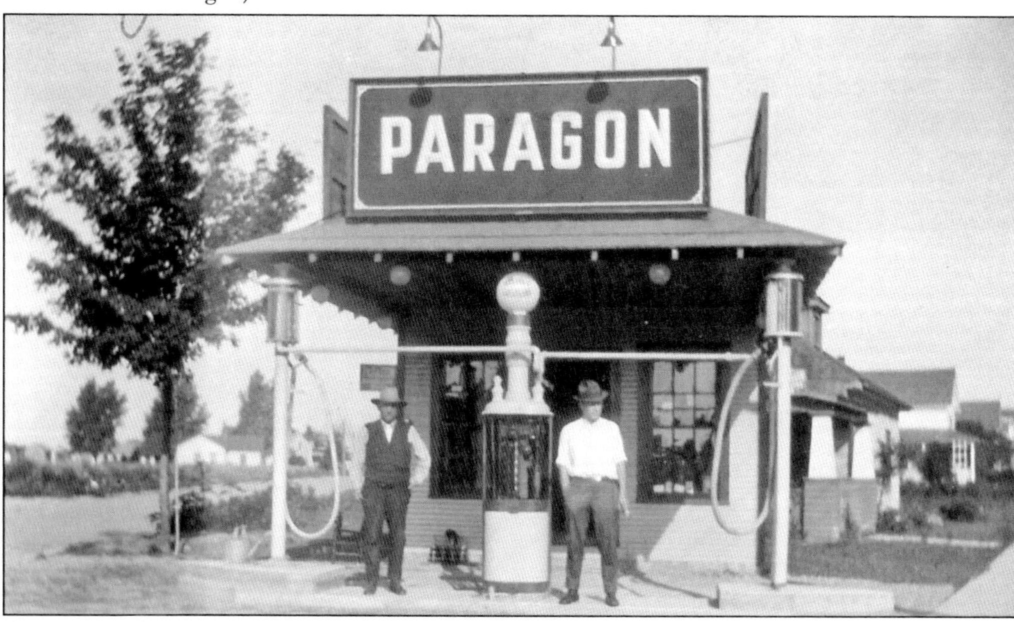

Gas stations became popular as more people owned automobiles in the 1920s. This gas station at the point of Bellefontaine and Benton is now the home of the popular Max's Dairy Bar. In the photograph, James Kantner and Oscar Ruck are ready to greet customers. (Courtesy of Norma Rickert.)

Considered a fine carpenter, Gus Koch built this barrel-shaped office in 1928 with the help of Sam Elsass and Leslie Koch. Located at the Burden and Koch sawmill on Jackson Street, it served as headquarters for a crate factory. Measuring 13 feet high and 20 feet long, it contains examples of hidden shelves and compartments. At the door are Gus's sons, Robert (left) and Leslie. (Courtesy of Julie and Lee Koch.)

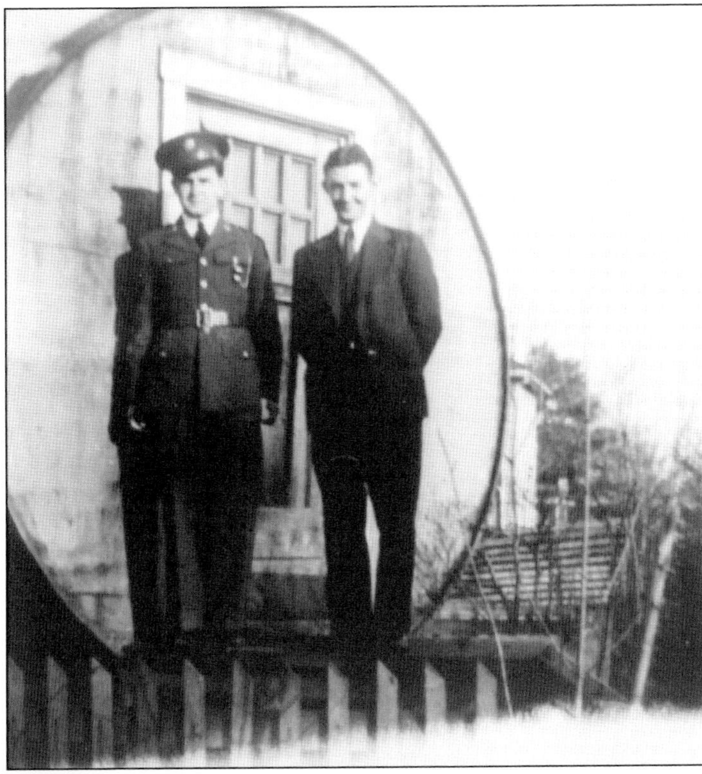

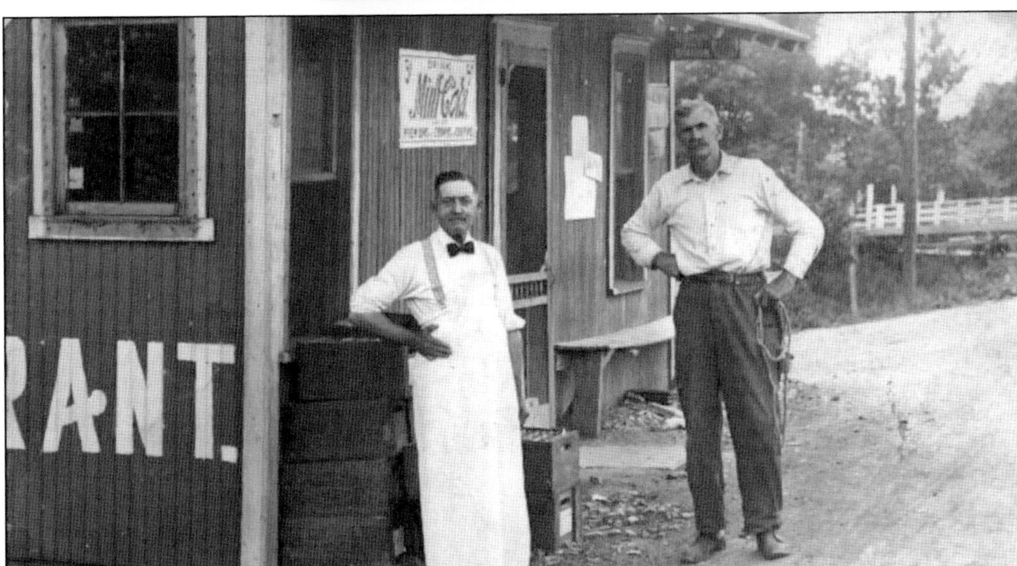

The "Old Lima Bridge"—located on North Dixie Highway, formerly U.S. Route 25 (Dixie Highway)—is seen in the background near a restaurant owned by Elmer "Belty" Hague in the 1920s. The bridge at this time intersected with State Route 67, and the little restaurant was positioned on stilts at the riverbank. The men shown here are unidentified. (Courtesy of Robert Hague.)

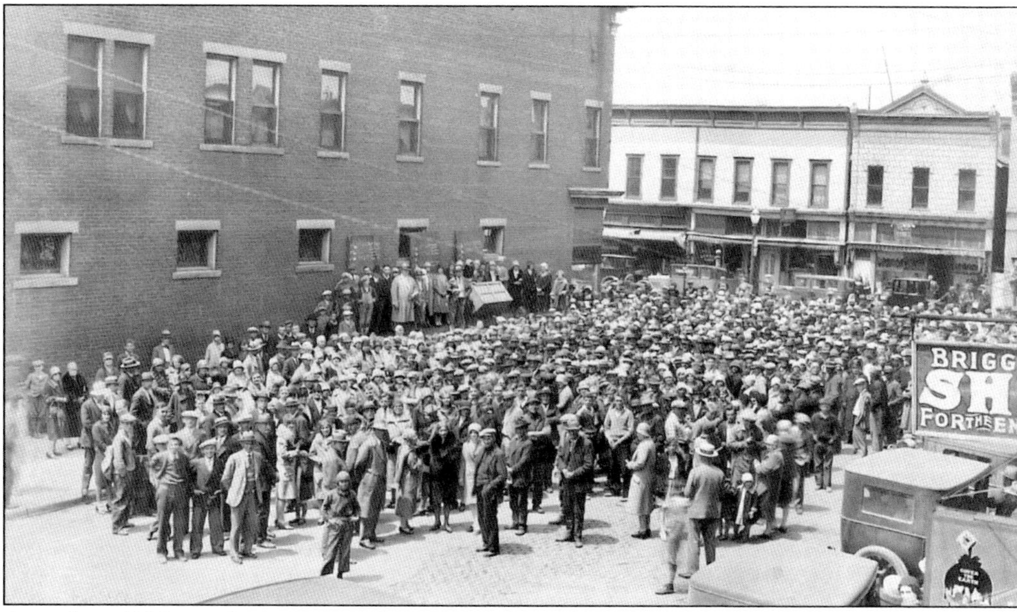

As early as 1926, merchants attracted patrons with "green ticket days" several times each year. With a purchase, business patrons received a ticket and the corresponding stub was placed in a large box. Sporting a tie and vest, businessman Harry Kahn is standing left of the drawing box at this 1930s-era green ticket day event held at Park and East Auglaize Streets. (Courtesy of Vernon E. Doenges.)

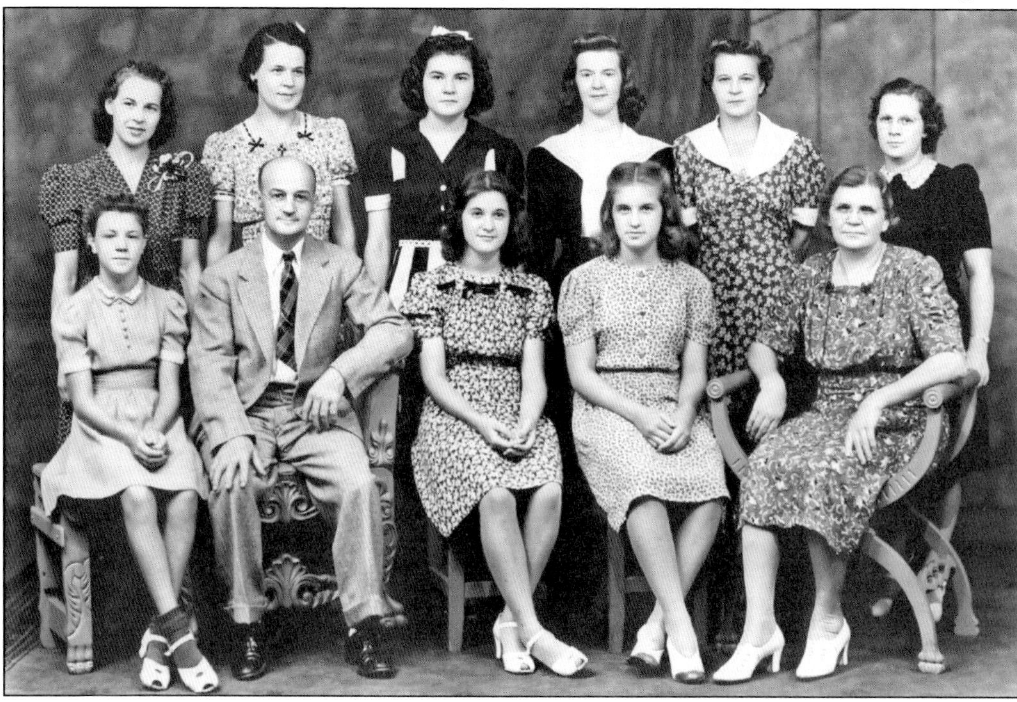

Large families were the norm in the early 20th century. As one example, the Albert "Brownie" and Louise Schneider family had nine girls. At one time, Brownie Scheinder had a small grocery in the first block of South Blackhoof Street. Descendants of this family remain in both Wapakoneta and Delphos, Ohio. (Courtesy of Richard Stearns.)

The wedding photograph of John and Alberta Schneider Helpling gives us a glimpse of the hairstyles and wedding fashions in 1936. Serving as witnesses are John's brother, Frederick "Fritz," and Alberta's sister, Pauline. John and Frederick were the sons of photographer Louis Helpling, and Alberta and Pauline were the daughters of Albert "Brownie" and Louise Schneider. (Courtesy of Richard Stearns.)

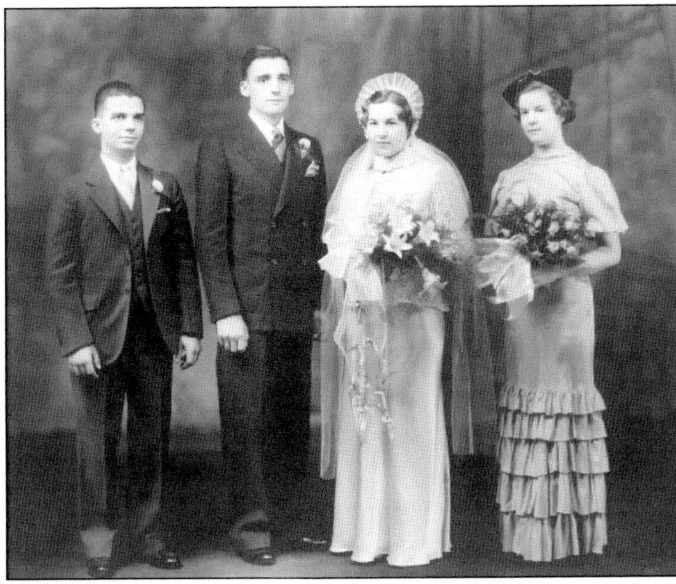

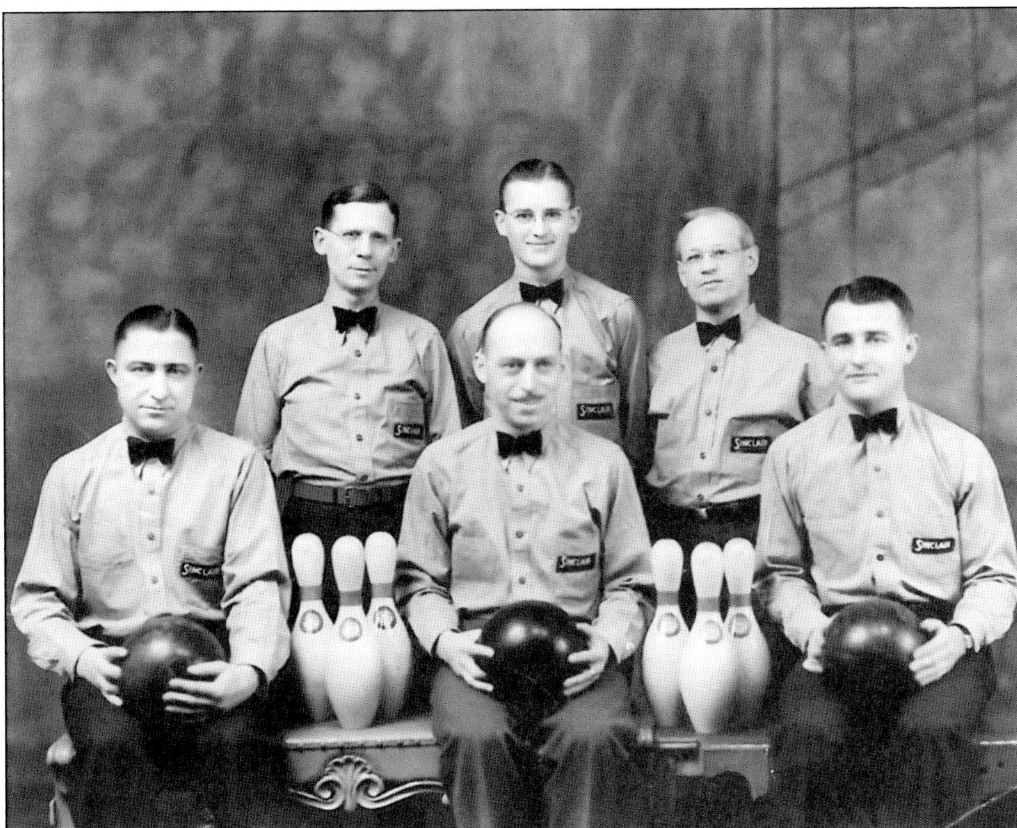

The Sinclair Gas and Service Station, owned by John Menges, was the sponsor of this 1935 City Bowling Championship team. Celebrating their win with this classic pose are, from left to right, (first row) Fred Bubp, Harry VanSkiver, and John Menges; (second row) Louis Helpling, Donald Foster, and Clem Hartman. (Courtesy of Bob and Nancy VanSkiver.)

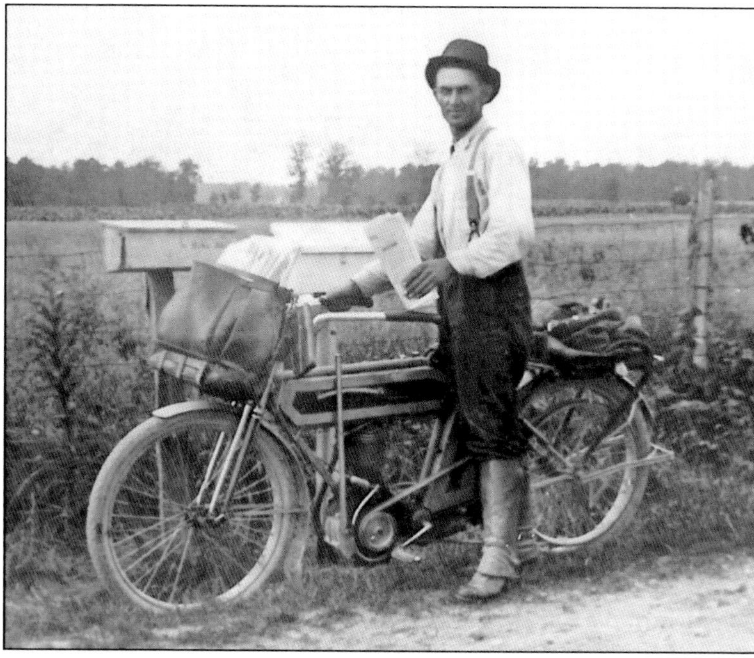

Wapakoneta had a federal post office when regular mail service began in January 1828 with Robert Boderick as the first postmaster. Here Wapakoneta rural mailman Ferd Lanning delivers mail in 1909. Serving with the U.S. Postal Service for many years, Lanning was well known in the community. (Courtesy of Bob and Nancy VanSkiver.)

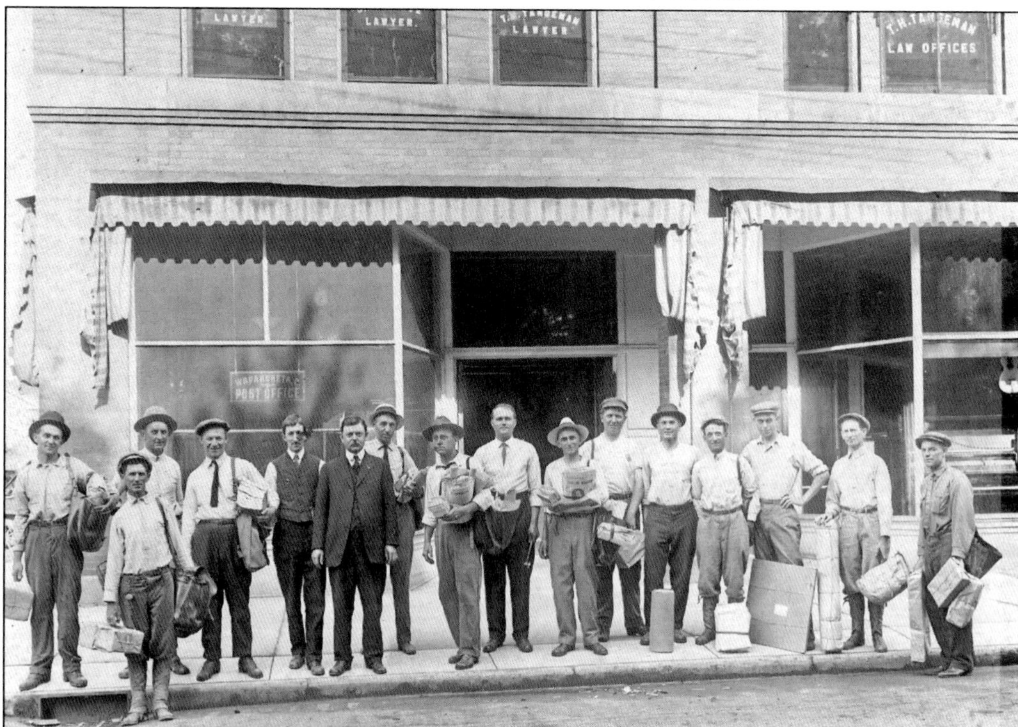

Originally at 1 West Auglaize Street, the post office moved in 1904 to the Brown Theater building. Taken about July 20, 1915, the postal carriers are, from left to right, Ferd Lanning, Frank Kerst, Charley Bush, Fred Swink, Almond Brown, postmaster Adam Schaffer, Fred Wiss, Earl Parish, Cornel Lanning, William Christler, Victor Fry, William L. Hasting, Henry Brockert, Howard Horn, Merle Kerst, and Albert J. "Dusty" Miller. (Courtesy of Eugene and Shirley Pohlable.)

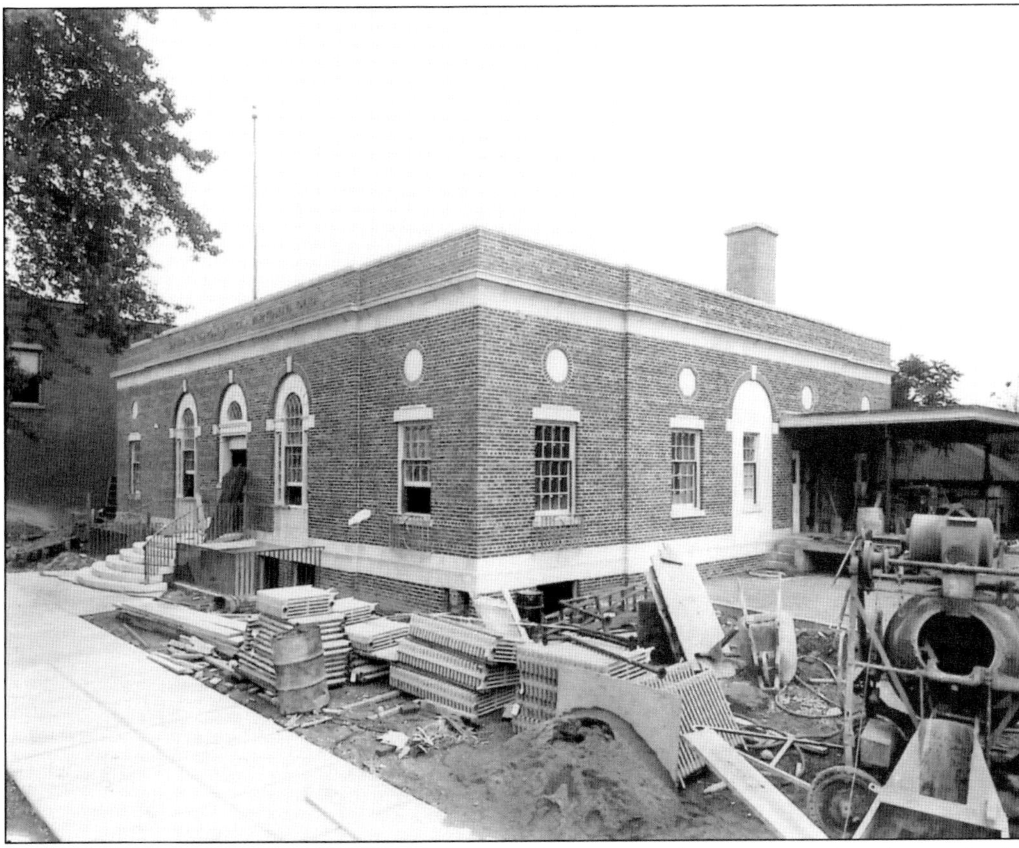

The Wapakoneta Federal Post Office had several locations as the town grew, but the one in the memory of most citizens is this structure that was dedicated on November 4, 1936. The photograph above shows the new post office under construction. This location still serves the community and remains a busy hub of activity. (Courtesy of Dennis Hague.)

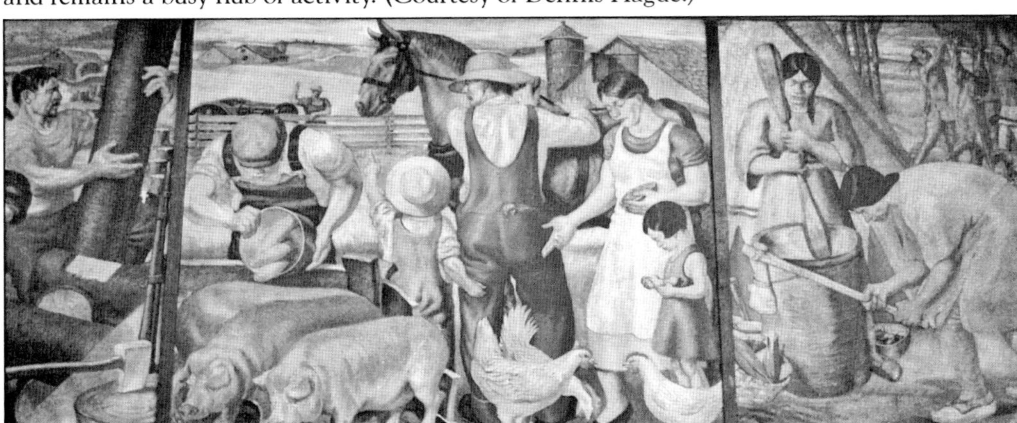

Wapakoneta's post office was built with WPA labor and features a mural of Depression-era artwork titled *Wapakoneta and American History* by artist Joseph Limarzi. This mural is located upward as one enters the post office lobby, so its significance can be overlooked. Known as New Deal Art, the mural was funded through commissions under the Federal Treasury Department's section of Painting and Sculpture. (Photograph by and courtesy of John Zwez.)

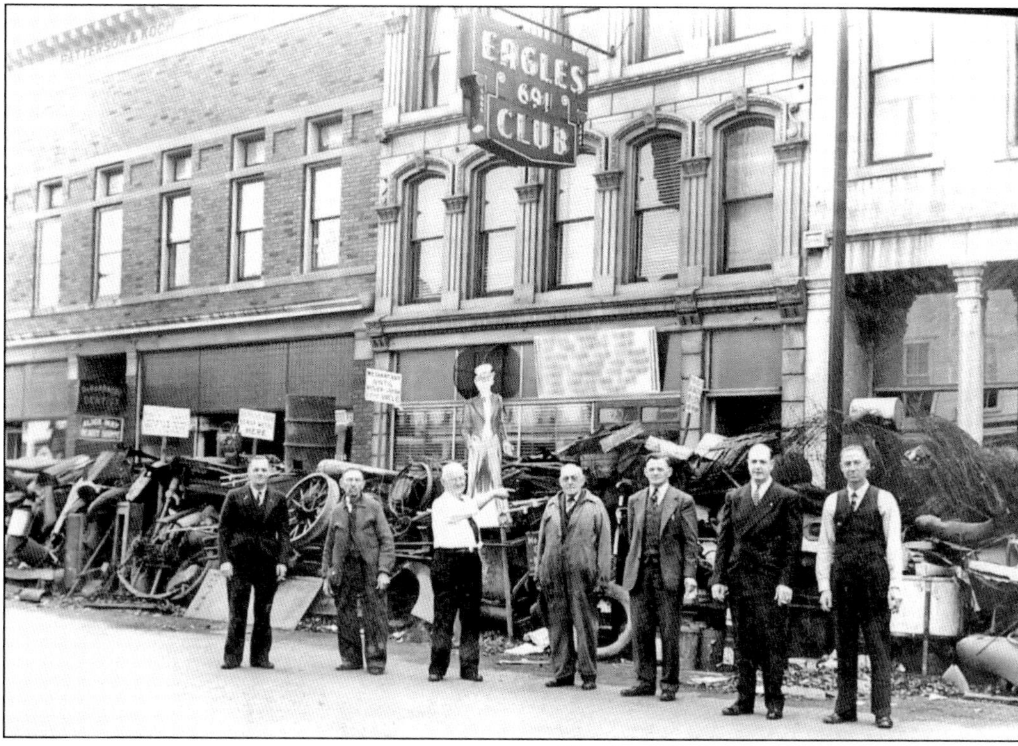

This business district effort to support World War II was held on East Auglaize Street. Scrap drives included collections by students in the 1940s, when many remember a large scrap pile was located behind Blume High School and added to larger town collections.

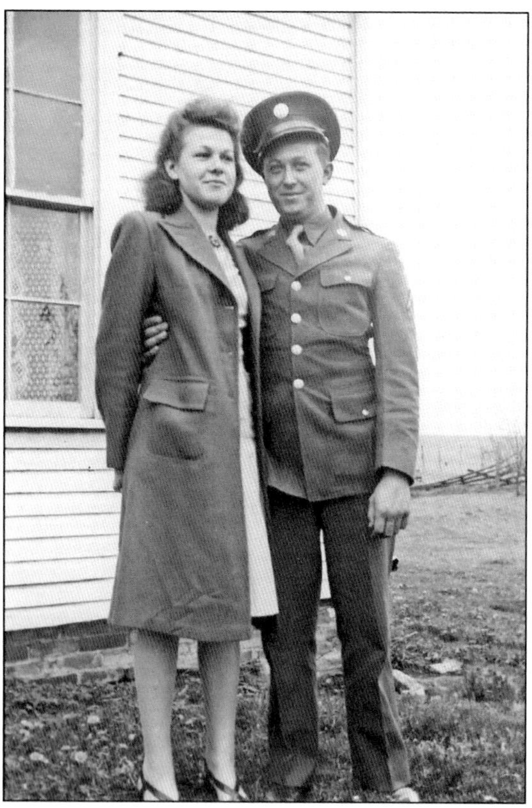

Representing all veterans, Harold E. and Venice Scott Zwiebel pose for this World War II–era photograph. Enlisting in August 1942, Harold served as a warrant officer for the duration of the war. His military service included driving an ambulance on the front lines and serving in India and the Asiatic-Pacific Theater. (Courtesy of Peg Zwiebel Schlenker.)

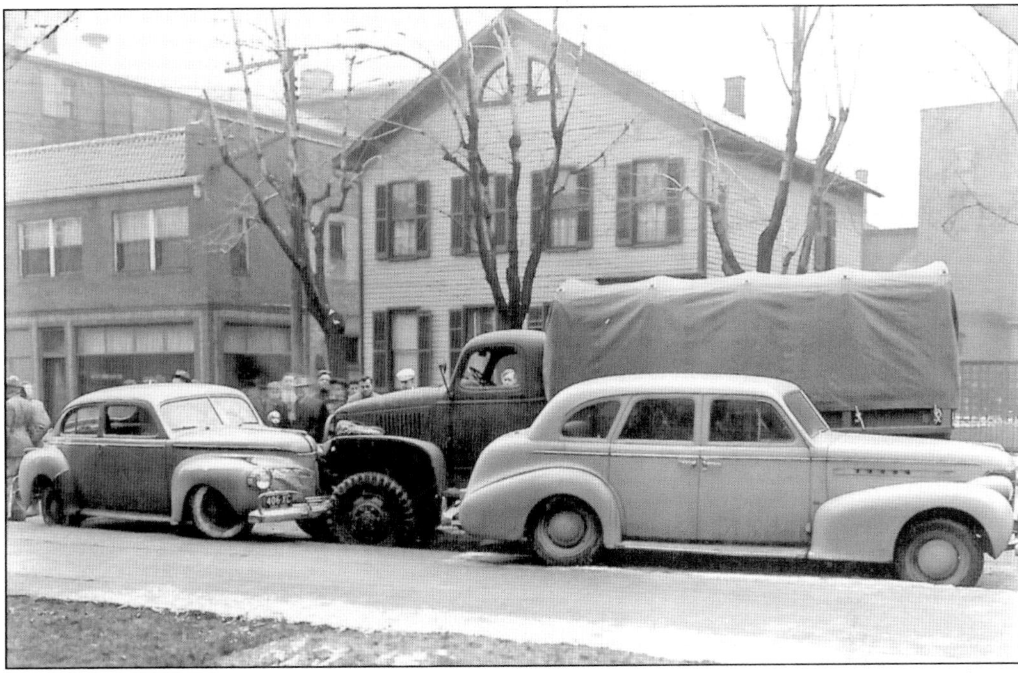

An Army truck missed the turn onto Willipie Street as it followed the jog of U.S. Route 25 (Dixie Highway) that weaved through town in the 1940s. The building across the street is now the law office of James Hearn. (Courtesy of Dennis Hague.)

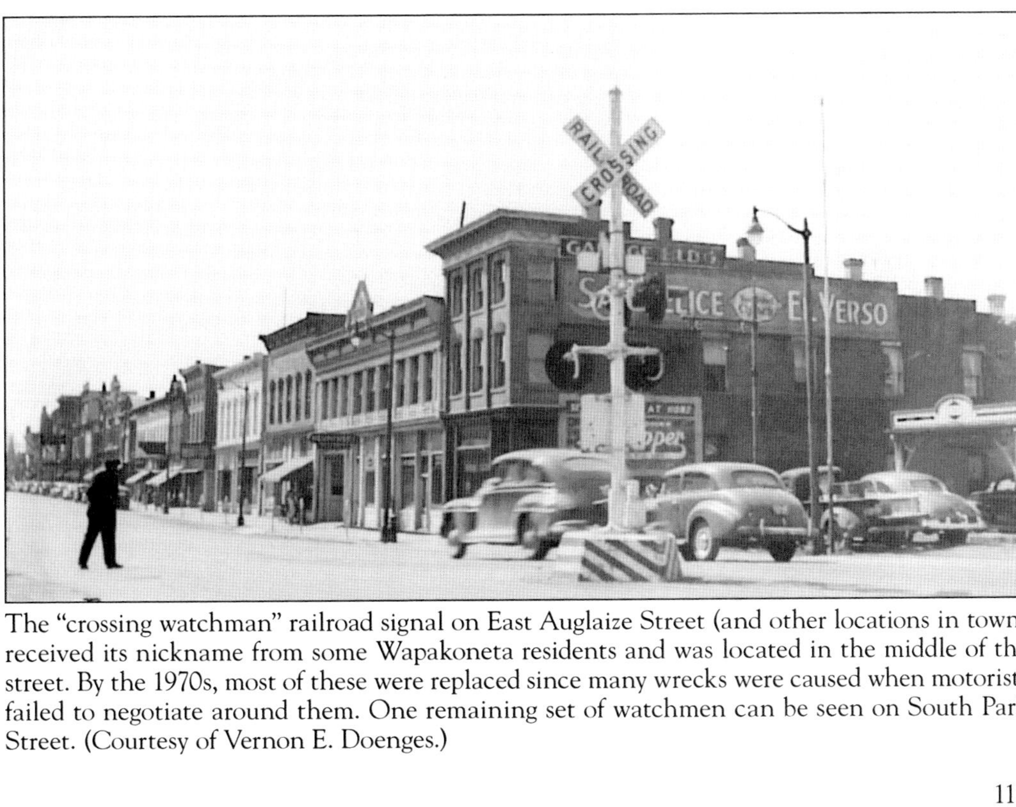

The "crossing watchman" railroad signal on East Auglaize Street (and other locations in town) received its nickname from some Wapakoneta residents and was located in the middle of the street. By the 1970s, most of these were replaced since many wrecks were caused when motorists failed to negotiate around them. One remaining set of watchmen can be seen on South Park Street. (Courtesy of Vernon E. Doenges.)

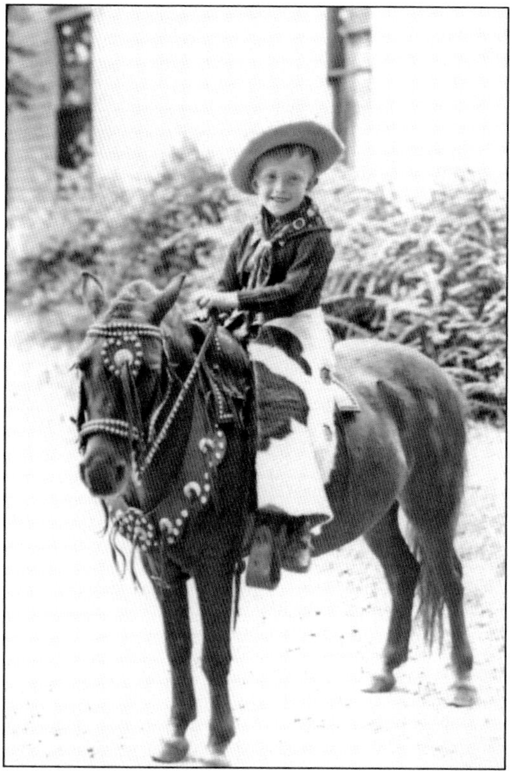

Many residents have photographs like this one in their family collections. It was common for door-to-door photographers to appear in the summer months with a well-appointed pony and cowboy gear to take photographs of the children. Taken sometime around 1932, Gene Pohlable represents the many happy children that could live the cowboy life, if only for just a few minutes. (Courtesy of Eugene and Shirley Pohlable.)

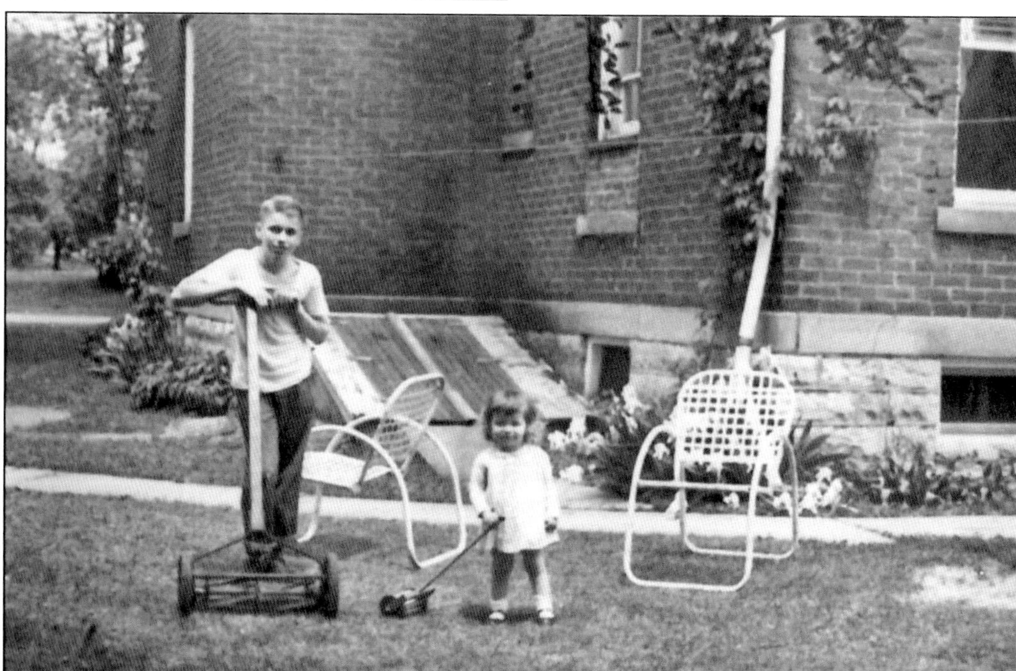

Children all over town played on the sidewalks and lawns near their homes. Siblings Jerre and Eloise "Ellie" Maxson enjoy a springtime moment at their 207 West Silver Street home around 1947. (Courtesy of Eloise Maxson Archer.)

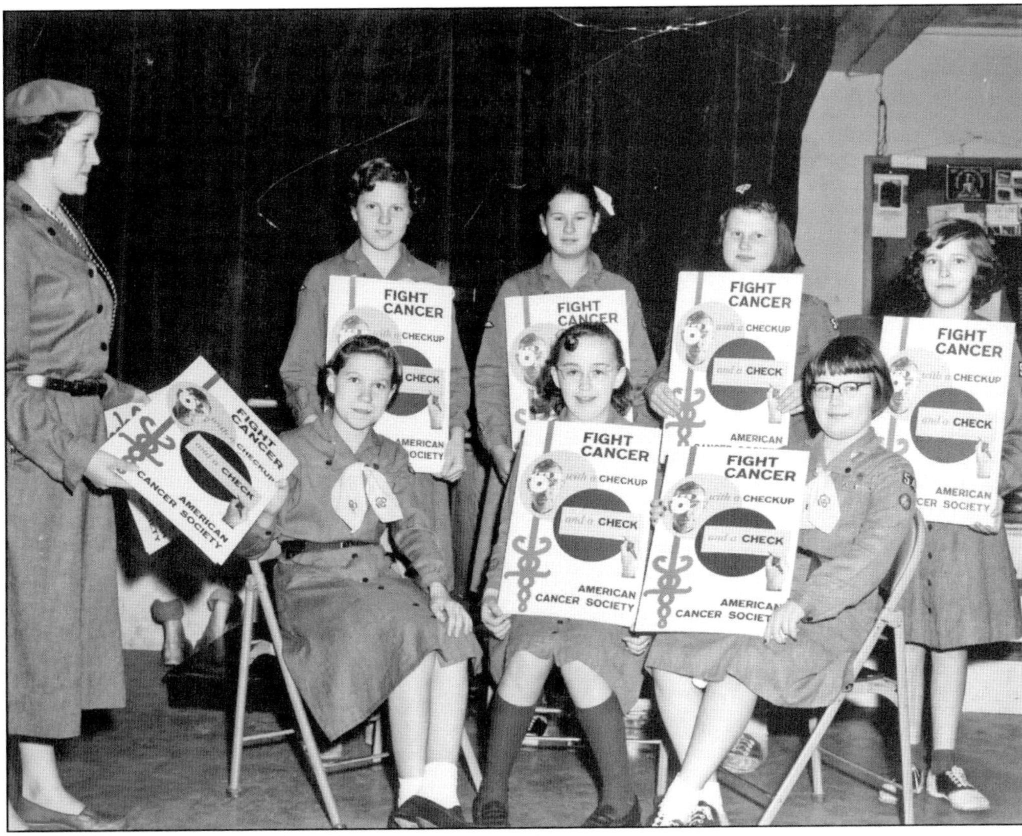

Always popular in Wapakoneta, the Boy and Girl Scouts have been actively involved in community and civic endeavors. Taken in the 1950s, this photograph shows leader Carolyn Maxson Layton enjoying a moment with Girl Scouts. From left to right are (first row) unidentified, Mary Ann Puetz, and Susie Earl; (second row) Sandra Wellington, Joy Fisher, Ann Briley, and Eloise Archer. (Courtesy of Eloise Maxson Archer.)

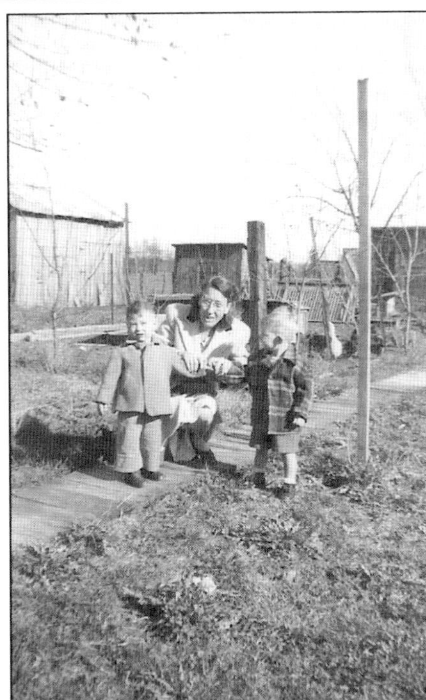

In the 1950s, Gladys Watt shares a loving moment at 210 Wagner Street with her grandson, Raymond Maxson (left), and son John. At this time, Wagner Street was at the edge of town with a new bowling alley next door. This view is looking east toward present-day shopping centers. (Courtesy of Terry Leudeke and Sue Fullerton.)

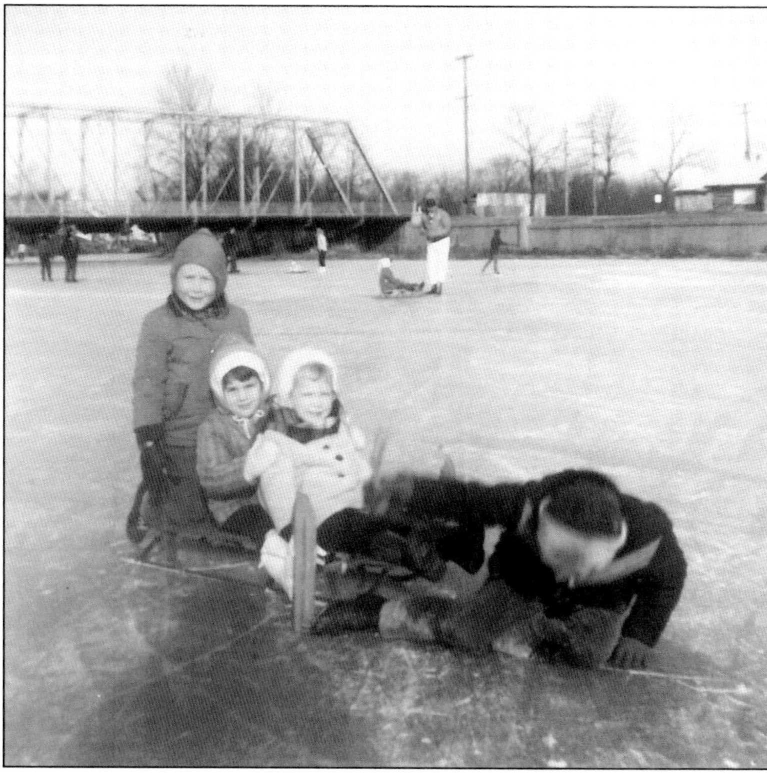

The Auglaize River was the site of many wintertime skating parties. This January 1966 winter party was recorded near the Harrison Street Bridge, recognizable by its steel trusses. The children on the sled are, from left to right, Kevin Ruck, Deb Copeland, and Jodi Ruck Groover. The boy in the front is unidentified. (Courtesy of the Larry and Pat Bell Thuman family.)

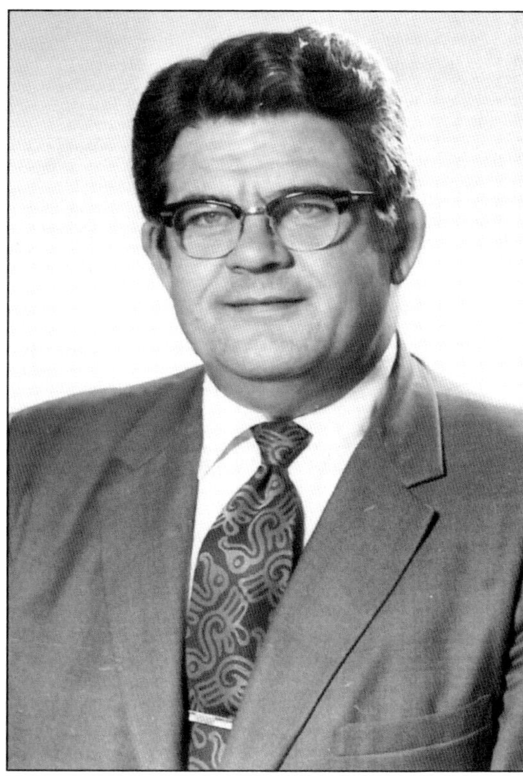

Recognized as "Mr. Historian," Vernon E. Doenges has written the Looking Back column in the *Wapakoneta Daily News* for over 18 years. Interested in all things Wapakoneta and Auglaize County, Doenges has been generous with his time and talents, providing access to his collections for research. Serving in a professional capacity as Auglaize County Auditor for 28 years, Doenges remains the longest serving elected county official to date.

Six

Fame and Footprints

Although Wapakoneta may be considered a small town, many people of achievement have called Wapakoneta home. Wapakoneta natives have become successful entrepreneurs, educators, and civic leaders. However, the city's most famous son is astronaut Neil A. Armstrong, who was the first person to step on the moon or, as Walter Cronkite quipped, became "the first tourist on the moon."

Beyond Armstrong being the world's most famous astronaut, Wapakoneta was the hometown of a Civil War Congressional Medal of Honor winner, nationally known vaudevillians, a prolific Oscar-winning screenwriter, an auto racing winner, and an early 20th century baseball star.

On July 20, 1969, State of Ohio governor James A. Rhodes pledged $500,000 and challenged the local community to match, dollar for dollar, the funds to build a museum dedicated to all Ohioans that have "sought to defy gravity" and space program history. Wapakoneta residents met that challenge and contributed over $528,000 for the Armstrong Air and Space Museum dedicated on July 20, 1972. At the dedication, Tricia Nixon Cox—representing her father, Richard Nixon—presented a moon rock for museum exhibition that was brought back to Earth from the *Apollo 11* Mission.

Also on exhibit at the museum site is a *F5D Skylancer* used by Armstrong as a NASA test aircraft, *Gemini VIII* spacecraft, *Gemini* space suit, *Saturn V* model, H-1 engine, space food, space personal hygiene items, *Apollo 11* space suits, *Apollo11* artifacts, and moon rocks. As space exploration has evolved, so have the exhibits at the Armstrong Museum. Welcoming visitors from around the world, the focus of the museum remains a repository of Ohio's aeronautical history and a monument to Ohio's contributions to aviation and space exploration.

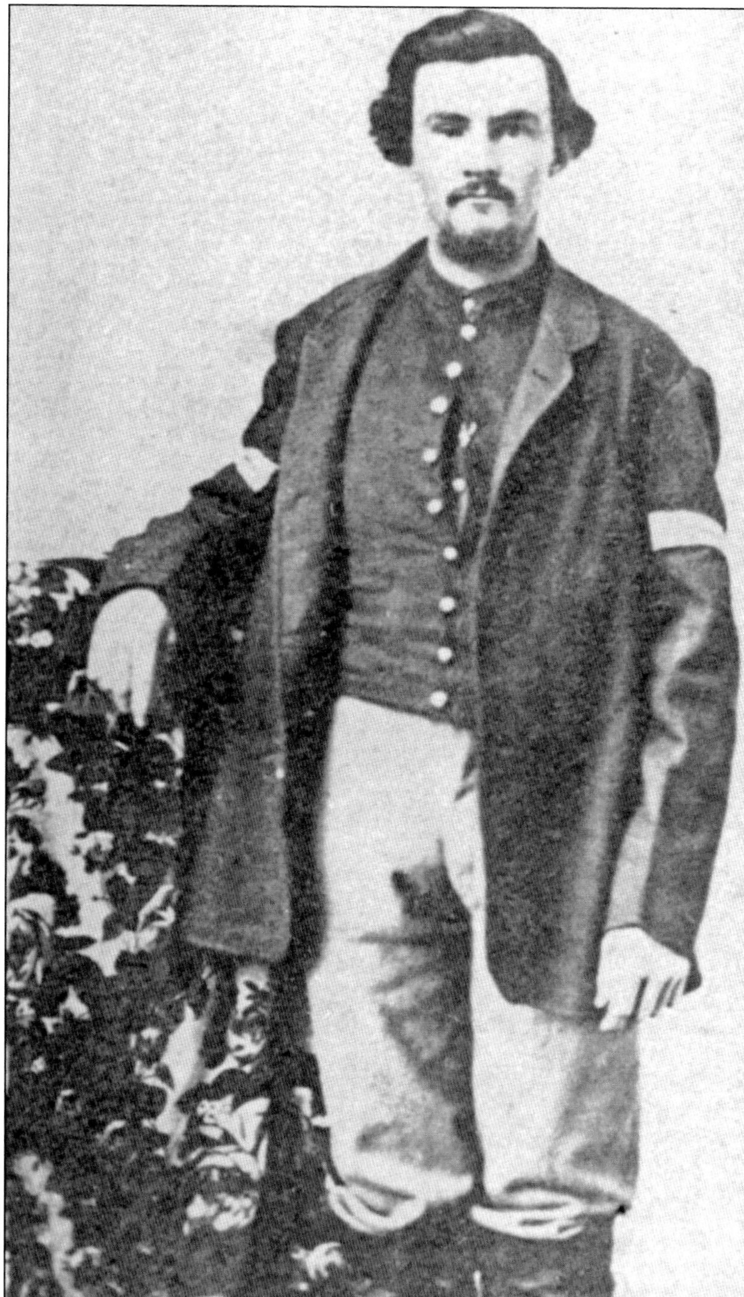

Born on February 19, 1838, in Virginia, Wapakoneta resident Cpl. Christian Schnell received the Congressional Medal of Honor during the Civil War for heroism during a storming party at the assault on Vicksburg on May 22, 1863. Corporal Schnell, Company C, 37th Ohio Volunteer Infantry, was one of 80 Union soldiers in this famous battle who volunteered to attack where the enemy force was greatest and most dangerous. The majority of Auglaize County soldiers served in the 37th, 45th, 99th, and 118th Regiments of the Ohio Volunteer Infantry. The 37th Regiment (Company C, composed of Auglaize County men) was the state's third German-speaking regiment, organized in October 1861. (Courtesy of Jim Bowsher.)

George "Long Bob" Ewing, a right-handed pitcher for the Cincinnati Reds, grew up near Wapakoneta, where he developed a pitching arm by throwing potatoes at a target. Playing sandlot baseball here and three years with the Toledo Mud Hens, "Old Wapak" was discovered in 1901 while playing the barn-storming Cincinnati Reds team in Sidney, Ohio. Ewing was inducted into the Cincinnati Reds Hall of Fame in 2001. (Courtesy of Jim Bowsher.)

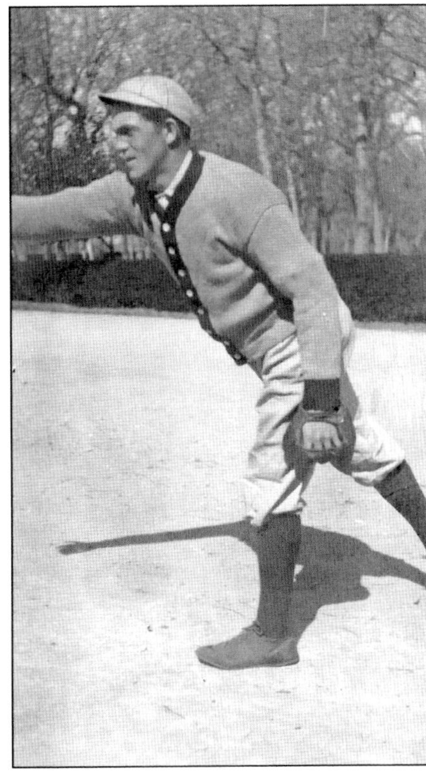

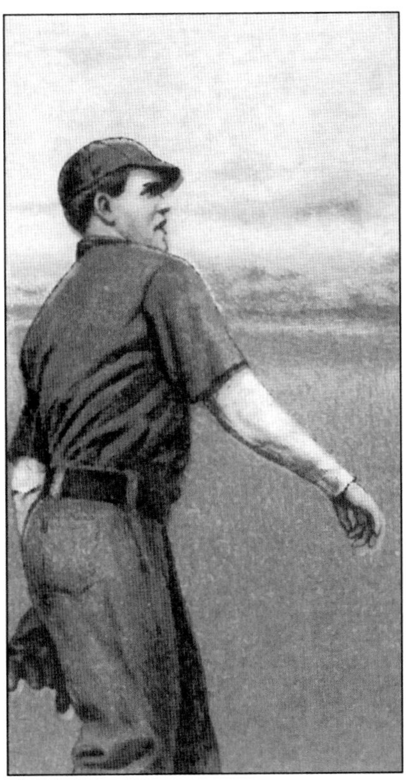

Appearing on a Piedmont cigarette baseball card in 1905, George "Long Bob" or "Old Wapak" Ewing has just completed a pitch. Retiring from baseball in 1913, Ewing was elected to a term as Auglaize County Sheriff in 1920, later operating the Brunswick Cigar Store, and engaged in other business endeavors in town. Wapakoneta was his home until he died in 1947. (Courtesy of Allen Elsass.)

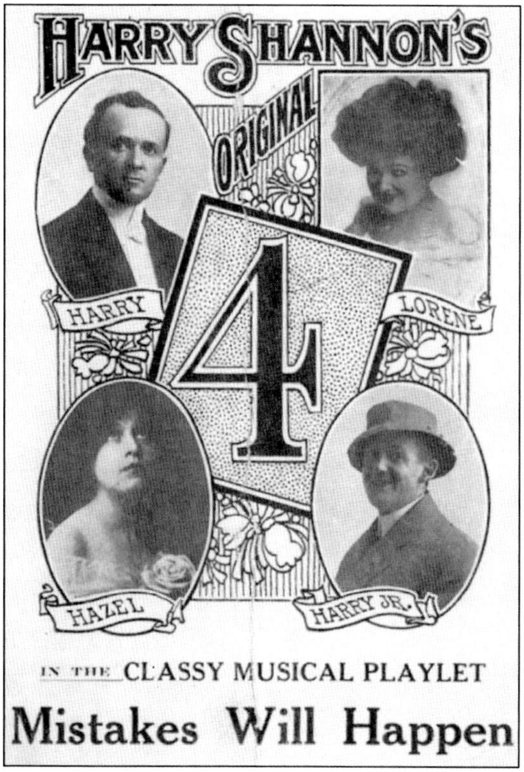

Col. Harry Shannon founded the Shannon Famous Players, a traveling theater company based in Wapakoneta from 1913 to 1938. The group included his wife, Lorene (more commonly known as Adelaide Stoutenburg Shannon), and children Harry Jr. and Hazel. When the Shannon Players were not traveling, the family and actors prepared for the next tour by holding rehearsals in the barn behind their home on West Auglaize Street. (Courtesy of Auglaize County Historical Society.)

Harry Shannon Jr. (first row, second from left); his mother, Adelaide Stoutenburg Shannon (first row, third from left); and his sister, Hazel (first row, fourth from left), are identified in this Shannon Players Stock Company photograph. The family and troupe would perform on stage or "under the canvas" in open fields. Ending their summer tour in September 1934, the Shannon's performed on the Tieben lot at East Auglaize and Wood Streets. (Courtesy of Jim Bowsher.)

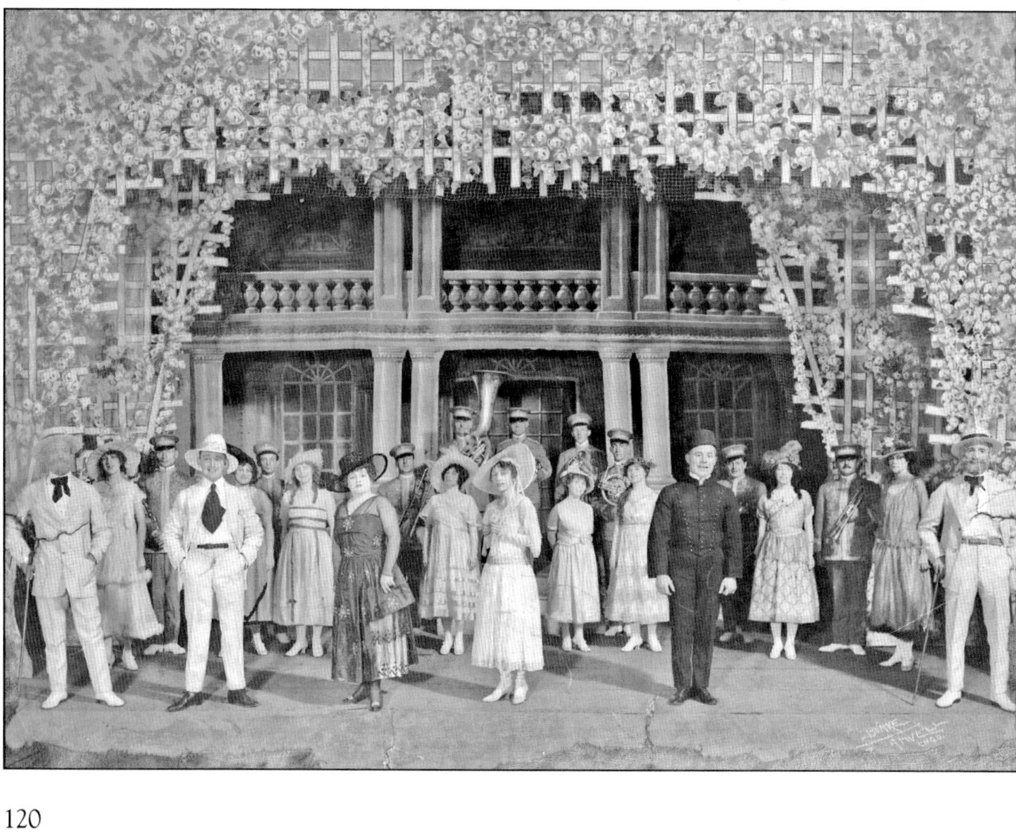

Locally born writer Dudley Nichols received an Oscar for his screenplay *The Informer* in 1936. A founder of the Screen Writers Guild, Nichols made history by being the first to refuse the Oscar in a stand to have independent unions recognized by the studios. As a varied and prolific writer, Nichols' other works include *Bringing Up Baby*, *The Bells of St. Mary's*, and *Stagecoach*. (Courtesy of Auglaize County Historical Society.)

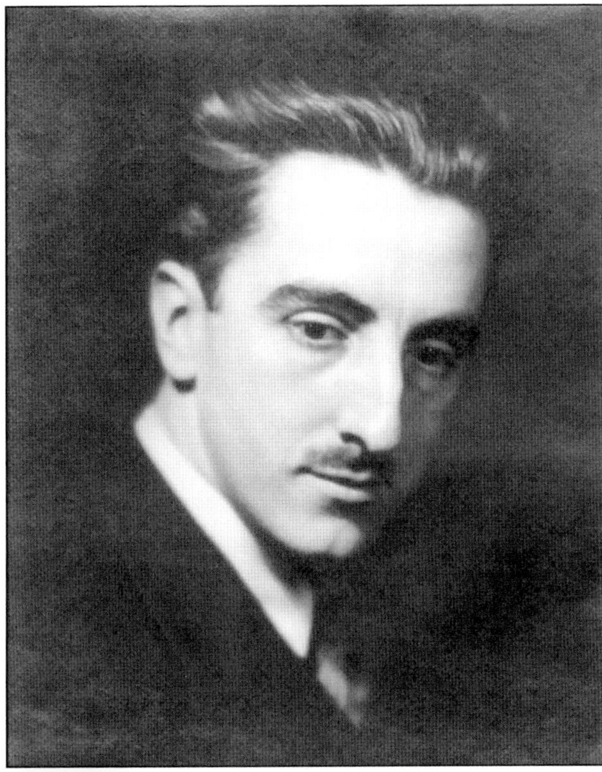

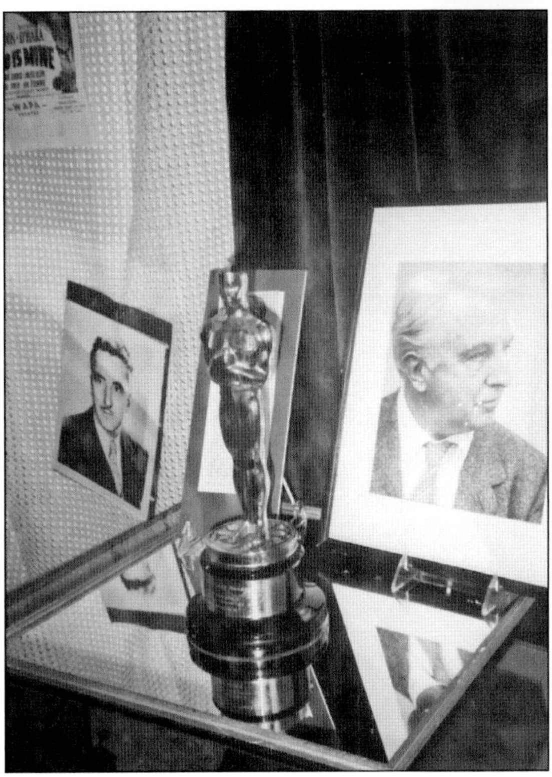

In 2003, an Ohio State Historical Society marker identifying the birthplace of Dudley Nichols was dedicated by the Auglaize County Historical Society, honoring Nichols for his body of work. At this time, the Oscar (sent to him after several refusals) was displayed at the local historical society museum, and special event showings of his films were seen at the Wapa Theater. (Courtesy of Barbara and Beverly Helmlinger.)

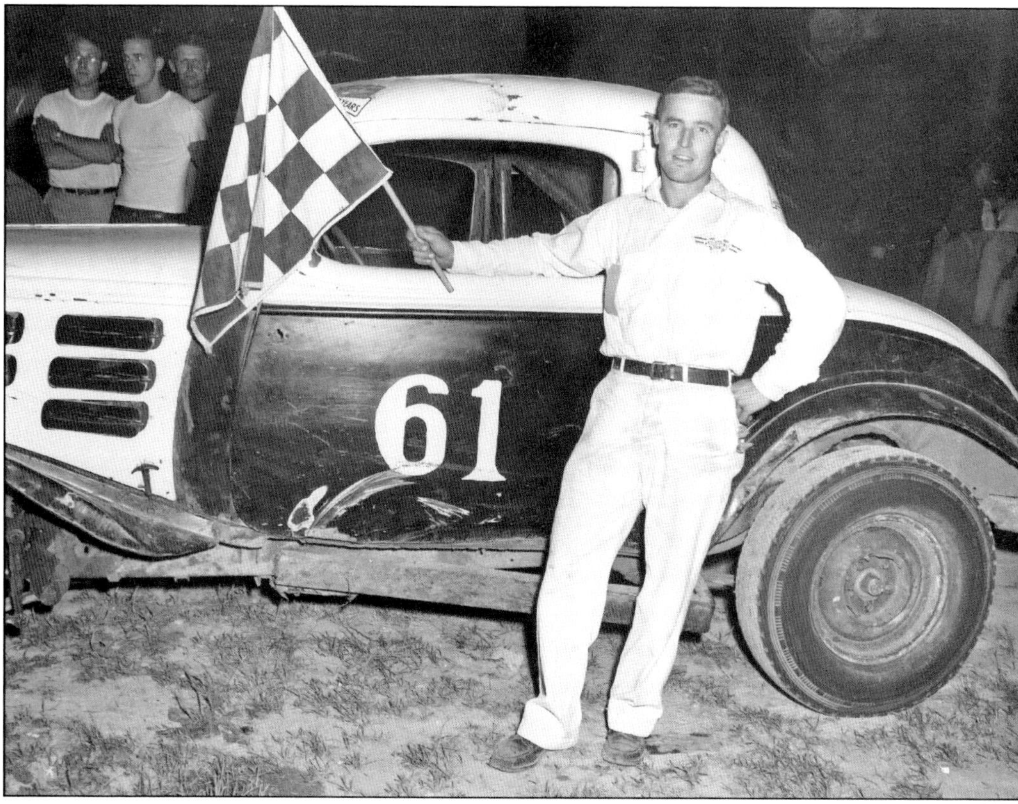

Leon Clum maintained a 20-year racing career at local and national tracks, setting many records. An expert mechanic, Clum worked for Clark Ford, spending his off hours racing all kinds of cars until he got his chance to drive in the Indianapolis 500. In 1961 and 1962, he qualified for the big race, serving his rookie year and becoming friends with A. J. Foyt. (Courtesy of Allen Elsass.)

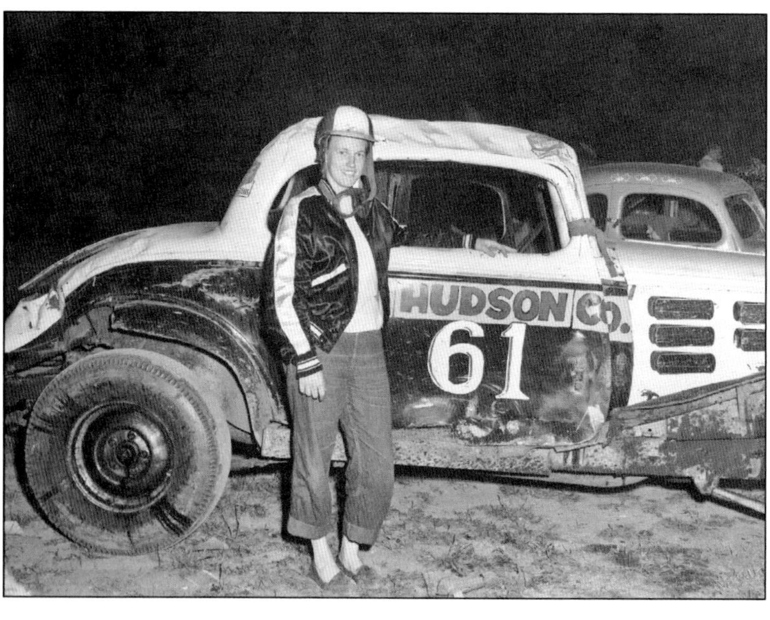

LaRue Clum, wife of Leon, was a winning race driver in her own right. She was one of the first female drivers who opened the door for women's NASCAR racing today. Participating in the ladies' racing tours of the 1950s, LaRue raced at Allentown Raceway near Lima, Ohio, and throughout the Midwest. (Courtesy of Allen Elsass.)

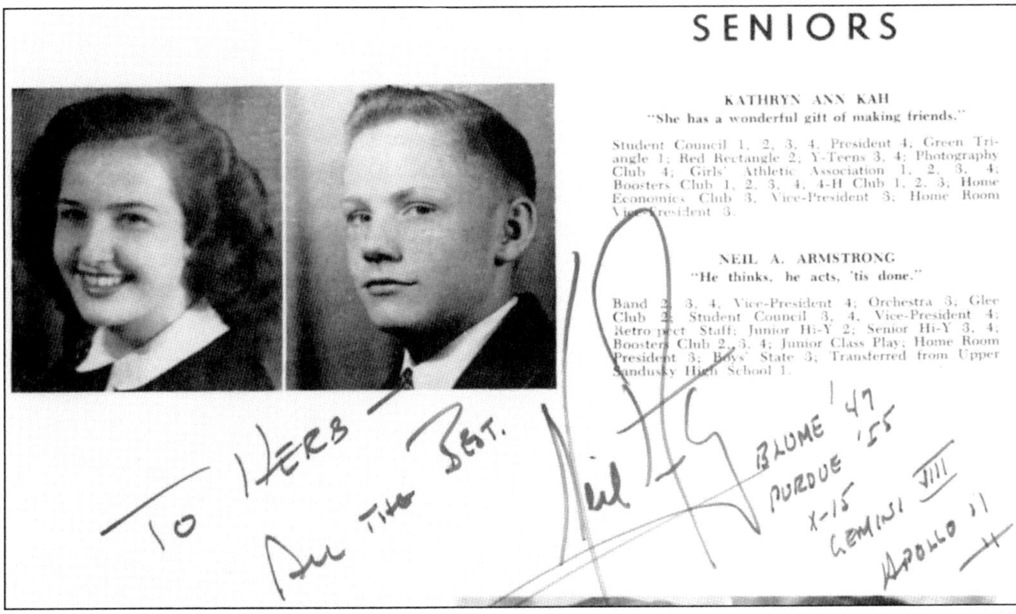
SENIORS

KATHRYN ANN KAH

"She has a wonderful gift of making friends."

Student Council 1, 2, 3, 4, President 4; Green Triangle 1; Red Rectangle 2; Y-Teens 3, 4; Photography Club 4; Girls' Athletic Association 1, 2, 3, 4; Boosters Club 1, 2, 3, 4, 4-H Club 1, 2, 3; Home Economics Club 3, Vice-President 3; Home Room Vice-President 3.

NEIL A. ARMSTRONG

"He thinks, he acts, 'tis done."

Band 2, 3, 4, Vice-President 4; Orchestra 3; Glee Club 2; Student Council 3, 4, Vice-President 4; Retrospect Staff; Junior Hi-Y 2; Senior Hi-Y 3, 4; Boosters Club 2, 3, 4; Junior Class Play; Home Room President 3; Boys' State 3; Transferred from Upper Sandusky High School 1.

Wapakoneta's most famous citizen, astronaut Neil A. Armstrong, was born August 5, 1930, on his grandmother's farm near Wapakoneta. He graduated from Blume High School in 1947 (yearbook photograph above) and Purdue University in 1955. Riding his bicycle to a local airport for flying lessons, Armstrong received a pilot's license before he could drive. (Courtesy of Herb Lunz.)

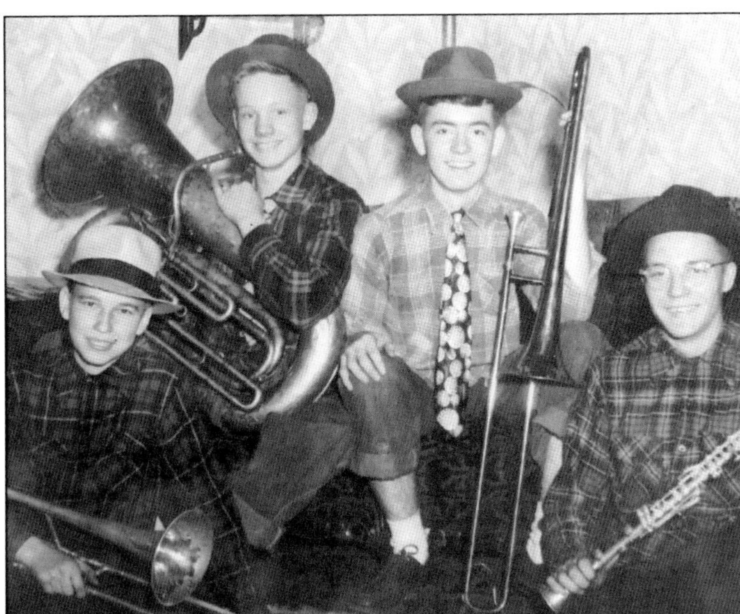

Armstrong was a busy teenager, participating in Boy Scouts, yearbook, school clubs, and community activities, as well as working part-time at a drugstore. Armstrong and fellow members of the Mississippi Moonshiners were part of Blume High School band. The quartet was, from left to right, Jerre Maxson, Neil Armstrong, Bob Gustafson, and Jim Mougey. (Courtesy of Stanley R. Maxson Jr.; photograph by Stanley W. Maxson.)

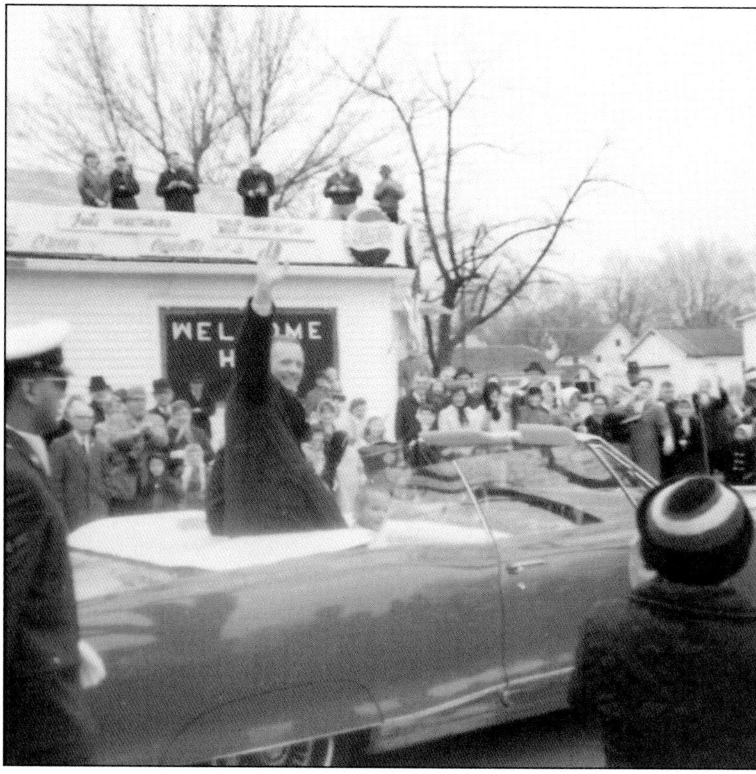

Former NASA test pilot and command pilot for the successful *Gemini VIII* mission, Armstrong was honored in March 1966 with a parade in his hometown. Memorable in the lives of city residents, the town population swelled with tourists and well-wishers. Among those standing on the roof of Wahrer's Grocery (later VanSkiver's) for a bird's-eye view are Bob VanSkiver and his daughters. (Courtesy of Terry Leudeke.)

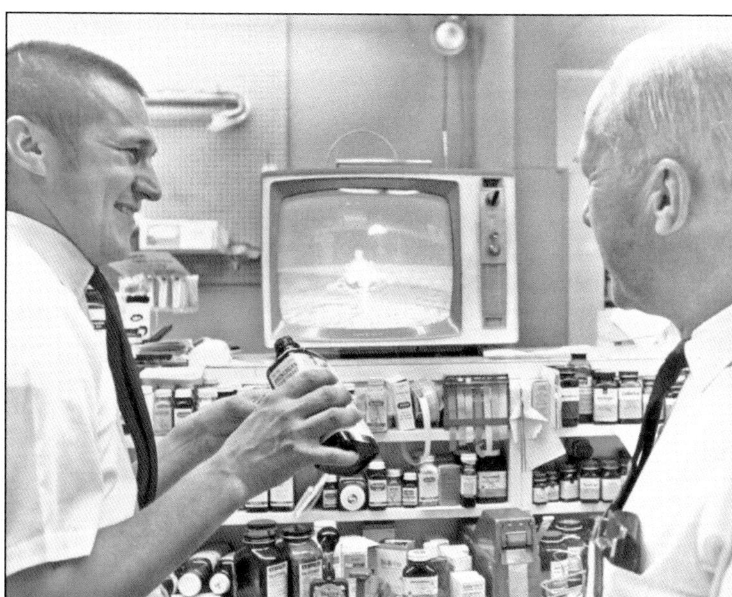

On July 20, 1969, as the world watched Neil A. Armstrong and Edwin Eugene "Buzz" Aldrin Jr. on the lunar surface, no greater audience was present than the family and friends gathered in Wapakoneta. Rhine and Brading Drugstore pharmacist Charles Brading (left) watches former drugstore student-employee Armstrong and astronaut Buzz Aldrin as they work on the moon's surface. (Courtesy of *Wapakoneta Daily News*.)

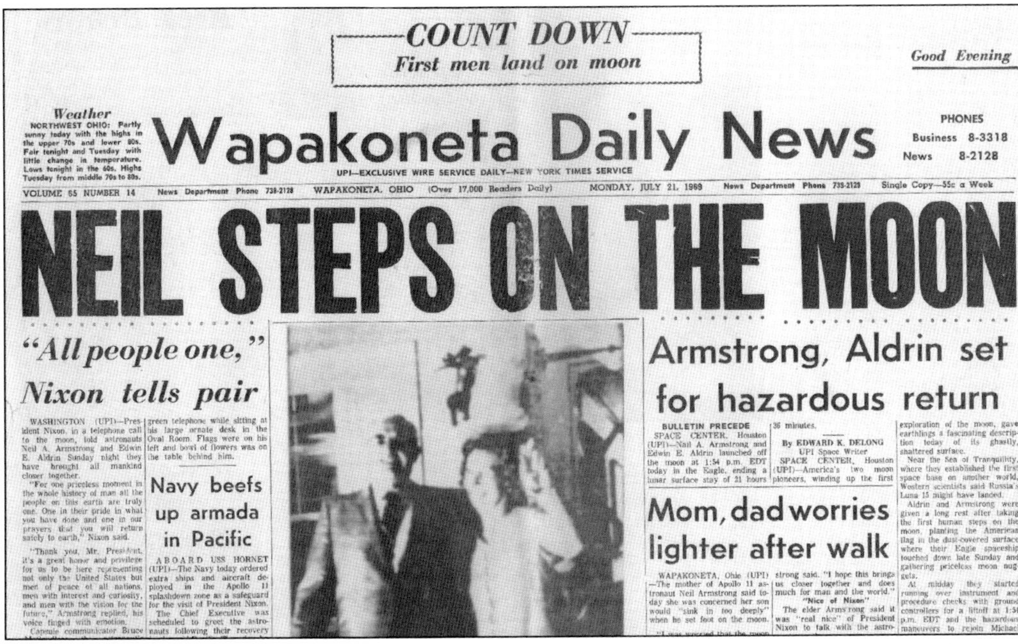

COUNT DOWN
First men land on moon

Good Evening

Weather
NORTHWEST OHIO: Partly sunny today with the highs in the upper 70s and lower 80s. Fair tonight and Tuesday with little change in temperature. Lows tonight in the 60s. Highs Tuesday from middle 70s to 80s.

Wapakoneta Daily News

UPI—EXCLUSIVE WIRE SERVICE DAILY—NEW YORK TIMES SERVICE

PHONES
Business 8-3318
News 8-2128

VOLUME 65 NUMBER 14 News Department Phone 738-2128 WAPAKONETA, OHIO (Over 17,000 Readers Daily) MONDAY, JULY 21, 1969 News Department Phone 738-2128 Single Copy—55c a Week

NEIL STEPS ON THE MOON

"All people one," Nixon tells pair

WASHINGTON (UPI)—President Nixon, in a telephone call to the moon, told astronauts Neil A. Armstrong and Edwin E. Aldrin Sunday night they have brought all mankind closer together.

"For one priceless moment in the whole history of man all the people on this earth are truly one. One in their pride in what you have done and one in our prayers that you will return safely to earth," Nixon said.

"Thank you, Mr. President, it's a great honor and privilege for us to be here representing not only the United States but men of peace of all nations, men with interest and curiosity, and men with the vision for the future," Armstrong replied, his voice tinged with emotion.

Capsule communicator Bruce

green telephone while sitting at his large ornate desk in the Oval Room. Flags were on his left and bowl of flowers was on the table behind him.

Navy beefs up armada in Pacific

ABOARD USS HORNET (UPI)—The Navy today ordered extra ships and aircraft deployed in the Apollo 11 splashdown zone as a safeguard for the visit of President Nixon.

The Chief Executive was scheduled to greet the astronauts following their recovery

Armstrong, Aldrin set for hazardous return

BULLETIN PRECEDE

SPACE CENTER, Houston (UPI)—Nail A. Armstrong and Edwin E. Aldrin launched off the moon at 1:54 p.m. EDT today in the Eagle, ending a lunar surface stay of 21 hours 36 minutes.

By EDWARD K. DELONG
UPI Space Writer

SPACE CENTER, Houston (UPI)—America's two moon pioneers, winding up the first exploration of the moon, gave earthlings a fascinating description today of its ghastly, shattered surface.

Near the Sea of Tranquility, where they established the first space base on another world, Western scientists said Russia's Luna 15 might have landed.

Aldrin and Armstrong were given a long rest after taking the first human steps on the moon, planting the American flag in the dust-covered surface where their Eagle spaceship touched down late Sunday and gathering priceless moon nuggets.

At midday they started running over instrument and procedure checks with ground controllers for a liftoff at 1:54 p.m. EDT and the hazardous maneuvers to rejoin Michael

Mom, dad worries lighter after walk

WAPAKONETA, Ohio (UPI)—The mother of Apollo 11 astronaut Neil Armstrong said today she was concerned her son would "sink in too deeply" when he set foot on the moon.

strong said. "I hope this brings us closer together and does much for man and the world."

"Nice of Nixon"

The elder Armstrong said it was "real nice" of President Nixon to talk with the astro-

The *Wapakoneta Daily News* headline captured the moment. As Armstrong's famous words, "One small step for man, one giant leap for mankind," became part of history, Armstrong's parents, Stephen and Viola, greeted reporters and newsmen at their home on what would later become Neil Armstrong Drive. On that day, Armstrong was probably the most famous person in the world. (Courtesy of Terry Leudeke.)

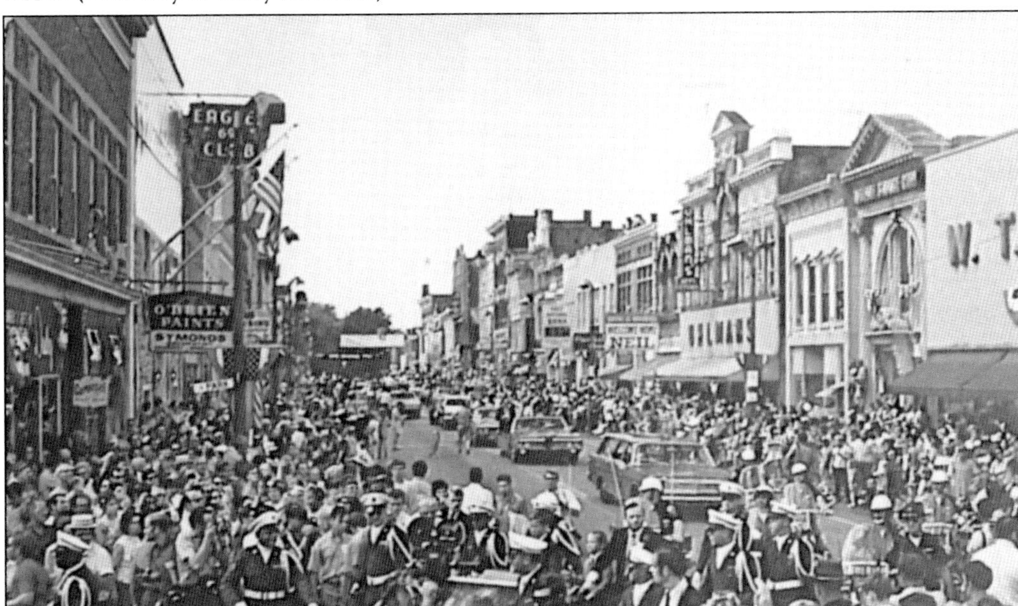

With hometown pride at a peak, a homecoming for Armstrong was planned for September 6, 1969. A local committee was organized for this grand event when dignitaries and celebrities were invited to participate in a reception, speeches, and parade. Drawing a crowd of over 80,000 to Wapakoneta, Armstrong led the parade that included celebrity Bob Hope. (Courtesy of Janet Schuler.)

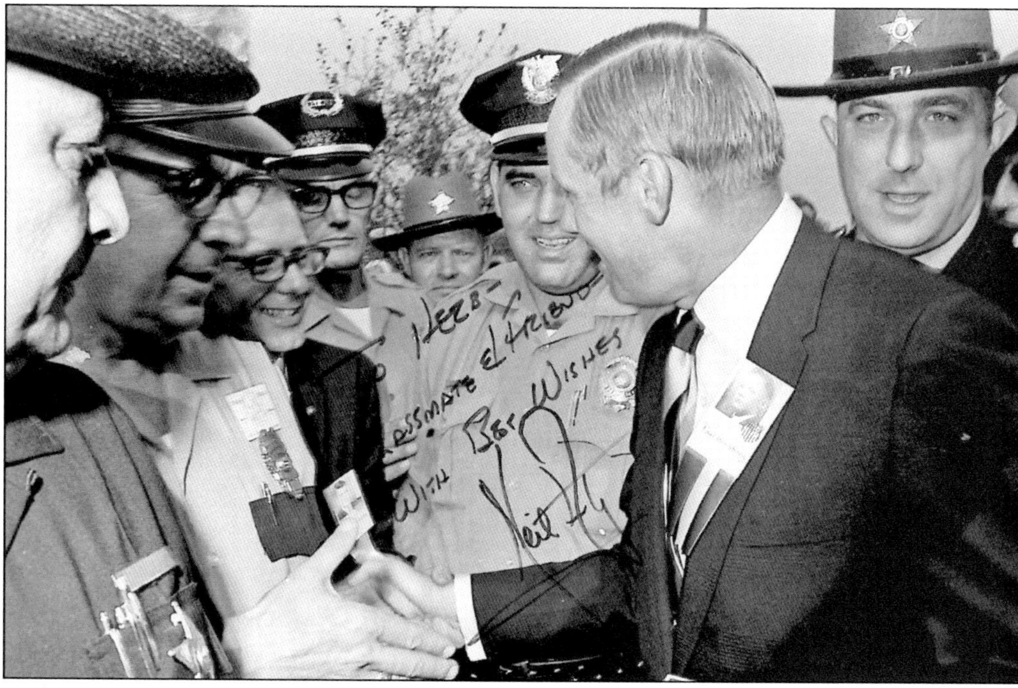

Neil Armstrong greets former high school classmate Herb Lunz in a throng of security before the Armstrong homecoming parade on September 6, 1969. Armstrong later autographed the photograph and was generous with his good wishes. (Courtesy of Herb Lunz.)

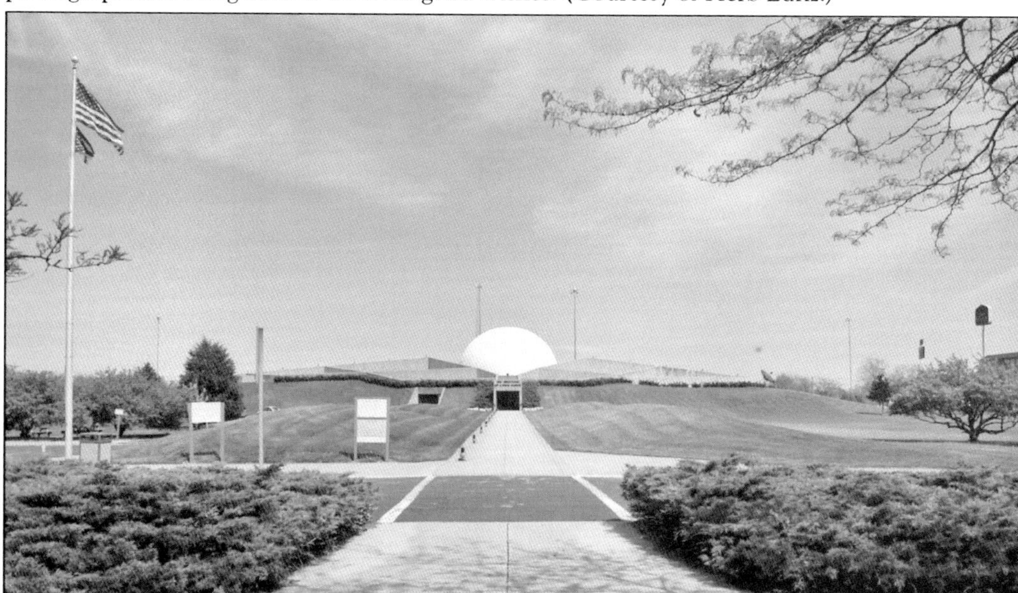

Wapakoneta native Arthur Klipfel was chosen as the architect for the Armstrong Air and Space Museum, which resembles a futuristic moon base. Accepting the challenge that Governor James A. Rhodes had proposed in 1969, Wapakoneta citizens raised over half the funds for the museum. Opened July 20, 1972, the museum features a domed astro-theater for multimedia presentations on space. (Photograph by and courtesy of John Zwez.)

Armstrong and Aldrin collected several lunar rocks during the *Apollo 11* mission, including this lunar sample on display at the Armstrong Museum. On loan from NASA, the moon rock is the cornerstone of the museum's exhibits. The museum collection also includes a *F5D Skylancer*, *Gemini VIII* spacecraft and artifacts, space hygiene items, and *Apollo 11* artifacts. (Photograph by and courtesy of John Zwez.)

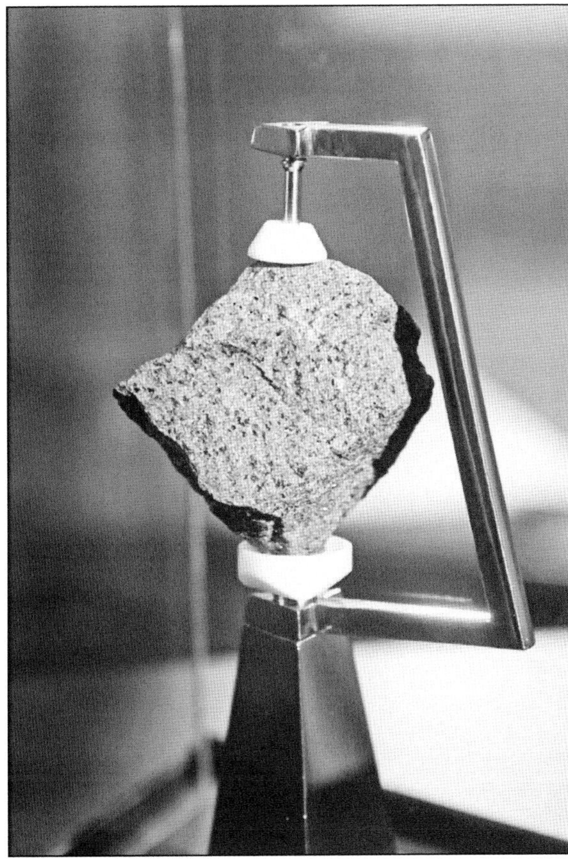

In celebration of the 40th anniversary of the *Apollo 11* mission, Wapakoneta celebrated with many events in the downtown business district and at the Armstrong Museum. One event was the Field of Honor, where organizations and individuals could place a flag in honor of local military veterans and first responders. Over 500 flags were placed in the Field of Honor on the Armstrong Museum grounds. (Courtesy of Jeff Pontsler.)

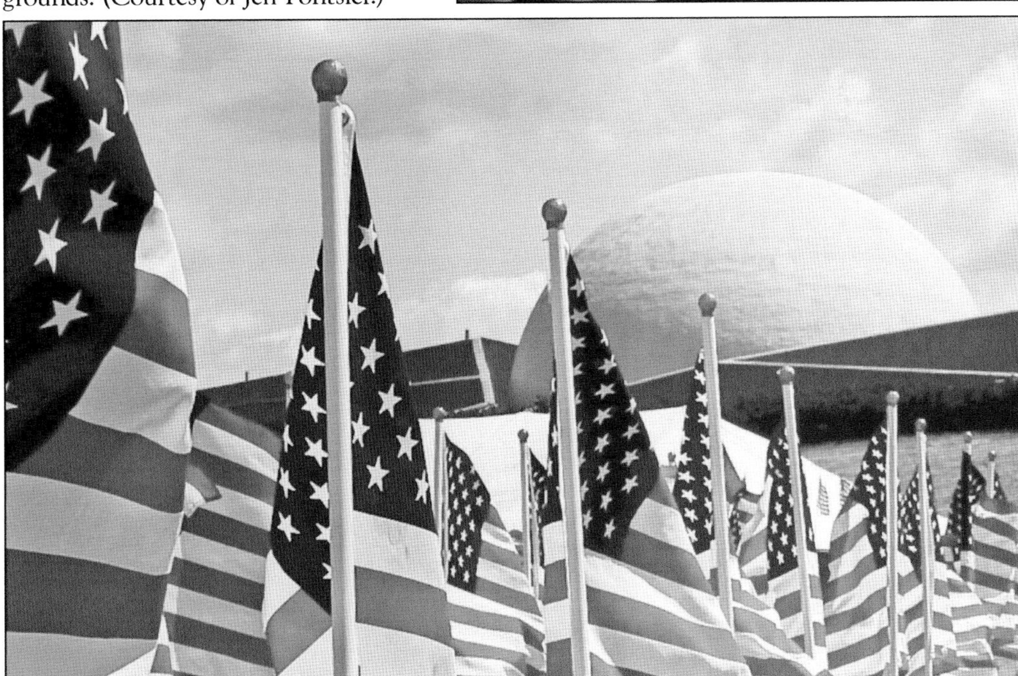

Consistent with our mission to preserve history on a local level, this book was printed in South Carolina on American-made paper and manufactured entirely in the United States. Products carrying the accredited Forest Stewardship Council (FSC) label are printed on 100 percent FSC-certified paper.